COVERT ENTRY

COVERT ENTRY

Spies, Lies and Crimes Inside Canada's Secret Service

ANDREW MITROVICA

RANDOM HOUSE CANADA

National Library of Canada Cataloguing in Publication

Mitrovica, Andrew
        Covert entry : spies, lies and crimes inside Canada's secret service / Andrew Mitrovica.

Includes index.
ISBN 0-679-31116-5

        1. Canadian Security Intelligence Service. 2. Police misconduct—Canada.
I. Title.

UB271.C3M57 2002   363.25'931'0971   C2002-902941-4

Jacket Design: CS Richardson

Text Design: Daniel Cullen

www.randomhouse.ca

Printed and bound in the United States of America

10 9 8 7 6 5 4 3 2 1

For Sharon, Sabrije, and S. B.

"Agitate. Agitate."
—FREDERICK DOUGLASS

CONTENTS

INTRODUCTION

This book is about secrets and spies. It is also an account of lies and crimes ordered and condoned by high-ranking public servants in the name of Canada's national security. *Covert Entry* had its origins in 1999, when as an investigative reporter at the *Globe and Mail*, I first cast a critical eye on Canada's spy agency, the Canadian Security Intelligence Service (CSIS).

I soon realized how little Canadians knew about the mandate, powers, resources and leadership of the intelligence service that is supposed to protect us from increasingly amorphous enemies at home and abroad. Beyond that depressing fact, I also discovered how difficult it was to pierce the culture of complacency that has grown up around CSIS. When the Berlin Wall crumbled, the Cold War and the cataclysmic threats the world faced seemed to vanish with it. In Canada, we took particular comfort in the reassuring but illusory notion that our international reputation as a peace-broker made us immune from the often costly consequences of terrorism and espionage. We also took comfort in the idea that Canada was, in a literal and figurative sense, a safe haven: it was unlikely that the architects of terror could, or would, export to North America the ugly conflicts that haunted the rest of the globe.

That all changed on September 11, 2001. Twenty-four Canadians were among the 3,054 civilians who perished when the political, entrepreneurial and military heart of the United States was attacked with such shocking ferocity. The onslaught on our doorstep jolted Canadians out of their stupor and revealed that in the netherworld of intelligence, the stakes can be very high. It also made clear that the safety and security of Canadians are dependent, in large measure, on CSIS's ability to detect, monitor and root out the dangers lurking in our midst. My unofficial tour deep inside the service's cloistered world does not inspire confidence.

Canada's intelligence agency was born in 1984 out of the discredited remnants of the RCMP Security Service. In pursuit of intelligence on Quebec's separatist movement, the service had been caught burning barns, stealing dynamite and committing other illegal acts. The final report of the McDonald Commission into RCMP wrongdoing, issued in 1981, laid part of the blame for the transgressions on an insular police culture and unaccountable police powers. It recommended that the Mounties get out of the intelligence business altogether and that, instead, the federal government establish a civilian spy agency—the Canadian Security Intelligence Service—whose mandate would be a kind of cross between the Federal Bureau of Investigation (FBI) and the Central Intelligence Agency (CIA) and whose focus would be domestic security.[1]

The new agency was invested with extraordinary powers in order to protect "Canada's national security interests and the safety of

---

[1] The RCMP was the subject of two inquiries in the late 1970s that examined law-breaking by the police force. Quebec Premier René Lévesque appointed Quebec City lawyer Jean Keable to investigate crimes committed by the RCMP in the province. To blunt the work of the Keable inquiry, Ottawa set up its own inquiry, headed by Justice David McDonald of the Alberta Supreme Court. Both inquiries found that the Mounties had broken the law for decades in the name of national security. They had opened mail without warrants, destroyed evidence, committed arson, perpetrated scores of thefts and illegal break-ins and engaged in misinformation campaigns.

Canadians."[2] In fact, CSIS's ability to invade the lives of Canadians is unmatched in government. If it decides, in secret, that you constitute a threat to national security, CSIS can listen in on your telephone calls at home and at work. It can deploy an army of watchers to monitor and record your every movement twenty-four hours a day, seven days a week. It can intercept and open your mail without your knowledge. It can break into your home and office and install state-of-the-art voice- and video-recording devices. If you become a target, your family, friends and neighbours can also be subjected to this suffocating scrutiny. Your life—past, present and future—is fair game. In effect, the act that created CSIS simply made legal the old service's tactics.

When the act was passed, however, Canadians were assured that in exercising these powers, CSIS would respect the rule of law. It would get rid of the renegades from the old service and usher in a new breed of intelligence officer who would be a model of probity for espionage agencies around the globe. The image was of newly recruited and eager university graduates with intellectual heft, trained to analyze the degree of risk posed to the country by foreign spies, terrorists, neo-Nazis, organized crime syndicates, as well as new immigrants determined to import their sometimes incendiary troubles to Canada. But in its haste to get up and running, CSIS turned to the Mountie "dinosaurs," who ended up running the show.

To watch over the new recruits and old veterans, CSIS is scrutinized by two civilian watchdogs: the Security Intelligence Review Committee (SIRC), which reports on the agency's conduct and performance to Parliament through the solicitor general, and the inspector general, who acts as the solicitor general's eyes and ears inside the service. Both

---

[2] The legislation creating CSIS (Bill C-9) was introduced in the House of Commons on January 18, 1984, by Liberal Solicitor General Robert Kaplan. The service's first director was Ted D'Arcy Finn, a career bureaucrat. His right-hand man was Archie Barr, a former senior member of the RCMP Security Service, who emerged from the McDonald inquiry with an unsullied reputation. The service's other top officials, including Ray Lees, Harry Brandes, John Venner and William MacIver, were also former senior RCMP officers.

have the power to audit the service's files routinely and to review judicial warrants and the affidavits upon which they were obtained.

On the ground, much of CSIS's $200-million annual budget and 2,100 employees are focused on two main branches: counter-terrorism (CT) and counter-intelligence (CI). Members of the physical surveillance units, or "watcher" service, (known inside CSIS as the "surveillant service" or SURs) regularly assist in operations conducted by intelligence officers assigned to the CI and CT branches. The service also posts liaison officers in Washington, London, Paris, Rome and Tel Aviv, and is permitted, on a limited scale, to undertake covert operations abroad.

Many of the recruits begin their careers in CSIS's security-screening branch, conducting background checks on government employees, or in the service's research and analysis branch, where they follow global developments to predict—with wildly oscillating degrees of success—emerging threats to Canada's national security.

Indeed, when relations between East and West thawed over a decade ago, CSIS shifted some of its resources away from ferreting out foreign spies to combatting terrorism. According to CSIS's current director, Ward Elcock, every major terrorist organization in the world has a presence here. Elcock insists that terrorists routinely use this country to raise money, set up bank accounts and plan operations. Elcock often reminds Canadians of that chilling assessment. In a June 2002 report to Parliament, he went further, declaring that Canada was no longer being used by terrorists for logistical and support activities but was becoming a possible "staging ground for terrorist attacks." He said that this country was "at risk of being targeted directly or indirectly by a terrorist network." As a result, more of the service's resources were being poured into fighting terrorism.

Another of Elcock's familiar refrains is that the intelligence service he commands is a professional, law-abiding operation that Canadians needn't fear or fret over; that under his direction, the service keeps its eye firmly fixed on its vital mandate and scarcely needs its oversight agencies to ensure that its unrivalled powers are wielded with caution and discretion.

Unfortunately, such reassurances about CSIS's conduct have little connection to what actually takes place at its fortress-like headquarters just outside Ottawa and throughout regional offices across the country. What I discovered behind the carefully constructed artifice is an intelligence service, still in its infancy, riddled by waste, extravagance, laziness, nepotism, incompetence, corruption and law-breaking. Far from being a shining example to sister intelligence services, CSIS and its imperious leadership remain wedded to its predecessor's destructive habits. As a result, the service's future and, ultimately, the security of Canadians are in jeopardy. In the aftermath of the terrible events of September 11, unearthing the truth about CSIS for this book left me shaken and very worried.

At its core, this book tells the story of a young man named John Farrell and his decade-long journey through Canada's intelligence community.

At thirty-four, Farrell has seen his share of trouble. The youngest of thirteen children who grew up in a housing project in Toronto's east-end, he has the physique of a light heavyweight boxer. His fights were waged not in the ring but on the street, in the schoolyard and in the tavern—usually after someone had crossed the invisible line that Farrell draws in the sand around him. His hands are scarred, but his face remains strangely undisturbed by violence. His temper, volcanic as it can be, is well-camouflaged by his manners and quick flashes of his engaging smile.

During his youth, Farrell's family was ravaged by drug abuse and alcoholism, and he found temporary sanctuary in the love of his mother, in school and in the Catholic church—the only constants in his life. But he also exacted his revenge on the world that wounded him. He and a small band of miscreants planned and executed scores of thefts. Their victims were neigbourhood businesses, delivery men, store clerks and the occasional passerby. The young thugs were devoted and loyal to each other. Their oath of secrecy was tested by parents and police, but they never wavered.

Farrell learned to live a double life, to act any part at any time. A natural chameleon, he could flit from one persona to the next and was able to persuade his teachers and priests to act as character witnesses when he was finally caught and sentenced for his crimes. Even now, he can be generous and kind yet brutish and selfish, dedicated and hard-working yet lazy and slovenly, open and warm yet secretive and cold, gregarious and bright yet conniving and stoic, learned and wise yet foolish and short-sighted. These are the very contradictions that made Farrell a gifted Canada Post and CSIS operative. So eager were Canada Post and then CSIS to recruit the former gang leader—and arrange his seamless move into the world of spies, safe houses and secrets—that his criminal record was expunged by Ottawa.

Farrell was a willing and enthusiastic conscript into the covert life. In 1989, as a postal inspector for Canada Post Corporation, the ex-thief learned that while senior executives shielded managers who defrauded taxpayers out of hundreds of thousands of dollars, they spent untold amounts of money to spy on postal workers and their union leaders. Appointed divisional intelligence officer for Canada Post in Toronto when he was only twenty-one, Farrell was charged with collecting information on troublesome union leaders and their families. He carefully built dossiers full of intimate details about them. And with the help of private security firms, he also entrapped gold-bricking postal workers. All of this was done, he insists, on the orders of his superiors.

In 1991, Farrell joined CSIS at the urging of his boss at the Crown corporation. For a spy service that publicly assured Canadians that it operated under the law, recruiting Farrell was an act of hypocrisy. He worked for the intelligence service until 1999. Throughout his eventful years with CSIS, he applied the tough and lasting lessons he learned in his youth. The only difference was that now Farrell was a government-paid thief.

He was assigned to work on some of the service's most sensitive and dangerous cases, including running the day-to-day operations of CSIS's top-secret mail intercept program in southern Ontario. He was good at getting things done quickly and without attracting unsettling attention—vital qualities for any intelligence officer. His ability to succeed when other CSIS officers failed, sometimes miserably and embarrassingly, also made him valuable to his bosses.

Farrell was welcomed into the very heart of CSIS's Special Operational Services (SOS). SOS is where the small, often unrealistic hope of almost every officer to play a part in the heart-thumping world of a John le

Carré novel is fulfilled. The elite corps is where the men and women of CSIS really do get to play at being spies. It's where the action is. For almost six years, beginning in 1994, Farrell worked with the unit in the largest, most target-rich region of the country: Toronto. Farrell became a close confidant of, and took his orders from, some of the service's most senior officers in Toronto, including Don Lunau and Ray Murphy, the veteran intelligence officers who ran SOS in the city.

Farrell had no trouble finding his place in SOS. His guile, charm, strength, cunning and insatiable thirst for a good payday were a perfectly calibrated mix of traits that assured his success with Canada's spy service. Farrell and CSIS were a perfect fit.

CSIS may want to distance itself from Farrell or to dismiss him as a minor figure who is now exaggerating the role he played for Canada's secret service. But Farrell was neither a source nor an informant; he was a determined foot soldier working in the agency's trenches, his membership in SOS known only to the other members of the unit and to senior intelligence officers in Toronto and Ottawa, including Keith McDonald, who is the national head of SOS, Ward Elcock and his former right-hand man, Tom Bradley.

CSIS knows that Farrell was a tireless member of its secret fraternity. It knows that Farrell has a prodigious memory, which is backed up by detailed notes, documents and other vital mementoes that he tucked away during his years with CSIS. It knows that Farrell is an extraordinarily bright man, who earned graduate degrees in criminology and education while working for the agency; it entrusted him to do its dirty work because the service believed that he would never utter a word publicly about his clandestine career. It was mistaken.

In over 150 hours of interviews conducted for this book, Farrell rarely speculated. He scrupulously described only what he knew, warned me when his memory wasn't clear and told me when he didn't know the answers to my questions. He made available meticulously catalogued documents that support his account of his time with Canada Post and CSIS. He travelled with me in search of the people and places that are central to his story. He gave me a tour of

Toronto that would be the envy of anyone interested in the world of espionage.

We visited the twelve safe houses that he rented for CSIS in and around Toronto under a variety of names and that were (in some cases that still are) used by the service to spy on suspected terrorists, intelligence targets and diplomatic missions. We also retraced the steps of two Russian spies who had assumed the identities of two dead Canadian infants and carefully built "legends" in Canada before being kicked out of the country in 1996. The undercover operation—code-named Operation Stanley Cup—ranks as one of the most famous capers in CSIS's short history, and Farrell was in the thick of it, keeping a close watch on the pair for the service for more than two years.

What prompted Farrell to speak out? At first, it was his sense of betrayal. In exchange for his loyalty and devotion, he says his bosses pledged that he would be rewarded with a permanent spot on the SOS unit as a full-fledged intelligence officer. He kept his side of the bargain, even working nights and weekends to secure a requisite university degree and complete recommended training courses. But he found himself pushed to the sidelines and then cut loose. "I did what I was ordered to do by this country's spy service without question or hesitation, and then they abandoned me," Farrell says.

But a sense of betrayal, however raw, is not enough to cause a person to take the profound risks Farrell is taking by exposing some of CSIS's most intimate secrets. In the end, Farrell decided that the public has a right to know the truth about an intelligence service that is charged with one of the most important responsibilities of any government: the protection of its citizens. And the events of September 11 confirmed his resolve to tell the truth, if only to appease his conscience. There may be those who suggest that the criminal acts Farrell was ordered to commit by high-ranking government officials, although troubling, are tolerable, or even justified, in the so-called war against terror. But if the government and its agents are permitted to unilaterally subvert the rule of law without fear of consequence or censure, the repercussions on our democratic system will be incalculable.

Farrell's tenure with CSIS shatters the illusion that it abandoned the criminal conduct that triggered the demise of the RCMP Security Service. His story is also an indictment of the leadership of CSIS and its political masters, who repeatedly assure Canadians that the civilian spy agency is built on a foundation of integrity, professionalism and profound respect for the rights and liberties of every Canadian.

Farrell knows, for example, how incompetent CSIS officers compromised some of the service's most sensitive cases, even its supposed triumphs. He knows of abuses of the public purse by senior intelligence officers, who put up their university-age children in apartments in Ottawa and Toronto that were paid for by the service as observation posts for top-secret, covert operations. He knows about the long bouts of on-the-job drinking by intelligence officers, which is tolerated by the service. He knows the identity of the highly placed CSIS officer who asked him to "obtain" a copy of an RCMP entry examination for new recruits to ensure that his daughter won a place in Canada's federal police force. He knows the identity of the senior CSIS officer who ordered him to steal a Crown key from a postal station in Toronto. (A Crown key is a special key issued to letter carriers that allows them to freely enter apartment buildings and office complexes.) The key was put to use by a string of CSIS officers.

He knows the identity of the senior CSIS officer who ordered him to intercept the mail of hundreds of Canadians without the necessary judicial warrants. He knows the identity of the senior intelligence officer who ordered him to steal the notebooks of another CSIS operative who threatened to blow the whistle on wrongdoing by the intelligence service. He knows how CSIS privatized the administration of its mail intercept program, essentially handing it to a former RCMP officer and Canada Post executive who ran the operation out of his home in a bedroom community of Ottawa.

And Farrell knows much more.

Ward Elcock and company cannot dismiss Farrell as an aberration, as a momentary lapse of judgment by CSIS or as the unfortunate residue of the service's "growing pains." The spy service's attraction to, and courtship of, Farrell was a natural consequence of a belief among senior intelligence officials that they are above the law and beyond real accountability.

While Farrell's story raises disturbing questions about the rectitude of Canada's intelligence service and its leadership, it is also an indictment of the watchdog agencies that repeatedly assure Canadians that they hold CSIS to account. In particular, it lays bare the naïveté and ineptness of SIRC and its leaders, who still cling to the belief that since its tiny cadre of investigators enjoy access to the service's files, they know precisely what's going on at CSIS. Like so much of the ambiguous world of espionage, SIRC's assurances are a mirage.

Farrell's tale of incompetence, corruption and law-breaking inside CSIS is an antidote to the chorus of voices who, in the raw residue of the atrocities of September 11, demanded that the spy service and the police be armed with even more resources to wage the war on terrorism. The fact was that despite all of their chilling powers, technical wizardry and multi-billion-dollar budgets, the alphabet soup of intelligence services in Canada, the United States, Britain and Europe had failed to prevent the catastrophe.

September 11 represented a calamitous intelligence failure. The terrorist attacks took years to plan, involved scores of co-conspirators on at least three continents and required a lethal mixture of logistics and fanaticism. Asked by U.S. Senator Richard Shelby to explain what went wrong, CIA Director George Tenet insisted that America's $30-billion intelligence infrastructure hadn't failed: "When people use the word 'failure,' failure means no focus, no attention, no discipline— and those were not present in what either we or the FBI did here and around the world." Shortly after he made these exculpatory remarks, ample evidence emerged that both the FBI and the CIA *had* failed to act on intelligence that may have averted the September 11 attacks.

Meanwhile, CSIS, the RCMP and Solicitor General Lawrence MacAulay, the minister to whom both agencies report, expressed relief that there appeared to be no Canadian connection to the events. Terrorists were able to strike on U.S. soil with precision and without warning, and stewards of the West's vast intelligence community have emerged unscathed.

In fact, the irony is that September 11 has been a boon for intelligence services, including CSIS. Intelligence budgets mushroomed in the aftermath of the terrorist attacks. Ottawa poured $334 million of new money (over the next five years) into CSIS and law enforcement coffers and swiftly passed its so-called anti-terrorist legislation, Bill C-36, which armed the police with new powers to arrest, detain and question suspected terrorists. For the first time in Canada, the police can make "preventive arrests" simply on the suspicion that someone is about to carry out a terrorist attack. Suspects can be detained and forced to testify before a judge at a secret "investigative hearing" even if they haven't been charged. The police are now able to detain terrorism suspects for up to seventy-two hours without laying charges and can arrest anyone they believe may have information relevant to their investigations. It has become much easier for police to obtain wiretap warrants. The police will certainly have to rely on CSIS's help to identify such targets and suspects. But Farrell's story provokes one unavoidable question: is the service up to the job?

In its zeal to rearm CSIS in the long shadow of September 11, Jean Chrétien's Liberal government repeated its own mantra: Canadians shouldn't worry that its civilian spy service or the police would abuse the potent powers they enjoy. That assurance was echoed by Maurice Archdeacon, CSIS's inspector general, who confidently reported in early 2002 that the spy service conducted its operations in compliance with the law and "in an effective and professional manner." Archdeacon did express some concern that the "rights and liberties of Canadians" might be at risk since CSIS emerged from September 11 more robust than ever. Farrell's career with the service makes crystal clear that, for years, CSIS has not only squandered resources but routinely broken the law, treating the rights and liberties of Canadians as no more than a nuisance.

In the months leading up to September 11, it was already clear that CSIS was in serious trouble. I wrote a string of front-page exposés revealing the depth and breadth of the crisis: that documents and computer diskettes containing top-secret information had fallen into the hands of drug addicts and passersby; that possible double agents lurked in CSIS's midst; that over one hundred current and former agents formed a company to sue the service for back pay and benefits; that a high-ranking intelligence officer illegally obtained confidential information about a CSIS employee; that a senior CSIS officer wilfully destroyed possible evidence related to the service's probe into the June 23, 1985, bombing of Air-India Flight 182, in which 329 people died; that a morale-sapping witch hunt had been conducted to root out agents leaking information to the press; that rank-and-file agents had accused senior officers of nepotism and favouritism in promotions; that the service's former chief psychologist had accused senior officers of pressuring him to release confidential medical information about troublesome employees; and that a thirty-five-year-veteran intelligence officer, Michel Simard, publicly called CSIS a "rat hole."[3]

Details also emerged about an intelligence debacle that placed the lives of many people in jeopardy—a lapse infinitely more serious than absent-minded spies. The service was apparently comatose at the switch while Ahmed Ressam, a thirty-three-year-old Algerian in Montreal, plotted to carry out the lethal orders of Osama bin Laden. The well-trained terrorist planned to slip into the United States from Canada and detonate a homemade bomb at the crowded Los Angeles International Airport as the final moments of the millennium ticked away.

It wasn't CSIS, but a U.S. Customs agent who stopped Ressam as he attempted to cross into Washington from British Columbia on December 14, 1999, in a rental car. Ressam's arrest, intelligence experts agree, was a stroke of luck in which CSIS played no role, despite the fact that the terrorist had been living in Canada since 1994, when he

---

[3] In May 2002, a federal tribunal ordered CSIS to repay Simard's lost wages after the service suspended him without pay for making his unflattering remark. In its ruling, the Public Service Staff Relations Board found that CSIS had acted too harshly when it suspended Simard and barred him from attending a ceremony honouring federal public servants who had completed 35 years of service.

arrived carrying a forged French passport. He then easily obtained a genuine Canadian passport under an assumed name. With his new passport in hand, Ressam was able to flit back and forth to Europe and Afghanistan at will without attracting too much attention from CSIS.

The stories I was writing attracted the wrath of Elcock and Bradley. Both men penned angry letters to my editors about the reportage. In late 1999, CSIS stopped answering my questions. My offence: while researching stories, I called CSIS officers at home to ask them questions after being ordered not to by the service's public affairs officials. Elcock and Bradley became so exasperated by the exposés that their chief spokesman once suggested that I and the *Globe and Mail* were pursuing a "vendetta" against the service.

Their reaction is instructive. It is rooted, I believe, in a siege mentality that increasingly defines CSIS and fuels its sometimes hysterical reaction to criticism and dissent. Public exposure of the service's soiled laundry—and there is much of it—is not tolerated by senior CSIS brass. They spare no expense to flush out officers who leak unflattering stories about the service to the press and carry out witch hunts that have wounded morale among rank-and-file officers—and done worse. In the early 1990s, Pierre Leduc, a veteran intelligence officer in Montreal, was accused of meeting with a French-language television reporter to pass on classified information. Leduc's pleas of innocence were rebuffed and he was suspended. CSIS only acknowledged its error when Leduc produced unassailable evidence showing that he was enjoying a round of golf on the day that CSIS insisted he was meeting with the reporter. But Leduc's belated exoneration came at a stiff price. He now suffers from a chronic and potentially life-threatening intestinal disorder triggered, in large part, by the service's now recanted accusation. CSIS never apologized.

Not content with silencing its own, CSIS has also attempted to silence journalists, trying hard to discredit legitimate reporting that raises serious and necessary questions about its management and direction. Its efforts are brazen. At the Canadian Association for Security and Intelligence Studies' annual conference in Ottawa in late 2000—which brought together intelligence officers, scholars and journalists from across the globe—Phil Gibson, a former reporter turned CSIS spokesman, encouraged attendees rankled by my reportage to write my editors and vent their displeasure. His unusual plea was greeted with enthusiastic applause and hoots from the assembled spooks and their academic allies.

There was one notable voice of dissent. Reg Whitaker, an authority on security and intelligence issues at Toronto's York University, blasted Gibson's entreaty as "appalling." When the *Globe* wrote CSIS to complain about the propriety of a civil servant attempting to engineer letter-writing campaigns, Bradley's response was curious. He claimed that Gibson's remarks were protected by Canada's Charter of Rights and Freedoms. "In summary," Bradley wrote, "no discipline, no apology, and no assurances will be forthcoming from this end."

The contempt of senior CSIS officials isn't reserved for inquisitive reporters. Members of Parliament who have, in the past, asked perfectly reasonable questions about the service's expenditures and conduct have been dismissed with curt, often perfunctory responses. Elcock has displayed a penchant for invoking that amorphous term, "national security," to refuse to answer their questions. At a particularly testy parliamentary hearing on May 26, 1999, Elcock had this telling exchange with Progressive Conservative MP Peter MacKay about who decides what national security means when it comes to answering questions by elected officials:

> *MacKay*: So you simply make a judgment call on whether it's
> a threat to national security to disclose the information.
> *Elcock*: Well, at the end of the day, Mr. Chairman, as the custodian of the information, if you will, I'm not sure who else
> would make the decision about whether national security is
> relevant or not.

There you have it: Elcock believes that he is the sole "custodian of the information." The keeper of the secrets is an unelected career civil servant and he alone decides what you can or cannot know about CSIS.

There has also been friction between Elcock and SIRC. Several of the watchdog agency's chairs have publicly expressed their frustration with his disdain for the review body. Speaking in 1999 at a conference organized by SIRC, Elcock embarrassed his hosts when he told the audience that the only good thing he could recall the watchdog agency having done for CSIS was to remind the intelligence service to construct new headquarters. For Ron Atkey, who had been SIRC's first chair, Elcock's pithy remark was not surprising; he found it perfectly in keeping with Elcock's view of the watchdog as a minor, almost irrelevant irritant. Atkey offered up this trenchant rebuke of the CSIS director: "Mr. Elcock appears to have shown precious little regard for the review process established by law, or for any kind of political scrutiny for that matter." Paule Gauthier, SIRC's chair and former president of the Canadian Bar Association, uses more restrained language to describe her prickly dealings with Elcock, suggesting that the busy CSIS director has his off-days. But she, too, has occasionally crossed swords with the self-described custodian of Canada's secrets.

Elcock's dealings with David Peel, a former CSIS inspector general, are perhaps the best example of the spymaster's scorn for agencies that keep watch over Canada's spy service. Peel's job was simple: ensure that CSIS abided by the law. His and Elcock's working relationship was so strained that the two barely spoke to one another during Peel's four-year tenure, beginning in 1996. Elcock was annoyed that Peel, a distinguished and respected career diplomat, had the temerity to insist that the inspector general be privy to information that he believed fell firmly within his mandate. Elcock refused Peel access to the information; the inspector general made his case to then solicitor general Herb Gray and prevailed.

Afterwards, Elcock refused to speak to Peel, leaving that chore to his second-in-command, Jim Corcoran. "I did have a particular problem with Ward Elcock," Peel said in a lengthy interview at his home in Rockcliffe Park, an exclusive Ottawa neighbourhood. "He didn't like it when it came down on my side, and we never really got along [after that]. He then stopped seeing me directly." Peel concluded that Elcock and other senior administrators resisted any meaningful oversight. "There is this sense that they [CSIS] can get away with things . . .

they were not open in the way they should be to scrutiny by somebody who should have been their friend," he said. "I felt that the inspector general should be someone who co-operated with the service and with whom the service co-operated; that it was in the best interest of both the service and the minister to have us working together rather than at daggers drawn."

Peel also insisted that Elcock often left the solicitor general in the dark about what the service was up to despite written instructions that the CSIS director had to keep the minister responsible for the service abreast of its clandestine work. "Part of my problem with him was that I didn't think that he was keeping the minister well enough informed about issues and problems and what the service was doing where the minister had, in general terms, given directives that he wanted to be kept informed about such things," Peel said. Elcock has publicly complained that CSIS is burdened with too many prying eyes, who consume too much of the service's resources and time. At the May 1999 parliamentary hearing, Elcock described SIRC's annual audit of CSIS as "onerous." His derision for scrutiny has been countenanced by a succession of solicitor generals who have effectively abdicated political responsibility for the actions of CSIS. They have preferred, instead, to place their blind faith and trust in Ward Elcock. Peel suggested that senior CSIS officers have successfully skirted responsibility for the failures of the intelligence service for years. "It's possible to evade personal responsibility when things go wrong," the former inspector general said. "I don't believe the service is as accountable as it should be."

Why has this happened? Part of the reason may be the stature of CSIS's political boss. The solicitor general is generally considered to hold a junior place at the cabinet table. Lacking any real weight, the job has attracted few politicians (perhaps with the exception of James Kelleher and to a lesser extent Herb Gray) with the intellectual vigour and determination to challenge the formidable bureaucracy that runs Canada's intelligence service. These junior ministers are often more inclined to take an interest in the workings and machinations of the RCMP, due to its much larger public profile. Although CSIS enjoys immense intrusive powers, for most Canadians the service has little, if any, connection to their everyday lives. In the myopic world of politics, since CSIS isn't on the public's radar screen, it's best to leave well enough alone. Like many of his predecessors, Lawrence MacAulay is a devotee of the "hear no evil, see no evil, speak no evil" school of CSIS oversight. His favourite tactic is to repeat, under questioning in or outside the House of Commons, that he can't get involved in the day-to-day operations of CSIS.

Our government routinely treats intelligence matters as though they are inconsequential or even silly. What secrets could Canada possibly have to protect? With his now familiar shrug, Prime Minister Jean Chrétien once told a gaggle of reporters that he couldn't understand why so much fuss was being made about CSIS's disconcerting habit of losing highly sensitive information, since most of Canada's secrets eventually leak out anyway. Chuckles all around. Chrétien's jocularity sends an unspoken but clear message to the public, the solicitor general, SIRC, the inspector general and journalists: spies, CSIS, secrets—it's all just fodder for a laugh. (When Chrétien was attorney general in 1982, he decided against prosecuting the Mounties for illegal mail-opening operations.)

On September 11 Chrétien and the country got a rude awakening. But after publicly assuring Canadians that Ottawa would join in the war on terrorism, shower CSIS and the police with more resources and powers, and appoint former foreign minister John Manley as the country's new security czar, the prime minister appears to have slipped back into a comfortable somnolence.

Chrétien's lack of interest in Canada's continuing role in the spy wars is, I believe, welcomed by the men and women who run CSIS. It signals to them that they enjoy free rein. Comfortably ensconced in their sixth-floor offices, CSIS's executive branch behave as though they are unimpeachable, safe from meaningful accountability, discipline or reform. This complacency has bred a culture of impunity at CSIS, founded on what is widely referred to at the spy service as the "Ways and Means Act": if you have a way to get things done, the means—legal or not—are justified.

As a dedicated operative in CSIS's covert war against terrorists and spies, John Farrell was a true believer in the "Ways and Means Act." He is also the first CSIS operative to openly discuss, in detail, his highly classified work for the service. Whether he is condemned or applauded for breaking his silence, Farrell is offering up his story so that Canadians can gain a clearer understanding of what actually takes place in the name of national security in the heart of Canada's spy service.

He knows the risks he is taking by stepping forward and peeling away the layers of deceit, folly and law-breaking which he witnessed and took part in at CSIS. The custodians of Canada's secrets have much to answer for.

1

JEKYLL AND HYDE

There are prisons that look more inviting than the housing project John Farrell once called home. And life in Parma Court, just off busy Victoria Park Avenue in east-end Toronto, can sometimes be as tough as any jail. In this crowded, garbage-strewn corner of the sprawling city, fear and intimidation often rule.

Built in the 1960s to offer shelter to poor families, the government-owned housing complex looks its age. Broken windows are boarded up with scraps of plywood, old newspapers or Canadian flags. Laundry hangs over balconies looking out onto large patches of grass that are slowly turning to dust. A small clan of neighbourhood toughs, milling about in a tiny courtyard, eye an interloper with suspicion. The scene inside the project's graffiti-laced walls is no more appealing. The scent of marijuana drifts aimlessly. The blare of televisions and heart-thumping music fills the halls. Angry voices and barking dogs occasionally pierce the electronic din.

As a young boy living here in the 1970s, Farrell would peer out of a window at 45 Wakunda Place and watch as men wearing ski masks to shield their identities did a brisk business selling drugs on the street. Parma Court's illicit pharmacy was always open, catering to Toronto's junkies. He saw quarrels erupt when drug deals went sour. Quick, bloody knife fights played themselves out below his private perch and sometimes gunshots echoed through the complex, followed by the ear-splitting wail of police sirens. "It was like the Wild West in Parma Court most nights. I grew up surrounded by drugs and crime," he says. "I knew, even as a seven-year-old, what was going down. I was born into that world."

When the mood strikes, Farrell still returns to his old home in Parma Court. On a recent visit, he came across the cobblestones he once laid in a small garden in front of his parents' home, a reminder of a not-so-distant past. He picked up one of the stones and dusted it off gently with his hands. More than once, he has knocked on the door of the home now occupied by strangers. But when someone answers, he never steps inside.

It was in this small, dull, impoverished world that Farrell's large family dealt with the vagaries of life. It was here, too, that Farrell honed many of the skills that would later serve him well in his secret work for Canada Post and CSIS.

John Joseph Farrell was a Remembrance Day child, born on November 11, 1967, at Toronto's drab East General Hospital. John's arrival—he is the thirteenth child in the family of Mary and Joseph Farrell—was celebrated with the excitement and wonder that welcomed each of his siblings. John followed nine girls, three boys and several miscarriages. For his parents, Catholics of Irish descent, children were the unconditional blessings in their harsh lives, who also gave them hope.

John's parents left Newfoundland in 1946 looking for a new and perhaps more promising life in Canada. Mary, a beautiful woman with a luminous smile and green eyes, travelled to Montreal in the vain hope of becoming a nurse. Joseph, who had served with the British navy during the war, joined his wife in Montreal after slipping into Canada illegally by boat. A strong man with a rugged, chiselled face, Joseph had a fondness for drink, fuelled in part by the toll the war had taken on his mind and body. An injured back became, in time, a patchwork of long, ugly scars, the unsightly residue of several operations. Constant pain often left him bedridden.

By the 1960s, the Farrells had moved on to Toronto in a fruitless search for work. The family was shoehorned into a four-bedroom, semi-detached house in Parma Court, where the government-subsidized rent was $180 a month. Fifteen people shared one bathroom, and makeshift beds filled the small home, leaving little room for privacy. Money was always tight. Joseph collected a $900-a-month disability pension from Veterans Affairs, and often that was all the family had to get by on.

The constant burden of an empty bank account followed the Farrells like a long shadow in the late-day sun. John experienced the soul-jarring humiliations that often accompany deprivation and want, the frayed hand-me-down clothes bought from a nearby Goodwill store. The weekly pilgrimage to Our Lady of Fatima church for a box of food and the occasional toy. The disapproving stares and whispered taunts of neighbours. Even in Parma Court, a family of thirteen children stood out.

Poverty bred a simmering anger that vented itself in ugly fights at O'Connor Public School, where the Farrell children were enrolled. John fought every day, in the classroom and during recess. He took on all comers of all weights, heights and grades. He was often badly beaten but he knew the lasting consequences of turning the other cheek: "You had to stick up for yourself, because if you didn't, you were walked on, you were rejected as weak."

At home, sharp bursts of frustration, shouts and recriminations were the norm, along with fisticuffs among the children over food and powdered milk. John often hid in the bedroom he shared with his older brothers, shielding his ears from the taunts his sisters rained down on their "lazy" father, who spent much of his time in bed popping pain medication.

Joseph Farrell was arrested several times for stealing meat to feed his family. Some of John's brothers and sisters began a slow, life-consuming descent into the fringes of crime and drugs. One brother stole cars to subsidize an expensive drug habit and also set fires and vandalized factories. When John was nine, that same brother robbed a Canadian Tire store and was jailed.

In time, his oldest sister, Carmelita, succumbed to the emotional and psychiatric wounds that marked her brief life. It was John who discovered her body in a blood-filled bathtub, surrounded by the cats she loved. Josephine, the next in line, ended her life, too, a victim of a deadly cocktail of drugs and alcohol. One day John found one of his brothers cowering naked in the darkness of a basement corner as he descended from a drug high.

Even as a young boy, John feared that he, too, would fall prey to the debilitating psychiatric maladies and dependencies that claimed several of his brothers and sisters. Public school didn't offer him a safe haven. Despite his quick intelligence, he was lumped into a special education class with many of his troubled friends. Just another poor, stupid kid from Parma Court, the silent message read. John used any ruse to avoid school, often missing as many as forty days a year. The police and school officials regularly visited his home, and he was often suspended for truancy and rowdiness. As he headed toward puberty, his fighting grew more intense, his mood more despondent.

His mother shipped him off to a Catholic school some distance from his home and, more importantly, from his wild group of friends, hoping that Our Lady of Fatima, with its daily dose of religious instruction, would guide her son to calmer waters. She was disappointed. His report cards routinely featured a long, dismal list of Ds and Fs.

He moved on to Heron Valley Junior Public School, and his truancy worsened. Then his father's health deteriorated and John went into a free fall. He failed grade eight miserably and began to dabble in petty crime, stealing groceries and pizzas with a pack of friends. Farrell was arrested after he stole a baseball glove from a department store. He was charged with shoplifting and received a suspended sentence and a temporary reprieve. A teacher told Mary that her son would soon be in jail or hanging on to the end of a garbage truck for the rest of his life. He offered no protest, accepting his fate, as if it had been ordained by forces beyond his control.

As a last resort, Mary had her youngest son repeat grade eight at

Our Lady of Fatima. And there, her hope and perseverance were rewarded. Farrell began to climb out of the morass that had marked his young life. But it wasn't a priest, nun, God or a decent education that pulled him out of the abyss—it was basketball.

Blessed with a deft and prodigious scoring touch, John finally discovered something he excelled at. He began to attend school regularly. In the hallways he was praised as the budding star of the basketball team. His coaches and teammates counted on him to shoulder the lion's share of responsibility for the team's success, and he rose to the challenge. His mood lifted and his grades began to improve. In his mother's eyes, it was a miracle, a gift from a patient and loving God. John wouldn't go that far. Behind the pictures of the young basketball star with the broad shoulders and gleaming smile lay another truth. John trusted no one and was convinced that his good fortune could not last.

John squeaked by academically to graduate from elementary school in 1983. At his mother's urging, he enrolled at Neil McNeil, an all-boys Catholic secondary school, where his brother Greg was a student. Founded in 1958 by the Spiritan Fathers, the school's Christian teachings seemed like redemption to John's mother, and the school motto, *Fidelitas in Arduis* (strength in hard times), seemed to perfectly describe his youth. School uniforms were mandatory and discipline and decorum were insisted upon.

The prospect of donning a burgundy blazer, striped tie and grey slacks each day wasn't particularly appealing to John, and the school's strict adherence to religious instruction and rules were anathema to a young man with a rebellious streak. One attraction tipped the scales. A Catholic all-girls school was a stone's throw away from Neil McNeil. Girls soon became Farrell's constant companions, attracted by his good looks, wit and thirst for adventure.

Wearing Greg's hand-me-down tie and blazer and a new pair of grey slacks, John stepped into Neil McNeil's church-like halls, lined with pictures of stern-looking priests and bishops. Other pictures portrayed the less formal, exuberant side of a school that barely contained the kinetic energy of a thousand young men. John Candy, the cherubic, forever-smiling comedian and Hollywood star, regularly visited his alma mater to sing its praises and seemed the perfect embodiment of a McNeil boy: polite, proper and courteous yet mischievous and rebellious.

John grew to like the school. He joined the bantam basketball team and emerged as a team leader. His marks were mediocre, but he applied himself, working hard to earn the respect of his demanding teachers. Traditionally, teachers at Neil McNeil have tried to impart a sense of a broader social conscience to boys usually preoccupied with sports, girls and cars. Charity, responsibility and righting social injustices are key ingredients of the school's curriculum.

Every Friday morning throughout grade nine, for instance, John put on his uniform and tie, plunked a homemade placard on his shoulders and headed off to nearby Kingston Road to protest the work of Litton Industries, an electronics firm in suburban Toronto involved in building the U.S. cruise missile system. He joined twenty to thirty schoolmates in rain, shine and snow to parade in silent protest against the firm's involvement in the weapons industry. At first he felt awkward pacing up and down the sidewalk with his placard—"Let the weapons fall from your hands," it read—as motorists and pedestrians streamed by. Truth be told, he knew little about the concepts of mutual assured destruction, weapons proliferation or disarmament. But he had a sense that what he was doing was right and important. He was stubborn, too, persevering when others lost interest.

His first and abiding love at his new school was basketball. His school yearbooks are filled with glowing descriptions of his prowess on the court—most valuable player, winner of scoring titles and championship trophies—and feature pictures of him suspended in mid-air as a basketball arcs off his fingertips toward the hoop.

Basketball is the game of the poor. A ball, a hoop and limitless energy are all it demands. At Parma Court, he played late into the night on a cement court dubbed the Black Square, next to the community centre, where the hoops were fashioned out of chain links. To others John looked like he was playing alone, but in his imagination he was almost always in the company of his basketball god, Larry Bird, the lumbering Boston Celtics star.

In the midst of his early high school days, one memory sticks out. On an early October morning when the fading sun hinted at the inevitable arrival of winter, Mary Farrell told her son that she wanted to go shopping. His reward, if he joined her, would be a half day off from school. John instantly agreed. They hopped onto the subway and headed toward Toronto's bustling Yonge Street. There, Mary took her son into a sporting goods store and bought him an expensive pair of sneakers and a new basketball. That day, there would be no hand-me-downs for John Farrell. "It was unbelievable," he says. "The shoes cost her $130. They were made in France. They were called Top Ten. Mom paid cash. I nearly cried right there in the store."

As school finally became a haven for John, the family's money woes intervened again. Joseph was thieving to make ends meet. Mary was working as a cleaner and taking in laundry from neighbours to cobble together enough cash to keep the household afloat. While the province picked up the tab for grades nine and ten at the Catholic school, tuition fees kicked in from grade eleven on, at $1,200 a year. It was doubtful that the Farrell family could afford to keep sending their two boys to Neil McNeil.

Bitter and resentful, John exploded on the court during a basketball game against rivals from W. A. Porter Collegiate. Driving to the net for an easy layup, he was pushed from behind and crashed into a wall. No foul was called. Incensed, Farrell confronted the referee. "He told me to shut up and called me a baby. I just went over and punched him in the head. He fell down and he started pulling my hair," Farrell says. "His nose was right there and I took a bite. I spit out whatever I bit into. The blood was pouring out all over the place, onto the court. It was a mess."

A melee involving both squads and many fans rumbled on and on until the police arrived. No charges were laid, but John was suspended from the basketball team for a year. The rewards of his labour had evaporated in an instant.

The two very different sides of John's temperament were laid bare on the court: the dedicated, industrious athlete who was beginning to excel at school and find his place among friends and teachers, collided with the seething, impatient young man from Parma Court who used his fists to settle scores. He was destined, it seemed, to have one foot firmly fixed in heaven and another in hell.

The worry over being able to afford tuition gnawed at him. He got into more bruising fights and his grades suffered. His brother Art, now a maintenance worker with the city, offered to chip in, but it wasn't enough. Then the school came to his rescue, giving Farrell a bursary to cover the school fees.

It was a turning point for John, who hated depending on others. He had worked hard at school and on the court yet still had to rely on charity. John decided then that if he couldn't make money he would just take it.

Mac Bromley, the director of the O'Connor Community Centre, was drawn to John Farrell. The kid was charismatic, Bromley thought, and had a beguiling way with children. In the summer of 1985, he gave Farrell a job minding the gymnasium after school and on the weekends while local kids played basketball. He was paid $6.80 an hour.

But Bromley's faith in Farrell was betrayed. With his buddies from Parma Court, Farrell broke into the community centre by smashing a door window. The gang stole anything they could get their hands on: money, peanut butter, milk, eggs. One of them sprayed the gymnasium with boxes of cornflakes and Rice Krispies. Bags of milk were ripped open and dishes were smashed. The food had been meant for children in a government-subsidized daycare centre next to the gym, but Farrell and his gang felt no regret. When the two-hour rampage was over, the centre was a shambles.

At sixteen, Farrell was the gang's natural leader. All eight members hailed from Parma Court. They weren't just neighbourhood toughs but determined hoods, who planned and committed a string of break and enters, assaults and robberies. They also trafficked in soft drugs. Farrell was an excellent thief—patient, adroit and imaginative, rarely betraying any nervousness. Once, using Halloween masks as disguises, the gang robbed a pizza delivery man in the lobby of an apartment building. When he resisted, Farrell took the lobby's heavy metallic telephone cord and wrapped it tightly around the man's neck. The man handed the pizza over, pleading with Farrell not to kill him.

Wielding crowbars, the gang smashed into a convenience store to steal lottery tickets and cigarettes. They ripped off a restaurant's roof hatch and slipped in to help themselves to case after case of beer. They lured yuppies and students who ventured to Parma Court looking for drugs into a vacant hallway where they would rob them of their cash and jewellery.

At school, Farrell was still a star, but on the street he was a crook. His teachers knew little about his double life, and his priest, Monsignor Colin Campbell of Our Lady of Fatima church, was also unaware of Farrell's Jekyll and Hyde nature. Every Sunday, Farrell would attend mass, often alone, and he would light two candles: one for his father and another for family peace. Though he regularly took confession with Father Campbell, he was circumspect about his damning and growing list of sins. At the insistence of a social worker, John and his family also tried secular counselling, but the sessions at East General Hospital degenerated into ugly, uncontrollable brawls where fists and insults were hurled. Yet John still lit his candles at church, the elusive goal of family harmony constant in his prayers.

He should have lit a candle for himself. The police were anxious to nab anyone responsible for the community centre break-in and suspected that Farrell was at the heart of it. At one in the morning on September 24, 1985, two police officers arrived at Farrell's door. The pounding and shouts woke his mother. Startled, she reached for her housecoat and slippers. Farrell bounded out of bed like a frightened rabbit. Farrell and his weary mother confronted the police. "I punched one cop in the face and the fight was on. I wasn't going anywhere with them," he says. The police had to call in reinforcements to subdue him.

Three other members of the gang were also rounded up in Parma Court, and all of them were hauled down to 54 Division, where they spent a few hours in jail. It was Farrell's first time in custody. He says he wasn't afraid—the jailing was a right of passage, like his baptism or losing his virginity. He and his gang were charged with a string of offences, including break and enter, robbery and theft. No one ratted anyone out. Farrell spent an uncomfortable night at the Regent Park jail, where he was fingerprinted and photographed. The following morning he was released on his own recognizance and walked home barefoot. His only regret was upsetting his mother. He knew that he would have to ask for her forgiveness and tell Father Campbell everything at confession. It was going to be a long one.

Farrell was charged as an adult offender and faced serious jail time. His brother Art was able to arrange for legal aid to pay Peter Scully, a top-flight criminal lawyer in Toronto, to defend him. Well-dressed and with Scully by his side, Farrell appeared before Justice Ted Wren at court. At Scully's urging, he told Justice Wren that he was remorseful and agreed to pay restitution. Father Campbell came to testify on John's behalf, as did Father Joe Kelly, Farrell's high school chaplain, who implored the judge to be lenient. A criminal conviction, he said, would prevent the gifted athlete and regular church-goer from winning a prized scholarship to attend school in the United States. Even Mac Bromley, the community centre's supervisor, had a kind word for Farrell, testifying that he was a diligent worker.

The charm offensive worked. Justice Wren dropped some of the more serious charges and allowed Farrell to plead out on others. In a pre-sentence report to the court, Farrell's newly appointed probation officer, Barbara Mancini, provided glowing testimonials from family, friends and teachers. She made particular note that Farrell was a "talented" young man who didn't use drugs and hoped to continue working with children in the future. On October 31, 1985, Farrell was given a conditional discharge and eighteen months' probation. He was ordered to meet Mancini twice a month and perform 180 hours of community service. While he had earned himself a criminal record, he was able to avoid the fate of his partners in crime, who were all sentenced to jail time.

Mancini was convinced that Farrell was back on the straight and narrow. "It seems the criminal justice system," she wrote in her pre-sentence report, "has had a positive effect on the subject and may act as a deterrent to further criminal involvement." Farrell's probation officer couldn't have known that Farrell would soon break the law again, only when he did, it would be on behalf of the Government of Canada.

His summer crime wave and subsequent arrest made Farrell think hard about the troubling direction his life was taking. When he returned to Neil McNeil to begin grade twelve, he threw himself more than ever into his first real passion: basketball. He spent hours practising, trying to perfect his game in the hopes that a U.S. college would offer him a lucrative scholarship. He thought basketball was his ticket out of Parma Court.

Farrell persuaded the long-suffering Mac Bromley to install a large night light on the Black Square court to allow him to play basketball after dark. But his neighbours began complaining that they could hear the loud thumping of Farrell's basketball until early in the morning. A timing device was installed that automatically switched off the lights at eleven each night, signalling the end of Farrell's basketball day.

Farrell was also filled with a renewed determination to do well in school. His teachers knew that Farrell had an innate intelligence but was impatient in class. His mind wandered aimlessly or rocketed from one idea to the next. Just as he had on the basketball court, he learned to slow the pace and concentrate. His improvement was reflected in his report cards. In grade eleven, Farrell's average had been sixty-one. His teachers remarked that although Farrell was "trying hard," he was "making little progress." A year later, his average was just over eighty and teachers were praising him as a "conscientious student" with a "clear commitment to learning" who was a "pleasure to teach." Farrell's school records show him missing just three days during grade twelve. It all led to the previously unthinkable: Farrell was being considered for the principal's honour roll.

While Farrell regained his footing at school, his home life was still abysmal. His mother was tired of the shouting and the nightly, violent arguments with Joseph and wanted to save herself and the three children who were still attending school—John, Greg and a daughter,

Mary Lou. Her solution was simple: move out. It was a huge risk for a single mother earning a meagre wage cleaning the homes and washing the laundry of strangers. Farrell fretted about moving away from the friends he had grown up with and could count on, but he decided to follow his mother into a two-bedroom apartment on Pharmacy Avenue. His brother Art was so angered by the separation that he trashed the home in Parma Court.

Now John had to help pay for groceries and rent. He scoured the want ads for a part-time job, circling an ad posted by the Hudson's Bay Company. The department store was looking for a loss prevention officer, or more plainly, someone who could catch thieves. The one-time gang leader with a criminal record called and arranged for an interview and was hired on the spot.

Who better to catch a thief than a thief? The job was a perfect match for Farrell. He and his gang had roamed many stores in Toronto looking for an opportunity to steal clothes, food, CDs, even appliances. They mastered their techniques under the ever watchful eyes of suspicious security guards. They worked alone, in pairs or in large groups. They were rarely caught.

Farrell knew the look of a thief. He could spot the nervous amateurs as well as the wily professionals. He knew their peculiar mannerisms, ticks, walks, telling glances, even the kind of clothes they wore to conceal their loot. He aced the short training course. His abilities weren't borne out of a how-to manual but from stealing from the very stores he was now assigned to protect. Farrell had switched sides, but it didn't offend his sensibilities. "I had the edge because I knew how to play the game," he says. "Now I was the warden. My thinking was, if you can't beat them, join them."

His inaugural assignment was the bustling Bay store at the corner of Yonge and Steeles in north Toronto. The store was a magnet for thieves. Secret surveillance booths and two-way mirrors were strategically placed to allow Farrell to spy on would-be robbers. He sat for hours, patiently waiting to nab his prize. He enjoyed the hunt, just as he had once enjoyed being among the hunted. His old friends laughed when they discovered his new job but were wise enough not to test him. Farrell was now a loyal soldier in the never-ending war on crime. He was eighteen and getting paid thirteen dollars an hour.

Farrell was transferred to the much busier Eglinton Square store near Parma Court. On his first day, the manager asked him to spend time flipping through a thick album that included Polaroid snapshots and grainy images, plucked from the surveillance cameras, of people arrested or suspected of stealing goods from the store. Many members of his immediate family and his friends were looking back at him from the pages of the album. Snapshots of his father, two brothers, a sister and a brother-in-law were all there along with members of the Parma Court gang. Farrell promised to be on guard against any of the culprits if they happened to visit the store again. The manager was pleased. Farrell was soon escorting a steady stream of thieves into his little office. Young and old asked for forgiveness and understanding. He was an ambivalent security guard who often gave the detainees a second chance, just as Justice Wren had given him.

Sometimes he was in a less charitable mood. Once, Farrell spotted four young men, including one sporting a hospital bracelet, sauntering into the store. Sure enough, the fellow with the bracelet slipped a pair of blue jeans under his jacket with a magician's dexterity, and then casually made his way out the door with his friends in tow. Farrell sprinted from his secret booth and nabbed him. As he was shepherding the shoplifter to his office, the man tried to bolt. Farrell pounced on him and flipped his jacket over his head. The struggle meandered wildly through the store as startled patrons looked on. The would-be robber pulled out a knife. Farrell grabbed his arm and veered intentionally into a large pane of glass. Some customers thought an action movie was being filmed and broke into applause as the pair exploded through the slim windowpane. Farrell escaped being cut as shards of glass rained down on him. The man was later charged by police.

Farrell believed that if a person's eyes darted about, something untoward was afoot. One evening Farrell noticed two men wandering through the store, their eyes dancing furtively, one of them carrying a large bag. He followed the pair into the store's washrooms, convinced they were thieves. He kicked open the locked stall door to find one man clad in dark leathers and chains with a face mask pulled over his head. The other was sitting on the toilet seat, waiting, presumably, to engage in one of life's pleasures.

Farrell was refining his already keen ability to observe and antici-pate the actions of others. He was a paid voyeur, discerning the capri-ciousness of human nature. These skills would certainly come in handy once Farrell left the world of petty thieves and entered the world of spies.

In his final year at Neil McNeil, basketball scouts from the United States and Canada were making the pilgrimage to the school to watch John play. In a game against long-time rivals from Cardinal Newman, Farrell scored sixty-two points—the feat still stands as the record for a high school basketball game in Toronto. He was routinely profiled in local newspapers and on television, awkward and uncomfortable in the spotlight. Other recognition started to flow his way. For being selected tournament MVP in the 1986 Father Troy Classic, Farrell won a custom-made ten-carat gold ring that featured a Tasmanian devil with a halo over its head. He was chosen the senior basketball team's MVP and finally won a coveted place on the school's academic honour roll.

Farrell had severed his links with Parma Court and his former criminal comrades. He didn't want to jeopardize his chances of win-ning a scholarship to attend university, where he wanted to pursue a degree in criminology. "I wanted a better understanding of where I grew up and how my family and Parma Court had shaped my mind," he says.

But the rigours of practising, the games and the travel to tourna-ments began to take a physical, emotional and financial toll. Farrell was worried that he couldn't sustain the unrelenting pace of school, work and sports. His mother was relying on him to help pay the bills. Basketball, the love of his life, might have to go—and halfway through the school year it did. He walked away from the game, even though his decision also endangered his chances at a basketball scholarship. It was an extraordinary sacrifice for a young man to make. Luckily, Farrell's athletic prowess still attracted the attention of a number of American colleges and universities. He chose, instead, to attend Simon

Fraser University (SFU) in B.C., the only university in the country to offer athletic scholarships at the time. It wasn't a difficult choice. His criminal record still haunted him and would complicate any move he made beyond Canada's border. With his mother's blessing, Farrell signed on with the university.

His future now lay in a school half a continent away. Before he departed, Father Campbell offered him some advice. "John, know always the great gifts that God has given you and use them to the full. God loves you," he wrote. The Hudson's Bay Company was sad to see him go. Farrell's supervisor at the Eglinton Square store wrote him a glowing letter of recommendation: "John Joseph Farrell is an intelligent, thoughtful, hard-working individual who has made an outstanding contribution to the Investigation Department," he wrote. He went on to praise Farrell "as a man of character" who possessed "great leadership qualities."

Farrell took the bus on a three-day cross-country trek out west. If he wanted to escape his past, SFU was an ideal hiding place. Sitting atop Burnaby Mountain with its broad, majestic vistas and surrounded by lush forests overlooking Burrard Inlet, the university's sprawling campus was idyllic. Still, Farrell's arrival on campus was an emotionally jarring experience. He was many miles from his family, friends and the church. He thrust himself into his studies, which included psychology and criminology. And Farrell was playing basketball again.

The practices were long, gruelling affairs. Exhausted, players would routinely throw up as they were pushed to their physical and psychological limits. The military-like regime slowly but inevitably began to drain Farrell of his enthusiasm for the game. The official team photo featured a beaming Farrell in the back row, dwarfed by the team's towering centres. But the picture was deceiving. By October 1987, Farrell was beginning to hate the game he had loved.

Then calamity struck. Farrell had just finished another draining practice when a coach asked him to join a men's pickup game. Fatigued, he lost his concentration for an instant as he tried to intercept a pass. The ball slammed into the pinky finger on his left hand, shattering it. A bone protruded from skin that had suddenly been ripped away. Farrell was in so much pain that he slipped in and out of consciousness on the long, winding drive to the local hospital's emergency room.

His coaches, including Canadian Olympian Jay Triano, wanted him to stay on. But Farrell decided that his basketball career at SFU was over: after only two months in British Columbia, he quit the team and the school. He prepared to head back to his mother's welcoming arms and tiny apartment in Toronto. Facing an uncertain future, he looked for work to help pay the bills. He sent his résumé to administrators at the Rotherglen Youth Detention Centre in Pickering, Ontario. (The centre later moved to Whitby.) Despite his record, Farrell was hired as a correctional worker dealing with young offenders.

Just before Christmas, he packed up his meagre belongings, bid a quick goodbye to his former teammates and SFU and hopped on a bus back to Toronto to begin work in, of all places, a prison.

Two days after arriving in Toronto, Farrell was making a daily, two-hour commute by bus and train to Rotherglen. Sitting on eleven hectares of land once occupied by a hockey arena, Rotherglen is home to young murderers, rapists and arsonists. The privately-run juvenile detention centre is a dangerous and volatile place where all of its inmates are doing "dead time"; that is, being held in custody before being sentenced by the courts.

Farrell identified with the young men on the other side of the bars. His affinity with the inmates, however, didn't shield him from their taunts, threats and assaults. At various times, he was attacked with a knife and a hockey stick and had a chair thrown at his head. He took it all in stride, but he was careful never to let his guard down. To make extra cash, he often worked double shifts.

Despite the risks, Farrell found the work challenging and rewarding. A patient listener, he spent hours talking to the inmates. He offered advice when it was sought, and in time, he became a confidant. He worried about the inmates' welfare. The centre's administrators were cutting costs by slashing mandatory remedial classes and serving up small portions of stale food. The penny-pinching measures upset

Farrell and he tried to do something about them, repeatedly butting heads with management.

In December 1988, an inmate from Smiths Falls, Ontario, a small town near Ottawa, was due to arrive at the centre. He had been charged with sexually assaulting and murdering an eight-year-old boy, who was discovered under a bridge, naked. The crime was horrific and word quickly spread throughout the centre of the impending arrival. Farrell and another correctional officer did the inmate's intake, conducting a thorough strip search and filling out the necessary paperwork. Farrell wanted to put the new arrival in a special cell, where he could be closely watched, both to shield him from potential retribution and to protect the other inmates. Administrators told him a cell wasn't available, even though Farrell knew it was. He threw his keys at his supervisor and quit days later.

But that wasn't the end of it for Farrell. Whether it was an echo of his practical lessons in social justice at Neil McNeil or his sympathy for the inmates that motivated him, Farrell was determined to expose what he believed was the mistreatment of the young men at the centre. With the help of another Rotherglen correctional worker, Farrell mailed brown envelopes of damning information to a number of newspapers in Toronto. The packages painted an unsettling picture of a high-security, privately-run detention centre that was poorly managed and understaffed, where medication was loosely controlled, where food was substandard, where escapes were common, where vandalism was rampant and where assaults against staff were reaching alarming rates. Taxpayers' money was footing the bills of a centre that was out of control.

Newspapers covered the allegations, and other stories soon surfaced about a former Rotherglen employee who was charged with gross indecency and sexual assault against a female inmate. The swirl of controversy triggered criminal investigations and an internal audit by provincial authorities.[1]

---

[1] The juvenile detention centre was the scene of more trouble in 1992 when ten residents went on a rampage on the eve of a strike by guards.

Farrell took pride in his accomplishment. He recognized that the press was a powerful tool and that whistle-blowers had to tread warily. One moment, reporters were on your side, solicitous, kind and empathetic. Then, when their interest waned or was diverted, they stopped taking your calls and abandoned you to the wolves. While his first brush with the media was an unqualified success, the experience taught him critical and lasting lessons: never risk being discredited by lying, never for a moment believe a reporter is your friend and, perhaps most important, always have the ammunition ready to back up your story. It was while dealing with the media over Rotherglen that Farrell began his fastidious habit of tape-recording conversations and keeping immaculate records of his dealings with his employers. It was a wise move, because he was destined to blow the whistle again.

2

THE PARDON, THE STING AND CANADA POST

The York Detention Centre is a dingy, sullen-looking edifice on George Street in the heart of Toronto. Seaton House, a warehouse for the city's homeless, is next door. Small bands of drifters, who have emerged from the shelter's showers, sit on the front steps or lean against trees, pondering another fruitless day. Down the street are tiny, well-kept row houses, dissident signs of comfort in an otherwise gloomy neighbourhood.

After quitting Rotherglen, Farrell landed a lucrative job at the jail as a provincial correctional officer. Getting an interview had taken weeks of bombarding a female supervisor with telephone calls. He'd had to agree, with some trepidation, to a background check. As expected, the Ontario Provincial Police (OPP) reported back to jail administrators that Farrell had been convicted of theft. His criminal record should have prevented him from working in a jail. It didn't. He persuaded the supervisor that he was a changed man, and was hired in May 1989.

The jail was in upheaval. Weeks earlier, seven boys had escaped after overpowering a female guard. Within hours of fleeing, five of the teenagers were killed in a fiery crash on Highway 401. With the OPP in pursuit, the car the teens had commandeered crashed head-on with a van. Questions were raised about lax security and poor training at the jail, and the quickest solution was to hire more guards.

Despite solemn pledges to improve the training of new guards in the aftermath of the tragic escape, Farrell's preparation for the job was brisk. He was given a few shifts to get a feel for the place, and then he was on his own. The atmosphere was dangerous and intimidating. Fights between inmates and assaults against guards were common, as were homemade weapons. Farrell braced himself. At twenty-one, he was only slightly older than the inmates he was now watching over. When he looked at them, he saw the same anger and frustration that marked much of his own young life. He and the inmates had come from the same place, and only the intervention of others—his mother, the priest, his teachers—had spared him from jail. For the first time in his life Farrell thought he was a lucky man. His fortunes were poised to take another turn.

Early one morning in late May 1989, Farrell accompanied a young crook to the bustling provincial courthouse in a strip mall at Eglinton and Warden in Scarborough. It would be over an hour before his prisoner would be summoned to appear before a judge. To relieve the tedium, Farrell dropped his charge into a holding cell and, on a whim, slipped into Courtroom 407.

An overweight man who looked to be in his mid-fifties, with a goatee, a paunch, a hearing aid and a garish tie, was testifying in a monotone. His name was Frank Pilotte and he was an investigator with Canada Post. Farrell was intrigued. When Pilotte finished his testimony, Farrell approached him to ask about the case. Pilotte tried to brush him off, but Farrell persisted. Pilotte finally told Farrell that he was a postal inspector, testifying in a case against a letter carrier accused of theft.

Postal inspectors are Canada Post's little-known in-house police force. Under the law, they are considered "public officers." That loosely defined term allows them to wield potent powers of arrest and seizure. The work of Canada Post's more than 120 postal inspectors falls under the auspices of the Crown corporation's well-monied and secretive Security and Investigation Services branch (now called Corporate Security). The unit's mandate is to probe any crime committed at the twenty-two postal plants and scores of postal stations across the country, involving the nearly ten billion pieces of domestic and international mail that Canada Post handles every year.

The postal sleuths look into everything from mail fraud, drug trafficking, forgeries, pornography, hate mail, theft by postal employees, welfare scams and black market stamp sales to letter bombs. They can intercept, scan and open mail without the knowledge or consent of the person or organization sending or receiving it if the target mail weighs over thirty-two grams and they can persuade a Canada Post executive that they have reasonable and probable grounds. Postal inspectors can also launch lengthy and expensive undercover investigations, and they routinely take the lead in joint probes with domestic and foreign police forces and other government security agencies. Inspectors drive unmarked cars and carry impressive-looking badges. About the only thing they aren't allowed to do is carry a gun.

Pilotte had the tired, forlorn look of an investigator who had chalked up too many kilometres chasing too many thieves in an endless game of cat and mouse. Farrell, on the other hand, was eager to learn more about the work and pressed for details. Who did he need to contact to see if he could make the grade? A little annoyed, Pilotte told Farrell he should join a police force instead. Farrell was already working double shifts on the weekends at the York Detention Centre, as well as doing part-time duty at the Hudson's Bay store at Eglinton Square, where he worked on undercover operations designed to stem the rising tide of employee theft.

Farrell thanked Pilotte for his time, picked up his prisoner and took him to face the judge, then headed back to the York Detention Centre and started dialling. He called postal stations across the city trying to find out more information about Canada Post's mysterious Security and Investigation Services branch. He struck out. Few people he spoke to were even aware of the branch's existence.

Undeterred, Farrell called Canada Post's human resources department and left several messages, inquiring about possible work as a postal inspector. His persistence paid off. Later that month, Mike Thompson, then Canada Post's divisional manager for Security and Investigation Services for York Region, which includes Toronto, called him back. He asked Farrell to send along a résumé and set up a time when they could meet.

Farrell was uncharacteristically late for the interview and hastily parked his car on the sidewalk right in front of Canada Post's offices at 20 Bay Street in downtown Toronto. As he rode the elevator to the seventh floor, he rehearsed his apology. Thompson's office featured floor-to-ceiling windows, a breathtaking vista of Toronto's waterfront, framed letters of commendation and pictures of him in his days with the Toronto Police Service's Mounted Unit. Thompson was a strapping, good-looking man in his mid-forties with a taste for expensive, well-tailored suits. Farrell thought he looked more like a corporate lawyer than a fourteen-year veteran of the city's police force.

Thompson seemed impressed by his résumé, with its eclectic mix of schooling and practical experience. The pair chatted awhile about the responsibilities and mandate of postal inspectors before Thompson asked Farrell if he had a criminal record. The job, he said, required top-secret security clearance. Farrell answered the question honestly, assuring Thompson he had mended his ways.[1] With that, the twenty-minute interview was over. Farrell was optimistic.

Farrell was called back for a second interview. This time Thompson was joined by Robert Letby, the then manager of security for the Security and Investigation Services and another top Canada Post

---

[1] As evidence of his transformation, Farrell offered up a recommendation of sorts from an unlikely source: the prime minister of Canada. On February 2, 1988, Farrell had received a Certificate of Merit from the government of Canada in "grateful recognition of your contribution to your community." The certificate was signed by the Right Honourable Brian Mulroney. Although the Prime Minister's Office hands out scores of such certificates every year, Thompson was nonetheless impressed.

manager. To prepare for the interview, Farrell had combed through the Criminal Code to study offences related to the mail and had memorized key sections of the Post Office Act, which sets out the powers postal inspectors can exercise under the law.

The officials peppered Farrell with questions. How do you make an arrest? Under what circumstances can you make an arrest? When does a postal inspector have the right to detain a suspect? Under what conditions is the use of force permitted? Had he ever made an arrest? What would he do if he saw a crime being committed on Crown property? Farrell fielded the questions easily.

Letby and Thompson then asked Farrell about his own and his family's many encounters with the law. He acknowledged that he hadn't been a saint and that most of his family had been arrested, charged, convicted and jailed for serious crimes, ranging from theft to drug trafficking. Thompson was sympathetic. He had grown up in a rough neighbourhood himself and understood that Farrell couldn't be held to account for his family's sins. Letby seemed less empathetic. After a ninety-minute interview, Farrell was asked to write a short exam, which he passed easily. But he still wasn't sure whether there would be room at the Crown corporation for someone with a criminal record.

A few days after the interview, Farrell's spirits were buoyed by a letter from Thompson, dated July 26, 1989. Thompson wrote that the Canada Post executives were "very impressed with you and your qualifications." He added that Farrell had been placed on a "very short list" of candidates who would be offered a job if an opening arose. The letter didn't mention Farrell's criminal record.

Two months later, Thompson called Farrell at home in the evening, asking him to come in for another meeting. When they met, Thompson was beaming. He pulled out a one-page contract, offering Farrell the position of "Officer, Postal Inspection, York Region." The starting salary was $33,600. Not bad, Farrell thought, for a twenty-one-year-old with a high school education. He was scheduled to begin work on October 2, 1989. There was one possible problem: "Confirmation of appointment," the contract read, "will be conditional upon receiving security clearance to the level of top-secret." The contract was signed by Thompson and Bob Stiff, a senior executive with the Security and Investigation Services in Ottawa.

Although his job hadn't even begun, Farrell was already making history at the Crown corporation. He was the first non–police officer to be considered for such a job and he was the youngest postal inspector ever appointed to the force. Other veteran members of the unit in Toronto, including Doug Lamb, Jim Troy, Brian Baker, Blaise Dobbin and Louis Ouellet, were either former police officers, ex–military police or internal hires. True to his cocky nature, Farrell wasn't the least bit intimidated by his brethren's credentials.

Farrell represented a much-needed injection of youth and energy into the unit. The pace his elders set wasn't particularly taxing, and he learned later that his hiring was intended to send a message that there were many young bucks out there hankering to replace them.

On October 31, 1989, George Clermont, vice-president of Canada Post, made Farrell's hiring official. In a single-page note, Clermont wrote, "In accordance with the provisions of Section 18 of the Canada Post Corporation Act, I am pleased to appoint, with pleasure, John J. Farrell as a postal inspector." Farrell was given postal inspector badge number 214. He had officially made the transition from crook to federal investigator. The new recruit understood that he owed his allegiance to Mike Thompson, and he was determined not to disappoint his new boss and, in time, to repay his faith in him.

As Farrell settled into his small cubicle on the seventh floor at 20 Bay Street, he sensed the wary and slightly suspicious eyes of his new colleagues upon him. He was given a cursory tour of the Security and Investigation Services offices in Toronto, and his training felt equally brief. There were a few manuals to be read and short courses on interviewing and note-taking to be weathered.

He was also given an eye-opening tour of the powerful databases that the postal inspectors often mined during their investigations. This included the RCMP-controlled Canadian Police Information Centre (CPIC) computer, which stores personal information on millions of Canadians. The computer holds details about individual criminal records, parole and bail conditions, the names of wanted criminals, and motor vehicle and driver registrations.

Before he could officially begin work, Farrell needed to obtain his top-secret security clearance. He filled out a questionnaire, listing his next of kin (which alone required three pages), his home addresses and workplaces over the past ten years and three character references. Gordon Bell, a veteran CSIS officer, was primarily responsible for Farrell's security screening.

A slim man with a stately bearing and a whiff of an English accent, Bell was well-mannered, well-spoken and well-dressed. He was in his late fifties, and had a crop of thick, sandy hair. Bell met Farrell at Canada Post's offices in Toronto in early 1990 and asked if there was a quiet corner where they could talk privately. Farrell ushered Bell into a small room adjacent to his desk. He had braced himself for a grilling, but the intelligence officer was only interested in the answer to one question: Why had Farrell lied about his criminal record on the personal questionnaire?

On the bottom of page two of the five-page declaration, was a simple yes or no question: Have you ever been convicted of a criminal offence for which you have not been granted a pardon? Farrell had placed a check in the "no" box. Farrell explained that since he was given a conditional discharge and he had met all of the conditions, it was his belief that he didn't have a criminal record. The evasion didn't impress Bell, who reminded Farrell that his criminal record needed to be expunged before he could entertain any thought of securing a top-secret security clearance. The only way to do that was for Farrell to apply for a pardon. With that, their meeting was over.

On March 26, 1990, CSIS reported that their CPIC and fingerprint checks on Farrell were "not favourable," but that he had a "favourable" credit history. CSIS also noted that "sources commented favourably on subject's loyalty, reliability and character. A favourable subject interview was also held." That "subject interview" with Bell had lasted all of five minutes. CSIS concluded that Farrell should be granted top-secret security clearance, with one important caveat: he had to win a pardon.

Farrell turned to his boss for help. Thompson had Farrell draft a one-page letter to the National Parole Board requesting that his pardon be expedited, and then Thompson signed the letter. "John's daily activities bring him into frequent contact with classified police and government information," the letter read. "To continue employment with Canada Post Security and Investigation Services, all postal inspectors require TOP SECRET CLEARANCE. The process takes approximately one year to complete and is granted by the Canadian Security Intelligence Service. John is presently at this stage and requires assistance in achieving his pardon as soon as possible."

Thompson's letter soon became moot. Canada Post didn't wait for the National Parole Board to render its decision before granting Farrell top-secret clearance. Farrell gained the prized security designation on April 12, 1990. Early in April, Farrell also received a glowing performance appraisal from Stiff and Thompson. "John has progressed extremely well . . . [he] has achieved significant success in his training and is contributing to the divisional objectives," Thompson wrote.

Six weeks after receiving his top-secret clearance, Farrell was granted his pardon. In a letter from Monique Cronier of the National Parole Board's Clemency and Pardons Division, Farrell was informed that Brian Mulroney's cabinet had granted him his pardon on May 17, 1990. "So, for a month I had my top-secret security clearance while I was still a convicted thief," Farrell says.

No one at CSIS rang any bells, warning the Crown corporation about hiring a young man with a criminal history. Canada's intelligence service didn't seem particularly concerned that a convicted thief would be privy to sensitive personal information about millions of Canadians and would, in fact, be conducting investigations in concert with major Canadian and U.S. law enforcement agencies.

Farrell's criminal record disappeared into history. His rap sheet was sealed, never to be reopened, courtesy of Canada Post and the government of Canada. Farrell could not believe his good fortune. He had joined Canada Post on a whim, in the hopes of making some extra cash while holding down two other jobs. He never imagined that his chance meeting with Pilotte would lead to getting his checkered past erased by the federal cabinet. "Christmas came early for me in 1990," he says.

Thompson's investment in Farrell paid dividends. His first big probe involved a Canada Post supervisor who was suspected of stealing money and expensive jewellery from registered mail. The inspectors originally assigned to the case needed more evidence. Farrell was asked to help out.

Farrell decided to ride shotgun on a garbage truck that picked up the supervisor's trash near the intersection of Main and Danforth in Toronto's east end. Perhaps the supervisor had ditched incriminating receipts for the valuable registered mail along with the eggshells, banana peels and old newspapers. Flashing his smile and his postal inspector ID, Farrell told a bemused garbageman that he planned to steal several trash bags on the street, clad in a pair of overalls and orange safety jacket. At a nearby underground garage, Farrell dumped the bags' contents and began sifting through the soaked, stinking mess. He struck out. Despite at least two other attempts, the garbage yielded no links to the crime. The eight-month probe ended when surveillance cameras caught the supervisor slipping the registered mail into his coat pocket. Still, Thompson loved Farrell's ingenuity. Stealing garbage would become a favourite trick, not only to glean information about crime but, eventually, to gather mounds of intelligence on union leaders.

For all his youth and energy, Farrell soon adopted some of his older confreres' bad habits. Farrell often spied other postal inspectors doing their grocery shopping, playing golf or getting haircuts in the middle of a workday. More than once, he bumped into his colleagues while they were enjoying a leisurely morning or afternoon, sipping coffee at shopping malls that dotted the city. Postal inspectors and Canada Post vehicles were also enlisted to help friends and family move during business hours. Farrell recalled that Thompson once ordered postal inspectors to help his mother-in-law move out of her apartment. A postal truck was used to ferry her furniture and other belongings to her new place. Farrell and his colleagues were determined to squeeze every conceivable dollar out of Canada Post's coffers with as little strain to mind and body as possible.

Thompson began to turn to Farrell whenever he had a thorny assignment. In early 1990, a woman registered the kind of complaint that gave Canada Post's public relations staff nightmares— she said a letter carrier had exposed himself to her while delivering the mail. Thompson wanted Farrell to settle the potentially damaging complaint before anything leaked to the media. Farrell hurried out to the woman's small home in west-end Toronto. She was distraught, still reeling from the incident, and she explained through a stream of tears that the letter carrier had often stopped by her home, wanting to make small talk. That morning, the postal worker had knocked on her door and when she answered, he opened his winter coat to reveal a brightly-coloured matching set of women's underwear.

Farrell spent two hours sipping tea, calming the woman and assuring her that the letter carrier would be dealt with swiftly and harshly. He recorded the conversation. When she recovered, she wrote Canada Post, thanking Farrell for his "kind and considerate manner." The deviant letter carrier was later fired, avoiding messy criminal charges and a possible lawsuit from the woman. Farrell had earned another star.

Though his fortunes were rising, Farrell was still low man on the totem pole. Another more senior postal inspector was hankering to return downtown, so in March 1990 Farrell was shipped out to the South Central postal plant at 969 Eastern Avenue. Thompson told Farrell that the move was a promotion, but Farrell wasn't convinced. The grey, utilitarian plant in Toronto's east end is one of the largest postal facilities in the country. Spread over fifteen acres, with more than a thousand inside workers, the plant handles a torrent of mail twenty-four hours a day, six days a week. Farrell was put in charge of fifteen security officers who roamed the plant. He briefly reported directly to James Bradley, Canada Post's chief of plant protection officers (PPOs) in Toronto. Farrell had been with Canada Post for less than six months. "Two days of training and they walk me around and I was lost," Farrell says.

But he quickly realized that the job wasn't as demanding as he had feared. Within days, he had settled comfortably into his large corner office. "I was a bit like the repairman in the commercial for Maytag," Farrell says. "It was a gravy train. I'd be sitting there with my feet up on the desk." Thompson was right, Farrell concluded; his move to the postal plant was a promotion.

Farrell occasionally made a slow tour of the plant on foot to assert his presence and authority. He attended numbingly long weekly management meetings. More often than not, he wasn't at the plant, sometimes working as little as twenty hours a week, while getting paid for forty. Other times, he invited a few friends over to the plant, ordered takeout and frittered away the hours racing around the plant on battery-powered scooters.

The South Central plant was where Farrell first encountered the wrath of militant postal workers, who viewed any Canada Post manager with suspicion and distrust. He was sneered at, called a "slime-ball" and worse. He arrived at the plant at a time of rising tensions between the Crown corporation and trade unions. Canada Post butted heads with two unions: the Canadian Union of Postal Workers (CUPW), who represented inside workers, and the Letter Carriers Union of Canada. In 1989, the two unions formed one bargaining unit to negotiate with Canada Post. The trade union's strikes routinely cost Canada Post millions of dollars in lost revenue. In time, Farrell would become an elite foot soldier in the seemingly never-ending feud with the postal union.

As a start, however, Thompson wanted to recruit Bill Marshall, a Halton Regional Police constable whom Farrell had befriended while working at a Bay store. With Thompson's consent and Ottawa's approval, Farrell walked into the plant's human resources department, flashed his badge and Marshall was on the payroll, ostensibly working as a mail sorter. But he was really there as an undercover intelligence officer, collecting information about union leaders and petty crime rings that were operating inside the plant. The unions would go ballistic if Marshall was exposed, but it was a risk Thompson was prepared to take. Marshall, however, turned out to be a dud. He lost interest in the covert work and eventually didn't even show up for his shifts at the plant. Farrell gave Marshall the boot.[2]

While Thompson's experiment with Marshall was a failure, it was a harbinger of a more systematic and coordinated effort to spy on union leaders.

While working at the mammoth South Central plant, Farrell stumbled onto word of a scam of equally mammoth proportions, which senior Canada Post officials hid from the public. The Crown corporation was defrauded out of millions of dollars by several large Canadian firms. Companies negotiated a fixed price with Canada Post to deliver a set number of pieces of mail—bills, advertising, promotional material and the like. Tractor-trailers filled with the bulk mail would back up to processing plants across the country and dump their loads directly into the ever-flowing mail stream. The firms, in some cases multinational behemoths, soon realized that Canada Post wasn't counting or even weighing the bulk mail. A light bulb went on in the minds of the sly corporate denizens. If no one was counting or weighing the mail, well, what prevented them from taking a free ride on Canadian taxpayers by topping up the volume Canada Post was delivering on their behalf for a fixed price?

Eventually, a light bulb also went on at Canada Post. The Crown corporation had been duped by seemingly responsible and conscientious corporate citizens who had conspired to defraud taxpayers out of millions of dollars. This is the kind of "victimless" white collar crime that usually goes unnoticed and unpunished by the legal system.

A special team of as many as seven postal inspectors was quietly set up to determine how big a financial hit Canada Post had taken. The hush-hush effort to tally the damage and recover some of the lost millions was given a benign-sounding, bureaucratic title: the Total Cost

---

[2] Marshall didn't go quietly. He called Farrell constantly, haranguing him about money he said Canada Post still owed him. The young police officer called so often that Farrell began recording his plaintive messages. Canada Post never returned the calls.

Revenue Management Program (TCRMP). Farrell got wind of the probe after he spotted several postal inspectors wandering around the postal plant wearing ID marked with a large red dot. They arrived unannounced. The red dot allowed them carte blanche access to the sorting facility.[3]

Despite the veil of silence, word spread throughout the plant about the unit's investigation. But it never reached the public, much to the relief of Canada Post.

Weary of impersonating the Maytag repairman, Farrell thought seriously about quitting. While he relished getting paid well, he was bored. Thompson came to the rescue. He decided to set up a major crimes unit and invited Farrell to join the new team. The cranky Frank Pilotte would take his place at South Central.

Thompson then sent Farrell to Ottawa to attend an investigators' course specially designed for postal inspectors. At least fifteen other postal inspectors from across the country attended the course, which offered new recruits basic training on how to conduct an investigation. There were classes on how to properly write a report and how to gather, analyze and chart intelligence. The Canada Post Act, postal security and laws governing the opening of mail were also reviewed.

To Farrell's surprise, the course was run with boot camp–like efficiency. Students were in class by 9:00 a.m. sharp, or else. Truancy and gum-chewing were not tolerated. Mornings were usually set aside to study the legal aspects of the work, followed by a fifteen-minute break at 10:30 a.m. After lunch, the young postal inspectors received hands-on training in the use of electronic surveillance equipment, interviewing techniques and making an arrest.

One of Farrell's four instructors at the training course was Alan Whitson, a balding, bilingual veteran Mountie and the national director of Canada Post's Security and Investigation Services. At six-foot-four

---

[3] Farrell knew some of the postal inspectors assigned to the secretive unit. David "Pickles" Martin and Marisa Napoleoni were among the unit's lead investigators. But both were very tight-lipped about the investigation.

and tipping 280 pounds, Whitson ambled about like a polar bear as he lectured students on interpreting body language during interviews.[4] Farrell pestered Whitson with question after question. "I irritated him, and I'm sure he considered me a huge pain in the ass," Farrell says. Years later, their paths would cross again—unhappily.

Fresh from his special training, Farrell joined two other postal inspectors, Blaise Dobbin and Tom Sheluck, in the newly formed major crimes unit. Thompson's brainchild was to create a small elite unit to tackle the most difficult and sensitive cases confronting Security and Investigation Services in Toronto. Farrell was the youngest member of the team. Dobbin had joined the branch just before Farrell was hired. Sheluck was the veteran and not shy about trumpeting his investigative talents.

In early July 1990, Thompson waved Farrell into his corner office and asked him to close the door behind him. Looking uncharacteristically serious, Thompson told Farrell he had a case that needed to be handled with discretion and diplomacy. Thompson handed him a manila envelope. Inside were the names of six senior Canada Post executives from headquarters in Ottawa, as well as their employee numbers, positions, years of service and copies of all their expense accounts. All six were making in excess of $100,000 a year. And all six were suspected, Thompson explained, of committing fraud by fudging their expenses.

---

[4] The new postal inspectors were videotaped by their instructors while they conducted mock interviews during role-playing sessions to assess their investigative skills. One of the videotapes featured Farrell. The poorly shot video shows Farrell interviewing another Security and Investigation Services member, who portrayed a postal worker who claimed to have been injured on the job. Farrell also featured prominently in a twenty-minute Canada Post training video prepared for "ad mail" workers. The delivery of junk mail—promotional flyers for local and national businesses—is a lucrative business for the Crown corporation. Much of the training video is devoted to warning new recruits of the stiff penalties they would face if postal inspectors discovered they dumped, rather than delivered, the ad mail.

Farrell went to work, putting the lessons he had learned in training to good use. He began by sorting the information that had arrived in a jumbled mess. He then drew up charts on each of the six executives, listing the date, location, amount and purpose of each expense. He also included a list of questions that popped into his mind as he examined the expense accounts. All of the expenses had been incurred in Toronto. Curiously, at least two of the executives shared the same corporate credit card. Farrell visited restaurants, bars and travel agencies in the city where the mandarins had racked up their bills. It was Gumshoe 101 stuff, but Farrell didn't mind at all.

His first stop was a small greasy spoon on Danforth Avenue, in Toronto's east end, where one of the executives had claimed a ninety-dollar steak dinner with dessert. There was one small problem, however: steak wasn't on the diner's menu. Farrell politely asked to speak to the manager. Flashing his Canada Post ID, Farrell asked to see the original receipt. The proprietor fidgeted nervously, worried that he was being audited by Revenue Canada. Farrell didn't disabuse him of that notion. The man disappeared into an anteroom for a few minutes and emerged waving the original receipt. As Farrell had suspected, the executive had added a zero to a nine-dollar tab.

The petty deceit was repeated over and over again. A $19 meal became a $190 feast. A $5 cab ride became a $50 fare. Farrell soon discovered that the executives had also pocketed thousands of dollars in bogus travel expenses. The ruse was simple. The executives visited travel agencies to purchase airline tickets. They held on to the credit card receipts. A few hours later, they cancelled the trips, getting a refund from the travel agency, but still claiming the expense. The executives were double-dipping.

Farrell methodically collected and charted the evidence: the fraud, he discovered, had gone on for years. He drafted a three-page report outlining the extent and nature of the scam and delivered it to Thompson. The investigation had taken him only eight days to complete. Farrell recommended that a variety of charges, including fraud and breach of trust, be laid against the executives. But Ottawa headquarters vehemently opposed the idea. The Canada Post brass weren't inclined to charge their own. They only wanted to amass enough evidence to force the executives out without attracting any bothersome public attention. It was becoming a familiar tune, and the hypocrisy infuriated Farrell. If a union member had committed such a fraud, retribution would have been swift and harsh and public. Farrell's boss shared his sense of frustration, but Thompson was powerless to change Ottawa's mind. The executives were booted from the Crown corporation, but on their way out the door, they were handed healthy severance packages to ease the sudden blow.

A few months after Canada Post conveniently chose not to charge the six executives who fleeced taxpayers out of hundreds of thousands of dollars, Thompson handed Farrell a file on a postal worker believed to be involved in his own brand of fraud. Thompson gave Farrell his latest orders in a two-page, typed report detailing accusations made by Canada Post's labour relations branch against the postal worker. Farrell understood that whenever Security and Investigation Services received a file from the labour relations branch, it meant that either a postal worker was up to no good or Canada Post needed to "dig up the dirt" on someone they had fixed in their crosshairs.

The corporation had an added incentive to dig up dirt on this particular letter carrier. He was suing his employer for $1 million, claiming that he had been badly hurt in an on-the-job accident three years earlier. He was already collecting a healthy stipend, courtesy of the corporation's disability insurance. The labour relations branch was convinced that the letter carrier was faking the injury, and they wanted Security and Investigation Services to prove it.

Farrell began by reviewing the letter carrier's existing file. The postal worker lived with his wife and young daughter in a small, two-bedroom apartment above the Kiss 'N' Tell lingerie and erotic tool shop at 2770 Danforth Avenue. Farrell went on a reconnaissance mission in his Pontiac Fiero, complete with its new government mobile phone. (Ottawa had granted Farrell a licence that allowed him to use restricted government radio frequencies to communicate with other postal inspectors.) For two days, he patiently camped near the Noah's Ark pub on the rundown stretch of the Danforth, spending hours in his car directly across from the lingerie shop, to watch, note and photograph the letter carrier's comings and goings. To relieve the boredom, Farrell invited friends to keep him company during the stakeouts.

Two days stretched into three weeks. Wherever the letter carrier went, Farrell was sure to follow. "If he took the subway, I took the subway. If he went shopping, I went shopping. If he went to the beer store, I went to the beer store," Farrell says. He avoided being spotted by the postal worker by using the skills he had honed as a thief-catcher at the Bay. Each day he wore different clothes, hats and glasses. He even altered his gait.

The gaunt twenty-six-year-old letter carrier walked with a cane and always carried himself as if burdened by the unforgiving body of a much older man. Farrell followed him to Postal Station F at 55 Charles Street East in downtown Toronto, where he regularly picked up his disability cheque. He tailed him to the bank and tapped a source inside the financial institution to obtain the letter carrier's banking records and conduct a thorough credit check. Farrell was now behaving more like a private investigator than a postal inspector.

Once he discovered the postal station that the letter carrier frequented, Farrell arranged a sort of early warning system with the branch's supervisor. Given their powers, postal inspectors were as much feared as respected by station managers. Farrell had no trouble persuading the supervisor to page him whenever his quarry walked into the station. Farrell didn't want to wait for the letter carrier to slip up; that could take months, even years. And Thompson was pressuring him to get results. If he wanted to nail the letter carrier, he had to get close to him, become his friend and confidant. So, he took the offensive, hoping to win the postal worker's trust.

It was snowing heavily the day Farrell got the call he had been anxiously waiting for. He raced to the station, parked, and began wiping snow off his car. The letter carrier emerged with his cheque, shielding himself against the worsening winter weather, and walked right into Farrell's web.

"It's bad out today, eh," Farrell said, smiling.

"Jesus, it is," the letter carrier replied.

They chatted a little longer before Farrell, feeling slightly uncomfortable, popped the question. "Look, do you need a lift? I'm headed up to Victoria Park and Danforth." Farrell, of course, knew that the letter carrier lived just blocks away from that intersection. His target jumped in. Farrell let him do most of the talking during the long ride across the city. People, he knew, often betrayed intimate details of their lives to strangers. The letter carrier was no exception: he rambled on about how fortunate he was to be on disability leave and how he loathed working at the post office. Farrell noticed the letter carrier's grease-stained hands. He saw an opening.

"Are you a mechanic?" he asked. "I have a car that needs some work."

The postal worker's eyes lit up. "I do a lot of work on cars," he replied. "I'm really handy."

"Really? I have a van that's acting up. I'll give you a couple hundred bucks if you can fix it, because it's hard to find someone you can trust these days."

"Sure thing," the letter carrier said, eager to help out his newfound friend.

The letter carrier invited Farrell into his sparsely furnished apartment, where he was greeted coolly by the man's wife and daughter. The awkward moment when an unexpected stranger steps into your home evaporated over a few cold beers. The two men exchanged phone numbers. Farrell gave the letter carrier his untraceable pager number.

To cement his friendship with the postal worker, Farrell often showed up at his door with a case of beer.[5] The letter carrier confided in Farrell, telling him that his lawsuit against Canada Post would yield his family a tidy windfall and pay for the new cottage that he and his wife had just bought.

While the postal worker cradled his drink, engrossed in a television

---

[5] Thompson gave him cash for the beer, but Farrell had to sign a receipt.

sitcom, Farrell excused himself to visit the washroom. On the way, he slipped into the postal worker's bedroom, where he rifled through cupboards and drawers looking for any potentially useful information. He scooped up telephone and credit card bills, as well as bank account records. The trap was set.

With the sting in sight, Thompson called in extra troops: Accu-Fax Investigations Inc., a controversial group of private investigators that has built a name for itself by offering clients what it calls "labour-dispute services." Accu-Fax has strenuously denied that the term is a euphemism for a blunt and sometimes brutal business—strike-busting—although the firm has readily acknowledged that, as part of its large menu of services, it arranges for busloads of scabs to replace striking workers and collects evidence for injunctions to neutralize picket lines.

Accu-Fax is popular with government departments and private firms looking to tame restive unions. Its small army of private investigators—over three hundred—are either former police officers, military personnel, prison guards or recent graduates of college law-enforcement programs. They constitute, in effect, a private police force that can gather intelligence on suspected criminal activity perpetrated by employees, including postal workers. Accu-Fax has come to the aid of over 350 Crown corporations and private firms who, it proudly boasts, are "our best reference." But finding those references can be difficult. While many of its clients admire Accu-Fax's expertise, they are not keen to express that admiration publicly. Canada Post is equally reluctant to discuss its controversial relations with the firm, fearing, no doubt, the angry reaction of its unions.

Canada Post tasted some of the union's wrath in 1991, when the head of the Canadian Union of Postal Workers, Jean-Claude Parrot, accused the Crown corporation of hiring detectives to bug a union strategy meeting at an Ottawa hotel. The union's own counter-intelligence discovered several suspicious-looking people leaving the hotel, carrying what appeared to be recording devices to a rental car. The union subsequently traced the vehicle to Accu-Fax. At the time, the company bristled at the suggestion that it was spying on the union or its members. It admitted that it had been enlisted by Canada Post, along with several other firms, to corral as many as three thousand scabs and to ferry senior postal managers by helicopter to avoid seething picketers. The firm's job was to help keep the mail moving in the Toronto hub, and that often meant putting up its people in hotels in Ottawa and Toronto during the strike. Beyond the enticing rental car clue, Parrot's suspicions remained precisely that, unfounded allegations, and the fracas eventually died down.

Farrell had met Accu-Fax's founder and president, Darrell Parsons, along with his younger brother Mike, at Canada Post's offices at 20 Bay Street and at a number of parties thrown by the postal inspectors. He also knew that Accu-Fax often supplied Canada Post with sophisticated surveillance equipment, including a van disguised as a Bell Canada truck. Despite his youth and relative inexperience, Farrell was the lead investigator on the undercover operation and he called all the shots.

His plan was simple: call the letter carrier and describe a phantom problem with his van, agree on a price and meet to fix the problem in the alley behind the target's second-floor apartment. Accu-Fax would set up surveillance equipment inside the fake Bell Canada truck, and film the disabled worker bending to lift heavy car parts.

Farrell and Accu-Fax left nothing to chance. They made a dry run the night before the rendezvous with the letter carrier, pinpointing where the surveillance truck needed to be parked to get the best vantage point to videotape the sting. Armed with high-powered cameras, two other postal inspectors would take scores of incriminating pictures of the letter carrier at work. Farrell pre-selected and weighed the car parts that the letter carrier would be asked to pick up and move. He had obtained the letter carrier's confidential medical records from Canada Post's human resources department, detailing the nature and extent of the postal worker's alleged back injuries. The medical notes were important because they allowed Farrell to ask the letter carrier to move in ways that would expose what he assumed was the fraud. Several weeks after Farrell's "chance" meeting with the letter carrier, the sting was set to go.

It was about one-thirty in the afternoon on a clear, crisp day. There would be no rain or snow to dampen their plans or obscure their lenses. Mike Parsons and another Accu-Fax investigator manned the camcorder in the Bell Canada van, while the postal inspectors sat in a car nearby with cameras in hand. Farrell parked the other van behind the lingerie store. He raced up the stairs to the letter carrier's apartment door and called out to his friend.

Out in the alley, Farrell told the letter carrier that he was having trouble with his alternator, a hefty piece of machinery that recharges a car battery. The letter carrier got to work. He lifted the hood with ease, bent over and dislodged the alternator. He also replaced the van's tires and changed its brake pads. For ninety minutes he worked hard to impress Farrell. The work required the kind of dexterity, agility and strength he claimed he no longer possessed. And it was all captured on film.

When the letter carrier finished with the van, Farrell slowly and deliberately paid out the five hundred dollars in plain view of the hidden cameras. Thompson had given Farrell the money to pay the letter carrier for the repairs. The serial numbers of all the bills were recorded and photocopied so they could be entered, if necessary, as evidence in court. Canada Post spared no expense on the undercover probe; Farrell estimated that the price tag for the sting topped fifty thousand dollars. But the videotape was all the evidence Canada Post needed to settle its potentially costly dispute with the letter carrier. It trotted out the tape at the letter carrier's Labour Relations Board hearing. During the hearing, lawyers for the Crown corporation admitted that Accu-Fax had worked on the probe. The letter carrier's lawyer also wanted to know who the young man was handing his client the money for the repairs in the videotape. Canada Post testified that he was "an unknown party."

The identity of the other man in the videotape was never revealed. The letter carrier and his lawsuit disappeared.

Farrell emerged from the caper as one of Canada Post's secret weapons in its internecine war against the union. He had proven himself to be a trusted, imaginative and determined agent in that battle. The time was ripe for him to hunt much larger game. And Farrell would not disappoint.

3

SPYING ON THE UNION

With every successful case, Farrell was scoring valuable points with his boss, Mike Thompson. When the postal inspectors assembled for their weekly meeting at 20 Bay Street, Thompson often walked over to Farrell, patted him on the back and announced that the kid was a prized member of the "at-a-boy!" club.

Farrell's reward: he briefly got to pick up Canada Post VIPs at the airport. To help spot the arriving "dignitaries," the Crown corporation supplied drivers with a photo album filled with eight-by-ten glossies of key executives, complete with their names and titles. Farrell replaced an absent-minded postal inspector who forgot to park in Canada Post's reserved spot at Toronto's Pearson International Airport. The car was towed away, leaving the bewildered postal inspector to ponder its fate and Canada Post's president, Don Landers, angrily cooling his heels.

Once, Farrell was sent to pick up Canada Post's vice-president of finance, George Clermont, from the airport in a luxury Buick. (It was Clermont who, a few months earlier, had signed off on Farrell's appointment as a postal inspector despite his criminal record.) Clermont was a powerful man in Ottawa with allies in Brian Mulroney's Progressive Conservative government. On the long ride downtown, Clermont and Farrell exchanged small talk. The number-two man at Canada Post asked Farrell how the Toronto office was faring. Farrell told Clermont that he had visited a postal plant that very morning and union members were talking openly about going on strike.[1] Clermont's face turned so white that Farrell thought he had been instantly embalmed. Clermont got on his cellphone, speaking rapid-fire French. By the time Farrell had parked and made his way back to the office, he had lost his membership in the "at-a-boy!" club.

Thompson and Letby laid into him. A burst of profanity and threats blew out of their mouths like a hurricane. Because of his indiscreet comment to this bigwig, they had all of Ottawa breathing down their necks. Letby had a warning for Farrell. "Next time you pick someone up and they ask you any questions, you answer using one word sentences, like 'Fine,' 'Good,' 'Okay.' Understood?"

But Farrell's stay in Thompson's doghouse was short-lived. In September 1990, a new position within the Security and Investigation Services was created for Farrell by Thompson: divisional intelligence officer for Canada Post's operations in York Region, from Toronto north to Newmarket, east to Oshawa and west to Hamilton. It was a big responsibility for a young man. Taken together, the postal stations and plants in the region represented the Crown corporation's largest, busiest and most critical hub for mail traffic in the country. And, perhaps most important, it was the home of militant union leaders and a fertile breeding ground for a new crop of activists who needed to be watched.

The timing of Farrell's appointment was significant. The beleaguered Crown corporation was facing a protracted, costly strike that might pose a threat to its financial viability and undermine the public's shaky belief in the reliability of the postal service. The already white-hot

---

[1] Farrell was right about the strike. Postal workers walked off the job in the summer of 1991. When it was over, the strike had cost the Crown corporation $100 million in lost revenue.

friction between management and the union only worsened in the months ahead. The following year, three top union leaders, Andre Kolompar, James Lawrence and Ron Pollard, were jailed after thumbing their noses at a judge's order banning picketing at three Toronto postal stations. Kolompar was the president of CUPW's seven-thousand-member strong Toronto local. Lawrence was its vice-president. The charges were triggered, not surprisingly, by a complaint from Canada Post.

Relations between Canada Post and its unions have been marked for generations by distrust, bitterness, anger, frustration, threats and suspicion. The victims in this postal cold war—which has outlasted the real one—are Canadians, who have endured numerous strikes and disruptions to the mail service. Canada Post has repeatedly and vociferously denied that it has ever spied on union members or executives. Accusations that the Crown corporation has been involved either directly or indirectly in snooping on its employees have been made but never proven.

As the new divisional intelligence officer, Farrell was at the very heart of Canada Post's espionage operations against union leaders, which were approved by his senior managers. He was not a lone ranger who embarked on these operations without the consent and encouragement of his superiors. He was entrusted with the work because his superiors believed that he would remain forever silent about the nature and extent of the spying. They were wrong. Farrell is the first member of the secretive branch to break the silence about how Canada Post has methodically gone about spying on its union.

Thompson told Farrell about his promotion in the boardroom at 20 Bay Street. Many of the other postal inspectors in Toronto were present for his christening. Farrell was embarrassed by the praise that Thompson lavished on him. His colleagues fell silent. The meeting made clear that as divisional intelligence officer, Farrell's abundant talents were now going to be put to use almost exclusively against Canada Post's arch-enemy—that is, its own employees and their union.

For Farrell, his new "intelligence" job was just that—another job. Thompson could have just as easily asked him to snoop on his fellow postal inspectors, and he would have done it for him. Beyond the occasional unfriendly encounter with rank-and-file members during his tenure at South Central, Farrell felt no animosity toward the union leadership.

Farrell's mission was simple: delve into the past, present and future of troublesome union leaders. He was free to use his fertile imagination and every tactic in his ever-expanding repertoire to collect intelligence on top union officials in Toronto. He was also responsible for identifying up-and-comers in union ranks who could, one day, emerge as the next generation of leaders. At the meeting to unveil Farrell's new job, the postal inspectors were instructed to immediately forward whatever information they had gathered on the union to the new divisional intelligence officer. "Thompson told everyone at the meeting that whatever union activity they were working on, whatever files they had, any information they had on names, targets, et cetera, they were to put that in a report and start feeding that information to me," Farrell says.

Some files on prominent union heads already existed. Farrell began drawing up new dossiers on others, including Kolompar and Lawrence. When he was through, Farrell had opened up fifteen to twenty files on key union members working in York Region—dossiers that included intimate details about their private lives, families, friends and associates.

"We collected lots of things," Farrell says. "Where they went to school. How many kids they had. The size of their house. Anything and everything you could use to build a complete file. So, when you had the dossier in front of you, you could say, 'Okay, this person, he went to this school. He got married on this date. He got divorced on this date. He's remarried now. These are his bank accounts. He owns this house. This is how much he has left on his mortgage. These are the phone calls he has made. These are his main sources that he is calling everyday. This is where he goes on his trips. These are his known associates . . .'"

The scope of Farrell's intelligence-gathering on the union membership was broad. He ran criminal background checks to determine if any of them had spent time in jail. Records of union executives' traffic or parking tickets also made their way into the dossiers. Through their contacts in various financial institutions, Farrell and other postal inspectors obtained banking records for most of the union leaders in Toronto. Credit checks were also done, showing the amounts each "target" owed to credit card companies as well as the size of any outstanding house and car loans. Motor vehicle registration and driver's licence checks were made. The make and model of cars the union leaders and their families owned were noted in the dossiers. Telephone records for key union members were also obtained by Canada Post—details of domestic and long-distance calls, as well as cellular phone bills. One surprising exception: Farrell said that Canada Post did not authorize or even contemplate tapping the phone lines of union leaders, either at their executive offices or at home.

An especially keen eye was trained on union leaders from the South Central postal plant, since it was a hotbed of union activity. Farrell knew the facility well from his days there as the senior postal inspector on site, and he says a few union leaders working at the plant were sometimes tailed as they made their way to their favourite haunts for a beer or two after work or an executive meeting. The hefty tabs they rang up while entertaining friends or visitors were of particular interest to Farrell's bosses. "We [the postal inspectors] would always joke," Farrell says, "if only the members actually knew how much their leaders were spending of their union dues to party with their friends."

Photographs were also taken, Farrell says, of some family members of union leaders and their homes—but not pictures of their children. However, the addresses and names of the schools the children attended were included in the intelligence files. As a postal inspector, Farrell had access to the personnel files of union leaders, which were stored in human resources offices at a variety of postal plants. "I would retrieve a lot of personnel files. Some of them were quite thick. I would just flip through the stuff, pulling out anything that might be of use," he says.

Provincial and federal courthouses, Farrell says, were scoured for documents that might yield intimate details about the personal lives of union leaders. Divorce proceedings were of particular interest.

Accusations of infidelity, physical abuse and financial problems were laid bare in explicit detail in the documents. Marriage licences were also collected for the dossiers.

Union leaders at Canada Post's Gateway postal facility in Mississauga were also prime targets of the Crown corporation's sanctioned spying. Spread over thirty acres, the plant is one of the largest in the country. An avalanche of domestic and international mail moves through the plant every day. At Gateway, Farrell says, he received help in his intelligence-gathering from Accu-Fax.

Farrell learned through Thompson and Robert Letby that Accu-Fax was running a major undercover operation at the plant. Unbeknownst to the union and most postal inspectors, Accu-Fax had placed at least three agents inside the plant to act as Canada Post's eyes and ears. That operation was already well underway, Farrell says, when he assumed his responsibilities as divisional intelligence officer. The agents were investigating rampant theft at the plant. Jack Riponi, a postal inspector for Toronto Region, wrote a brief outlining the extent of the theft, which usually involved big-ticket items, such as Rolex watches, that were being shipped through the mail.

But the private investigators were also busy, Farrell says, funnelling information to him through Thompson, about brewing union activity and its militant leadership. Farrell says that he was not privy to the identities of all of the Accu-Fax agents. However, he soon learned (again through Thompson) that Canada Post had also planted a former OPP officer, Mark Gemus, as an undercover operative at the plant. The ex-cop was hired on as a postal inspector and put to work gathering intelligence at the plant, posing as an inside worker who paid his dues and could find out what the union was up to. Canada Post moved him out of the Gateway plant to perform other duties. Accu-Fax's undercover agents remained in place, posing as drivers or mail clerks. (Gemus eventually left Canada Post and now works for CSIS.)

As a strike loomed, the tension between Canada Post managers and their employees worsened. In a show of force, most of the Toronto postal inspectors were ordered to march en masse into the Gateway

plant wearing matching windbreakers with Postal Inspector emblazoned on the backs in large, bold type. Their mission was to arrest a
handful of postal workers whom Accu-Fax had identified as suspects
in the sophisticated theft ring. Farrell says the arrests and the very public display of Canada Post's strength and resolve were a ruse to deflect
attention away from the real purpose of his and other postal inspectors' covert work at Gateway and South Central, which was to amass
intelligence about union activity.

Farrell was authorized to intercept and scrutinize every piece of
mail delivered to the homes of union leaders. In intelligence circles,
the term used to describe this highly controversial practice is "mail
cover check." The "check" involves photocopying both sides of each
piece of intercepted mail without opening it. The information derived
from the checks was invaluable. For instance, a credit check paints
only a partial financial picture. The mail cover checks permitted
Farrell to fill in that incomplete picture by arming him with information with which to mine his contacts at the credit card agencies and
banks, to pry loose monthly statements on each of the cards. Conducting
mail cover checks that weren't authorized as part of a criminal investigation or under judicial warrant was illegal.

There were also ways to unofficially scrutinize the contents of the
mail. Postal inspectors had access to cans of See-Through spray; a shot
on an envelope rendered it transparent enough so they could read the
contents, and the spray dried without a trace. Another trick involved
inserting a needle with an elastic around it into the top corner of the
flap. Deft twirling wound the contents of the envelope around the
needle, which you could then pull out, read, twirl and reinsert. "I
couldn't get the hang of that," says Farrell.

Canada Post's quest for intelligence about union leaders, Farrell
insists, was simply insatiable. And he was full of ideas on how to secure
information discreetly. A scheme to set up a bogus carpet-cleaning
company to get into the homes of union leaders generated a lot of
interest at Canada Post but never got off the ground. Farrell did, however, resurrect garbage detail with Thompson's enthusiastic blessing.
Home addresses of his targets in hand, he began by calling municipal

offices. He told clerks that his family had recently moved into the neighbourhood and he wanted to know when garbage pickup day was. Unfortunately, pickup fell on the same day for many of the union leaders. That meant Farrell had to wake up at 4:30 in the morning to begin his garbage runs to Mississauga, Brampton and Toronto. Battling fatigue and the occasional hangover, he zigzagged across the city in a frenzied bid to get to the prized refuse before the real garbagemen showed up.

At first, he was in such a hurry that he just stole the garbage. It was an unusual lapse for the young inspector who prided himself on his near-obsessive attention to detail. Stealing the garbage was bound to attract the attention of suspicious neighbours. Without time on his side and with so many garbage bags to inspect, Farrell had little choice but to take the calculated risk. In the event he was caught, he had rehearsed several plausible explanations for his peculiar interest in other people's garbage. His favourite: he was a health inspector, checking to see if any potentially hazardous material was being left unattended, which could pose a risk to children or pets.

Farrell worried that eventually one of the targets or their neighbours would notice the missing garbage bags and start asking some ticklish questions. To limit the odds of exposure, he began substituting dummy bags filled with old newspapers for the original garbage bags. Other times, he brought along his own garbage (which he sifted through to make sure it contained nothing that could be used to identify him) or used a neighbour's garbage to exchange at the scene. If Farrell sensed he was being watched, he pulled over, reached for his powerful binoculars and made a quick check of the neighbourhood.

On some mornings, he stuffed as many as twelve leaking garbage bags, each marked with the target's name and address, into his small car. As he whizzed along the city's highways, Farrell attracted the stares of passing motorists, who sometimes chuckled at the sight of a compact car stuffed with garbage bags, the car's driver cupping a hand over his nose as protection against the pungent odour.

Farrell's patience was often tested. He occasionally arrived at a union leader's home to find that the garbage had not been put out the night before. Then he'd have to sit in his car and wait until either the target or an unlucky member of the family emerged from the house carrying the garbage to the curb.

A few union leaders lived in apartment buildings. This posed a big problem. Tons of garbage ended up in large bins in the basement. Sifting through the mountain of refuse to pluck out the target's bag seemed like an impossible task. That is until Farrell came up with a simple, ingenious solution. He convinced Canada Post to buy specially coloured garbage bags and deliver them for free to union leaders as part of a bogus business promotion.

To avoid any possible connection to Canada Post, Farrell says, the work was contracted out to private investigators. "We didn't want to get too involved directly," Farrell recalls. The investigators visited the homes of union leaders pretending to be conducting a consumer survey on a new brand of garbage bag featuring bright colours, as opposed to the standard dark green. The union leaders were asked to fill out a form listing their likes and dislikes regarding the new product in exchange for a free supply of bags. Not one of the targets, Farrell says, turned down the enticing offer, and eventually, the special bags made their way into trash bins and were retrieved by the private investigators.

Farrell routinely took the trash to a quiet corner in the underground parking lot at his apartment building at 22 Walpole Avenue, where he dumped the contents, one bag at a time. Wearing latex gloves and a surgical mask, Farrell combed through the refuse. Apart from the occasional ATM withdrawal slip, the information retrieved from the garbage runs turned out to be of little use. All of the material culled from the trash was stored, however, in the secret dossiers.

Even though it was his idea, Farrell hated almost everything connected with the garbage runs, from being forced to roll out of bed so early in the morning to the noxious odours that clung to his clothes and body for days. But part of him revelled in the hunt and the prospect that some morsel of information might be gleaned from the messy business. It was that thirst to challenge himself, to test his limits, that propelled Farrell.

Farrell didn't ask many questions about how the sensitive information he was collecting was actually being used. All he knew was that the dossiers were sent to Ottawa. Beyond that, he didn't want to know, and didn't ask.

Spying on union leaders and their families was a clear violation of the Privacy Act, which prohibits the unauthorized collection, use, disclosure, retention and disposal of personal information about identifiable individuals. The intelligence gathering also violated an internal Canada Post "Do's and Don'ts" directive concerning the Privacy Act, distributed to postal inspectors and their managers throughout the country. That exhaustive list included prohibitions against keeping secret files on individuals, asking for or collecting unnecessary personal information or circulating such information.

Every one of these so-called cardinal rules was broken by Farrell with, he says, the consent, knowledge and encouragement of Mike Thompson. In an interview with the author, Robert Letby, a senior Canada Post official, confirmed that postal inspectors have gathered intelligence on union officials. Letby acknowledged that "under some circumstances" postal inspectors collected personal information on union officials, including "licence plate [numbers] and that."

Farrell's spying on the union leaders was another example of the contradictory sides of his temperament. On the one hand, his clandestine work for Canada Post offended his Christian sensibilities and the teachings of his faith and his religious schooling. On the other hand, the thief in him had a natural affinity for the work and liked the fact that he made a tidy sum of money to boot. Farrell was no victim or stooge. At the time, he was a willing and energetic accomplice in Canada Post's war against its unionized employees.

Canada Post's Security and Investigation Services was, in effect, a law unto itself. There were no oversight bodies such as police service boards or review committees to keep a watchful eye on the unit's actions or its managers. The small, little-known army of investigators enjoyed extraordinary powers of search, seizure and arrest that rivalled those of any police or security agency in the country, and yet they were effectively accountable to no one outside of a few Canada Post executives. Given the vacuum, it didn't surprise Farrell that a sense of immunity pervaded the unit. The postal inspectors and their bosses, Farrell says, believed that they could do whatever they wanted, whenever they wanted, to whomever they wanted and get away with it.

The unit's campaign of spying on Canada Post's own employees and their families was a powerful example of the secretive unit's belief that it was above the law. But it wasn't the only one.

In the fall of 1990, Thompson told Farrell by telephone that he had another special assignment for him. "We need to get inside certain cars out at Gateway," he said. The owners of the "certain cars" were no mystery to Farrell.

"This was the planned method of attack against the unions," Farrell says. "We wanted to get into union leaders' cars out there while they were meeting inside the plant."

Thompson was coy on the phone, so Farrell got to the point.

"What do you need me to do?" Farrell asked.

"We have to get in," Thompson said.

"I'll get some slim jims," Farrell said.

A slim jim is a handy but difficult-to-acquire tool. Popular among tow-truck drivers, the thin metal ruler can, in expert hands, unlock car doors within seconds. For this reason, they are wildly popular among thieves. Farrell had never mastered the use of the slim jim. Now, with Canada Post's encouragement, he was about to become an expert.

He knew he wasn't going to find a slim jim on sale at any hardware store, so he approached some friendly tow-truck drivers. "I bought a couple of slim jim sets off a tow truck driver. I gave him a couple hundred bucks in cash. He didn't know who I was or what I did," Farrell says.[2] The cash also bought Farrell lessons in how to use

---

[2] Thompson had given Farrell the cash to buy the slim jims. The money came from the Security and Investigation Services' small, silver petty-cash box.

the tool. In time, he mastered a variety of techniques to unlock passenger and driver car doors with ease.

He then trained other postal inspectors and at least two Security
and Investigation Services managers on how to use the device. The
training sessions took place, Farrell says, at Canada Post's parking lot
at 20 Bay Street. Several cars were used during the training sessions,
including Farrell's Fiero and a Reliant K company car. Each postal
inspector and manager took a turn gently manoeuvring the slim jim to
unlatch car locks. Everyone treated the exercise, Farrell says, like a
challenging puzzle.

A week after the training sessions ended, the slim jims were put
to use on cars owned by union leaders at the Gateway plant.
Thompson, Farrell and another senior postal inspector climbed into
an unmarked Canada Post car at 20 Bay Street and made their way to
the plant. There was little chatter on the way. They pulled into an
industrial parking lot a few blocks shy of the plant, and all got out.
Each inspector took a final turn using the slim jim on the company
car. They then donned surgical gloves to avoid leaving incriminating
fingerprints on the union leaders' cars or documents found in the
cars. Each inspector also carried a hand-held radio tuned to a secure
government frequency to be used if they were spotted by a postal
worker. A lookout was posted inside the plant. A cover story was prepared: if a passerby happened to stop and ask questions, the one using
the slim jim would claim that he had left his keys inside his car.

The plan was to break into three union leaders' cars parked on an
industrial road that rimmed the large postal plant. Thompson, Farrell
says, knew precisely where the union leaders parked. "I think they
scouted the location of the cars before we headed out," he says. Thanks
to Farrell's dossiers, they knew the licence plate number and the make,
model and colour of each vehicle. The team parked their car a few
spots behind the first target vehicle. As an extra precaution, Farrell
slipped a pair of thick leather gloves over the surgical gloves he was
already wearing. Thompson, Farrell says, urged him to be careful
because the caper could cost them their jobs.

On Thompson's command, Farrell slipped out of the car and

walked slowly toward the union leader's car. The others remained behind, silently keeping watch. He slid the slim jim into a rear passenger door. Within seconds, he was inside, snatching up whatever documents he could find. He gave Thompson the documents, and his boss hurriedly made notes while Farrell searched the car's trunk. Nothing of interest was found. Thompson gave the documents back to Farrell, who carefully replaced them in the union leader's car. He then moved on to the next car, parked a short distance away. Using the slim jim again, he broke into the car through a rear door. An unlocked briefcase and other documents were taken from the second car and given to Thompson, who spent about ten minutes riffling through the pages and making notes. Again, the trunk was searched and the documents returned. Farrell moved on to a third car—it was unlocked. Nothing of use or interest was found. Breaking into the three cars took about half an hour.

Little was said on the long drive back to 20 Bay Street. When they arrived, Thompson reminded them to keep their mouths shut. "Remember, this never happened."

They nodded in silent agreement. They could all imagine the consequences, and everyone did keep their mouths shut—until now.

A week after the break-ins, Farrell was summoned to Thompson's office. Thompson's secretary had booked Farrell on a return flight to Ottawa, leaving from the Toronto Island Airport. Thompson told Farrell that he wanted him to courier a briefcase that contained a manila envelope filled with highly sensitive documents to Canada Post headquarters. "Under no circumstances," Thompson told Farrell, "are you to allow anyone to open the briefcase."

If questioned about the briefcase's contents by airport officials, Thompson told Farrell to flash his Correctional Services peace officer badge, not his Canada Post ID, and say that the documents dealt with confidential prisoner information. Once he'd handed over the briefcase in Ottawa, he was to call Thompson immediately to tell him that the mission was accomplished. Farrell made the trip and delivered the package. He used his government calling card to call Thompson to confirm that the briefcase had indeed been handed over.

Asked about the slim-jim affair, Thompson denied any involvement. When former SIS manager Robert Letby was asked if he could recall the incident, he replied, "When are you talking? No one would ever authorize anything like that to happen." He then volunteered that he'd discussed the matter with Thompson and another former postal inspector. Questioned further, he said, "I don't think I want to explain anything."

Despite the praise and promotions, Farrell was getting restless.[3] He was tired of the work and sick of the other postal inspectors, who resented his success. He hoped to return to Simon Fraser University to renew his studies in the criminal justice system. He wanted to become a probation officer. But he also worried about leaving the financial security of the job behind him. He needed someone, or something, to nudge him out the door. The push came from an unlikely source.

Farrell's already strained relationship with some of the other postal inspectors in the unit worsened dramatically with the arrival of Ron Flemming, a short, prickly Newfoundlander, who had been transferred to Toronto to replace a departing manager in Security and Investigation Services. The pair took an instant dislike to one another. Farrell thought Flemming was an arrogant little bully. The Newfoundlander, in turn, thought Farrell was a young punk who needed a good, swift kick in the rear end. And he was determined to deliver it.

Somehow Flemming found out that Farrell and Thompson had hired a police officer at the South Central postal plant without going

---

[3] Thompson had also sent Farrell for intelligence training at the Ontario Police College in Aylmer, Ontario. The two-week course at the famed police college, which is about 190 kilometres west of Toronto, brought together under one roof seasoned police officers from all over the country and a rainbow of police forces. There were twenty-five investigators in all, from every stream of law enforcement—drug agents to intelligence officers. For Farrell, it was a chance to make indispensable and lifelong contacts in police forces and other government security services. Those friendships were sealed during long days of courses on how to properly conduct interrogations, how to identify and chart patterns of criminal behaviour and how to uncover links between major crime syndicates with broad roots in Ontario.

through the proper channels. So Flemming asked Farrell to get his friends and relatives jobs at the plant. Farrell told him to get lost.

The friction between the two men erupted on a Saturday evening outside the South Central postal plant. A group of postal inspectors, including Farrell and Flemming, had just finished installing surveillance equipment inside the plant as part of an undercover operation. It was 3:35 a.m. and they were milling about in the parking lot. Farrell needed a lift back to a friend's place in Whitby, so he asked Flemming for a ride since he was headed that way. Flemming refused.

Farrell exploded. He raced toward Flemming, who sought refuge inside his car, quickly locking the car doors as Farrell pounded away on his hood. Blaise Dobbin, a slightly-built postal inspector, tried to restrain Farrell, but it was no use. Farrell kept up the assault as Flemming cowered in his car. Finally, Flemming hammered his foot on the accelerator and sped out of the parking lot, barely missing Farrell.

The following Monday, Farrell was summoned into Thompson's office to explain himself. Flemming wanted Farrell booted out of the Security and Investigation Services unit immediately. Thompson reluctantly sided with Flemming. Farrell saved them all the trouble. He quit.

Farrell submitted a short, typed letter of resignation to Thompson on January 21, 1991. In his letter, Farrell thanked Thompson and senior Canada Post managers in Ottawa for "giving me the opportunity and experience in working with your Investigation Department." He added, rather presciently, "During my time of employment, I have gained positive and valuable experience that will be applicable to career opportunities in the future."

In a letter accepting his resignation, Thompson reminded Farrell to keep his mouth shut once he stepped out the door. "You are reminded," he wrote, "of your obligation and compliance with the Official Secrets Act and/or the Government of Canada Security Policy of maintaining confidentiality in any matter arising from your employment with Canada Post Corporation's Security and Investigation Services."

Thompson knew that Farrell had seen and done things that would be highly embarrassing for Canada Post and the Government of Canada if they were revealed publicly. Farrell was now the keeper of some very troubling secrets. If Farrell decided to tell all, there would be stiff consequences. Thompson may have been his friend, but the letter made clear that the divisional manager for Security and Investigation Services in York Region owed his allegiance to Canada Post.

Farrell's last official day with Canada Post was February 17, 1991. Before he left, Thompson wrote Farrell another letter—this one of recommendation—pointing out that Farrell was "responsible for the investigation of criminal activity directed at the Corporation and/or committed by employees of the Corporation. Due to the sensitivity and confidentiality of the position, John received Government security clearance to the level of Top Secret." Thompson omitted any reference to Farrell's spying on union members and their leadership.

He added that Farrell had "an inquisitive nature and very creative approach to complicated investigations which led to successful results." Thompson concluded his letter by saying, "[I am] optimistic that the training and exposures John received have enhanced his skills and talents in the security and investigations field."

Their last meeting was very much like Thompson's letter—polite and to the point. Thompson asked Farrell what he intended to do next. Farrell told his boss of his plans to return to school. After a brief but awkward silence, Thompson blurted out a curious question. "John, what do you know about CSIS, the Canadian Security Intelligence Service?"

Farrell said he had heard snippets of disparaging gossip about Canada's spy service from the other PIs and law enforcement agents he had met at the police college and in Ottawa. Thompson told Farrell that he had received a call from a friend at CSIS who was looking for someone "creative" to join the intelligence service. He asked Farrell if he was interested in Thompson setting up a meeting with his friend. Farrell was interested, but his heart was still set on resuming his studies. Thompson assured him that the unique work would allow him plenty of time to pursue his degree and to make a load of money.

What was the nature of the work? Farrell asked. Thompson was guarded but said it involved intercepting mail. Although Farrell had been with Canada Post for less than two years, he certainly knew his way around postal facilities in and outside the city. Thompson handed him a small piece of paper with a name and phone number.

Farrell warmed to the idea. He had the experience, and he needed the money. He mulled the proposal over for a few hours before he stepped into Thompson's office later that day and agreed to a meeting. The lure of cash proved irresistible.

Thompson wished Farrell well. "I'm sure you have the world ahead of you, John," he said. "You have your talents. Use them well."

Farrell thanked Thompson as he handed in his badge. Then he glanced down at the note. The CSIS officer that Thompson had arranged for him to call was Don Lunau.

4

CSIS AND THE MAIL

John Farrell had first heard about CSIS in 1984 when his brother Art happened upon a job ad that the fledgling spy service had placed in the *Globe and Mail* to attract recruits, and jokingly encouraged him to apply. Farrell laughed him off. Now the prospect of joining CSIS didn't seem so laughable. But Farrell also wanted to return to school, become a probation officer and perhaps even start a family. He swung back and forth like a pendulum. He decided, in the end, that Mike Thompson's suggestion was too attractive not to check out. With a hint of trepidation, he dialled the number Thompson had given him. Farrell had, for better or worse, taken the plunge.

Don Lunau picked up after a couple of rings and mumbled hello. Most CSIS officers don't immediately identify themselves on the telephone for fear that an unfriendly party may be lurking at the other end of the line. Lunau was particularly cautious, since he was a senior member of CSIS's Special Operational Services (SOS) in Toronto. SOS members are certain that they are the intelligence service's elite band of operatives, assigned to the most high-profile and sensitive cases.

Their swagger often invites the scorn of fellow intelligence officers, who bristle at the suggestion that SOS members are a more accomplished breed. At times, SOS work is sexy and exciting. More important, while some intelligence officers are chained to their desks conducting tedious computer searches, SOS members are often out of the office on covert operations, racking up thousands of dollars in overtime every month. Any officer with an ounce of ambition or thirst for a good payday pines after work in SOS. Lunau loved it.

Lunau knew who Farrell was and promptly got down to business, inviting the young man to meet him at 277 Front Street West, CSIS's Toronto headquarters.

The spy service occupies three floors in the concrete office tower beside the Metro Convention Centre and near the SkyDome, where a motley collection of rickshaw drivers, ticket scalpers and peanut vendors often loiter on the busy sidewalk in search of gullible tourists. Small groups of chain-smoking CSIS officers can also be spotted in front of the building's revolving-door entrance.

Space is scarce in the non-descript building that the service calls home. About 125 counter-intelligence and counter-terrorism officers, senior administrators and technical support staff are bunched together like children in an overcrowded schoolroom. The only relief from the monotony of the metal desks that litter the floor are large, green, potted plants, and tinted windows that offer up a view of the busy boulevard below. There is little privacy. The claustrophobic quarters force intelligence officers to duck awkwardly behind their desks or cup their hands over phones to make personal calls. New hires soon learn that there are no secrets inside a secret service.

Farrell dressed for the meeting in his version of business casual: a pink polo shirt with a tie. Lunau arrived at the reception counter just as Farrell was signing in. The commissionaire at the desk wanted to see some ID, but Lunau waved him off: "Don't worry. He's with me." A brawny six-footer, Lunau had a shock of dark, curly hair, a neatly trimmed moustache and a disarming smile. The pair shook hands firmly. In search of some privacy, Lunau ushered Farrell into a large boardroom—dubbed "the bullpen"—overlooking bustling Front Street and the new, monolithic CBC headquarters. Farrell was immediately conscious that Lunau was watching him quite carefully, perhaps searching for any mannerisms that would silently betray a lie. Farrell had been taught about reading body language during his investigators training course in Ottawa months earlier. Direct eye contact, for example, suggested confidence, while touching of the mouth, ear or nose or shifting body position implied nervousness and evasiveness. Farrell trained an equally keen eye on his inquisitor, looking for similar but ultimately elusive clues.

Lunau told Farrell that his former boss had spoken highly of his work in the Security and Investigation Services. He explained that, among many responsibilities, he ran CSIS's mail intercept program in Toronto. He stressed that the service always secured the necessary federal warrants before intercepting and opening the mail of targets deemed to be a threat to Canada's national security. The warrants also allowed CSIS to eavesdrop on targets while they were on the phone and, if necessary, to break into their homes and offices.

Lunau peppered Farrell with questions about how he would go about intercepting a target's mail. Farrell parried the queries easily. Lunau appeared impressed by the breadth of Farrell's knowledge and by how self-assured the young man seemed. He later told Farrell that he'd seemed mature beyond his years.

For his part, Farrell felt a connection with Lunau, just as he had with Thompson. Both men were street-smart, confident and charming, at ease in each other's presence. The meeting lasted fifteen minutes. By the time he left, Farrell was sure the job was his. Precisely what that job was remained a mystery.

Later that day, Lunau reached Farrell on his cellphone while he was at home with his mother. (To save money, Farrell had converted the tiny solarium in his mother's government-subsidized seniors' apartment into his bedroom.)

"Are you near a land line?" Lunau asked.

"Sure."

"Call me right back."

Farrell found a phone and did.

"We want you on our team," Lunau said. "We're going to send you out for a bit of training. Is that okay?"

Without waiting for a reply, Lunau told Farrell that he would be paid twenty dollars an hour plus expenses and earn twenty-seven cents a kilometre when he used his own car for government business—the going rate. He gently warned Farrell that the work meant getting up early in the morning and that he would be on the job for fifteen to twenty hours a week. His title would be auxiliary postal inspector, or API. The task was straightforward: travel to postal stations to intercept the mail of CSIS targets and, a few days later, return the letters into the mail stream without attracting any undue attention.

Then Lunau told Farrell to call Kenny Baker, a veteran member of CSIS's mail intercept operation. "He's a good man. He's going to show you around. You two will get along just fine."

Despite Lunau's reassuring tone, Farrell had doubts. It took weeks, an exhaustive background check and two interviews to get hired on at Canada Post. Canada's spy service hired him on the strength of a fifteen-minute meeting and a recommendation. What kind of security service does business in such an amateurish fashion? Farrell wondered. Other questions were percolating in his mind. What precisely was the relationship between Canada Post and CSIS? Who was Don Lunau? Who was Kenny Baker? Why was CSIS interested in him? For Farrell, first impressions were important, and he'd liked Lunau, but he had doubts about CSIS. Still, Farrell was curious and, as always, looking to make a quick buck. So he picked up the phone and called Baker. What did he have to lose?

A week after his meeting with Lunau, Farrell met Baker outside Farrell's sister's house, a large, brick, split-level home in Scarborough. Farrell wasn't anxious for Lunau and Baker to learn that he was living with his mom at a seniors' apartment, and he was determined to protect his own and his mother's privacy.

It was the early morning of February 27, 1991, and bitterly cold. Farrell shuffled his feet, waiting impatiently for Baker to arrive. At 6:30 sharp, a Mercury Grand Marquis rounded the corner onto the quiet, tree-lined street. Baker turned out to be a small, waif-thin man in his late sixties with wispy, grey hair, whose fedora-topped head was barely visible above the dashboard. Tiny as he was, Baker was fond of large, audacious North American–made cars.

Farrell hurriedly waved him down and hopped in, grateful for the car's heater.

A genial chatterbox, Baker immediately started to ramble on about his past, present and hopes for the future. He was married with two grown children. His wife and daughter worked for Canada Post and he had worked as a postal inspector for nearly a quarter of a century before being lured over to CSIS by Lunau two years earlier to work on the mail intercept program. Given his age and health, Baker had wanted a less hectic pace—working for the intelligence service was a good and lucrative marriage. "If you play your cards right, you can make a nice bit of change," he said. Finding ways to rack up extra mileage was the key.

Farrell soon realized that Baker had been hired on at CSIS for precisely the same reasons as he was: he knew his way around postal stations and enjoyed top-secret security clearance. Baker also told Farrell that he kept a daily diary of his work on behalf of the service in small black police notebooks that featured wraparound elastic bands to hold the lined pages firmly in place. Baker tucked his notebooks inside a slightly worn leather satchel, which he always stowed in his car. In his florid penmanship, he noted the time of his departure every morning, the names and addresses of targets, the number of kilometres he clocked each day, the number of pieces of mail he intercepted and the location of postal stations he visited. If there was anything approaching a bible on the mechanics of the service's mail intercept program, then Kenny Baker was its author.

On that February morning, however, Farrell was preoccupied with another of Baker's habits: he was an atrocious driver. Heading out to a postal station in Brampton along busy Highway 401, Baker gingerly navigated his way into the collector lanes and then slowed right down. Farrell urged Baker to speed up. He didn't respond. Other cars roared past, their angry drivers honking wildly and gesturing rudely. Eyes fixed on the road ahead, Baker ignored them, too. He drove twenty kilometres slower than the speed limit, because the longer he was on the highway, the more money he earned. Relief washed over Farrell when Baker pulled off for coffee.

As he slowly sipped his coffee Baker gave Farrell a primer on how to intercept mail. Secrecy, he said solemnly, was paramount. No union members inside the postal stations were to become privy to the fact that he was actually working for CSIS. If that fact became common knowledge, Baker warned, there would be a chain reaction that would inevitably lead to a blow-up of nuclear proportions. The unions would point to the presence of CSIS-paid operatives on site at postal facilities as proof that the intelligence service was spying on their members. Farrell didn't mention that he had already spied on union leaders at the behest of Canada Post's Security and Investigation Services and was sitting on a time bomb of his own.

Baker's modus operandi, he said, was to walk confidently into a postal station, go up to the letter carrier handling the target's mail, flash his Canada Post–issued ID and say he was investigating a kiddie porn ring. Outraged that someone on his route might be part of the vile trade, the letter carrier would happily co-operate, without asking too many questions. Baker would sift through the mailbags as slowly as he drove, searching for the target's mail. Farrell thought the ruse would attract rather than deflect attention, but Baker was set in his ways. "Your routine is going to be different than mine," he said to Farrell.

After the forty-five-minute coffee break, Baker drove Farrell to a small postal station on Queen Street in downtown Brampton. Along the way, he reminded him that secrecy and vigilance were key to any successful undercover operation. Once inside, he introduced Farrell to the station's supervisor.

"Oh, is this another top-secret friend of yours?" the supervisor joked, pointing to Farrell.

Baker then walked over to a letter carrier who blithely handed him a packet of five or six letters held together with an elastic band.

Back in the car, it took a while to break the uncomfortable silence. "You know, John, it's not supposed to happen that way," Baker whispered.

"We're supposed to go through the mailbags ourselves, but my eyes aren't so great anymore, and I can't possibly leaf through a few thousand letters looking for a name, address or postal code. It's impossible."

Farrell smiled wanly. He was being tutored by a kind old man who had taken a dangerous shortcut: Baker gave letter carriers the names of CSIS's top-secret targets, and they fished out the mail for him. And it turned out Baker had a novel solution when it came time to dump the letters back into the mail stream: he handed the target's mail back to the letter carrier. Occasionally, he didn't return all the intercepted mail within the three-day limit that the federal warrants allowed. The delay usually prompted the nervous letter carrier to ask about the whereabouts of the missing mail. "Ah, we aren't finished with it yet," Baker would reply.

Lunau had said that Kenny Baker was the man to watch and learn from. Farrell certainly did a lot of watching, but it was debatable how much he learned. After one day on the job, Farrell did take away one important and disturbing lesson: the so-called secrecy surrounding the program was routinely compromised by Kenny Baker.

He found out later that the letter carriers had nicknamed Baker "Maxwell Smart," and even cracked jokes about his phantom shoe phone. Joking aside, Baker was committing a colossal transgression. To get a warrant to open the target's mail, CSIS had to go before a federal judge and likely had to present highly classified evidence showing that the target either directly or indirectly posed a threat to Canada's national security. Based on that evidence—probably culled from human sources and electronic eavesdropping—the judge issued the warrant, allowing CSIS to take the extraordinary step of intercepting and opening the target's mail. The service also required the approval of the solicitor general before it could break into targets' homes, plant electronic listening devices, or tap telephone lines. That approval process was shrouded in secrecy for several important reasons, including the protection of sources and ongoing intelligence operations. Then Baker exposed the top-secret investigations by sharing the names and addresses of targets with letter carriers, their supervisors and God knows who else.

It was clear to Farrell that Baker had been taking this convenient shortcut for years; Lunau and CSIS were either oblivious to it or countenanced it. Either way, Farrell thought, it was a peculiar and troubling way to run a spy service.

Farrell and Baker slowly made their way from Brampton to another small postal station in Bridletown in Scarborough, to pick up more target mail. Farrell watched in silence as his guide was handed another batch of mail by a compliant letter carrier. "I was thinking, 'Oh my God! I can't believe this. Here we are working on a top-secret project and it's no secret at all. Everybody knows about it.'"

Their next destination was Canada Post's administrative office at 1200 Markham Road in Scarborough. CSIS rented a room on the fourth floor of the office building as a kind of safe house where intelligence officers would rendezvous daily with Baker and the other auxiliary postal inspectors to exchange mail. That afternoon, Jeff Yaworski and Jack Appleton, two counter-intelligence officers, made the drive up from headquarters to handle the mail swap. The small, windowless, L-shaped room was next to the postal inspector's office. Save for a phone, chair, small desk and a locked briefcase, the room was empty. To keep interlopers out, CSIS had installed a high-security lock on the office door. Their presence was supposed to be a well-kept secret. The building housed personnel files on every postal worker in the city; if word leaked that CSIS officers, including a former divisional intelligence officer for Canada Post's Security and Investigation Services, were a stone's throw from that sensitive information, the ensuing controversy could well have buried the program.

Working the mail intercept beat was a rotating, mundane gig for intelligence officers in the Toronto office. Yaworski and Appleton appeared to take the work seriously. The pair of SOS officers embodied the schizophrenic makeup of the civilian intelligence service. Yaworski was twenty-five and a recent university graduate. A burly six-foot-five, the former collegiate football player and correctional officer was an intimidating figure, representing the type of officer that CSIS was trying to attract. Later, Yaworski was given a plum posting as the service's liaison officer in London, England, where he was responsible for maintaining good relations with British intelligence services.

Appleton was old guard. The fifty-four-year-old former RCMP officer was married to a policewoman; his life and family were steeped in police work.

The drill to swap the mail was simple. Baker and the other APIs put an elastic band around their letters and slipped into CSIS's office at the administrative building. The API unlocked the secure briefcase and dumped the freshly intercepted mail into it. Later, intelligence officers would retrieve the mail, leaving behind letters that had been examined and needed to be returned promptly to the mail stream.

As a general rule, any intercepted mail that arrived from overseas or was particularly tricky to open was sent to Ottawa to be dealt with. Some intercepted mail, for example, would be sealed with layers of Scotch Tape to foil CSIS. Sometimes a correspondent taped a tiny, almost invisible hair under the back flap of an envelope. If the hair was disturbed or lost, it would alert the target that the mail had been tampered with. The service always shipped such intercepted mail to Ottawa by same-day courier. The letters, Farrell says, were addressed to the post office box of a fake environmental firm that the service had set up to reduce the chances of Air Canada Cargo employees getting wind of the undercover operation. Farrell or an intelligence officer would hand-deliver the intercepted mail bound for CSIS's front company in Ottawa to the Air Canada Cargo counter at Terminal 2 of Toronto's Pearson International Airport.

When the packages were sent out, an intelligence officer would page or e-mail CSIS in Ottawa with the flight information and waybill number. In Ottawa, the letters ended up on the desk of the service's technical experts. Despite the precautions, Farrell says that mail often went missing or was left unattended for hours, sometimes days. And it didn't take long for airport personnel to figure out what the intelligence service was up to.

All domestic mail was handled in Toronto. CSIS's little-known cadre of technicians has perfected a variety of techniques to open and close mail without leaving any signs that the letters or packages have been tampered with. They also carefully scan the letters and stamps for concealed coded messages that can only be revealed under the gaze of powerful microscopes. The envelopes and their contents are photo-copied, translated if necessary, and distributed to the appropriate counter-intelligence or counter-terrorism officers for review. A federal warrant usually permitted CSIS to hold on to the letter for seventy-two hours before returning it to the mail stream. The service tried not to hold on to the mail for longer than three days to avoid rousing suspicion among its targets. Timing was critical. Often, however, CSIS failed to meet that deadline. Lunau told the APIs they could destroy or not deliver the letters if they posed a threat to national security.

Farrell spent nine days "training" with Baker. For the most part, he kept his own counsel. Following Baker on his mail runs coached him on precisely what not to do. He rejected almost every bit of advice Baker offered up during their travels together, save one: keep detailed notes.

He was pleased, however, that the clandestine work translated into a healthy paycheque: twenty dollars an hour plus mileage and over-time. Three days into the training, Farrell told Baker that he wanted to follow him in his own car so he could begin claiming his mileage allowance. Baker was impressed.

"You're a smart boy," he said.

Lunau, Baker and CSIS would soon discover how ingenious John Farrell could be.

His strange, occasionally unnerving orientation with Baker over, Farrell met Don Lunau on March 19 at Timothy's, a small coffee shop nestled just off the entrance to CSIS's Front Street headquarters. It's a haunt of CSIS officers, who often stop in to grab a coffee and a Danish before heading up to work. Farrell had no idea what to expect at the meeting with his new boss. When Lunau asked how the training with Baker had gone, Farrell lied, insisting that yes, Kenny Baker was an old pro.

In the midst of the conversation, Lunau slipped Farrell a plain enve-lope. Inside was a lined three-by-five-inch index card. On the card were Lunau's handwritten instructions for Farrell's first assignment. Farrell was surprised that Lunau was doing business so openly, particularly since they were constantly being interrupted by Lunau's colleagues who were drifting into the shop for their morning caffeine fix. Farrell glanced down at the card to find a name, a home address including postal code and the location of a postal station in Port Credit, a small bedroom community near Toronto. There were no other details. Lunau didn't tell Farrell why the mail had to be intercepted, how long it had been intercepted or what risk the target posed, and Farrell didn't ask.

Farrell's silent meter was already ticking as he left the coffee shop. A return trip to Port Credit would easily top seventy-five kilometres. He could intercept the mail, catch a few hours of sleep and do a shift at the York Detention Centre, where he was still working part-time as a guard.

Despite his own inclination to take Baker-like shortcuts, Farrell resisted the temptation. Lunau had impressed upon him the need to shield the program, and Farrell prided himself on his professionalism.

The next morning he arrived at the postal station at seven, introduced himself to the supervisor as an investigator and flashed his now defunct Canada Post ID. But prudence was futile. Courtesy of Kenny Baker, many of the supervisors he was to meet at the postal stations were well aware of what CSIS was up to. But supervisors were management and therefore unlikely to raise a ruckus about CSIS's work. The real threat came from letter carriers who might alert their union leaders about the intelligence service's presence at postal stations.

To reduce the risk of exposure, Farrell turned on his charm. He befriended Herman Roberge, a dedicated letter carrier with an unblemished career who was handling the target's mail at the Port Credit postal station. Delivering the mail was Roberge's one and only job. His daughter was studying biology at university with the hope of becoming a forensic scientist with the provincial government. Clearly, Roberge wanted to avoid any trouble that might jeopardize his job and his children's futures. Farrell exploited that insecurity by hinting broadly that he was conducting an investigation into mail fraud, and as a result Roberge kept out of Farrell's way and didn't ask any questions.

Other letter carriers Farrell encountered worried that he was really conducting a probe into the common practice of "red boxing." To shorten their workload and workday, some letter carriers would take a batch of perhaps two hundred to three hundred pieces of mail, discard the elastic band that bound them together and dump the letters into a red mailbox (especially on a Friday). The letters spent the next few days winding their way through the mail stream again. The stunt could shorten a letter carrier's day by two or three hours. Red boxing is a serious offence, often inviting a lengthy suspension or, in some cases, a pink slip. Farrell often threatened to clamp down on the practice in order to prompt jittery letter carriers to co-operate.

On his first few visits to a new postal station to pick up a target's letters, Farrell would only do a mail cover check—photocopying both sides of each envelope and then slipping the letters right back into the bag. Some veteran letter carriers had an uncanny sixth sense about when their mail bags were a letter or two short. "Some of these guys were crazy like that," Farrell says. "They would know if a letter had gone missing or if their precious bags had been tampered with."

When he was sure that the letter carrier was comfortably unaware or utterly uninterested in what he was up to, Farrell would begin to "borrow" the target's mail. As a final precaution against possible detection, he always retrieved at least three mail bags. He didn't want the letter carriers to be able to guess which bag contained the target's mail. He took the bags to a quiet corner of the postal station to carefully unseal and unpack them, making sure to return the packets of mail in the exact sequence he had found them, sorted by postal code. He flicked through the mail until he found the matching postal code, then zeroed in, searching for the name and address of his target.

He would seal the target's mail inside a manila envelope and head for CSIS's safe house at Canada Post's administrative offices, where Yaworski or Appleton retrieved the mail from the secure briefcase.

Farrell soon learned that he was CSIS's latest recruit into a top-secret program code-named Operation Vulva. He had no idea why the intelligence service named its mail intercept program after female genitalia. But the code names intelligence services or law enforcement agencies attach to their clandestine work seem to be either jingoistic clarion calls—like Operation Enduring Freedom—or sophomoric inside jokes. The fact that Farrell and his family harboured lengthy criminal pasts didn't seem to trouble Lunau and CSIS at all. In time, Farrell would become a valued member of Operation Vulva.

Farrell certainly didn't epitomize the new breed of recruit that the service was trying to attract. At the time, he lacked a university education and wasn't bilingual. But he did have a valid driver's licence, a creative mind (as Thompson so aptly put it) and top-secret security clearance. Farrell was also affordable, convenient and experienced. He knew his way around postal stations and had already conducted scores of sensitive investigations with Canada Post. He was a wonderful find.

With the co-operation of Canada Post, CSIS had also worked out a way to conceal the payments to Farrell and the other APIs involved in Operation Vulva. Canada Post essentially acted as a front company for CSIS. The APIs worked for the intelligence agency but were being paid, on paper, through Canada Post. The deal was struck so that CSIS could publicly claim that its operatives were not intercepting mail at postal facilities, plants or stations. That job, according to the paper trail, was being done by Canada Post "contractors." CSIS was applying for the warrants. The API time sheets all had CSIS warrant numbers until Farrell convinced Lunau to delete them for security reasons.

To complete the ruse, beginning in 1992, CSIS had Farrell sign a series of contracts with Canada Post Corporation. (Before that, there was no contract covering Farrell's employment.) Marked secret, the contracts laid out the terms and conditions of employment in Operation Vulva. Under those terms, Farrell was not considered an employee of Canada Post but rather an independent contractor—a contractor who was executing judicial warrants. The contracts stipulated that Farrell was to be paid "professional fees" of twenty dollars per hour, with a minimum charge of three hours per day, just as Lunau had promised. "The corporation shall reimburse you for meals, mileage and incidental expenses incurred by you solely in connection with the performance of your obligation under this contract," it read.

The title of auxiliary postal inspector was a subtle but significant variation from his earlier one of postal inspector. The "auxiliary" reference was designed to suggest that Farrell was providing assistance to Canada Post when, in fact, his boss was no longer Mike Thompson but Don Lunau. "Training and work shall be performed in close liaison with the Divisional Manager S&IS or an authorized representative," contract number 584269 read. The "authorized representative" was Don Lunau.

Not surprisingly, all the contracts Farrell signed had one overriding condition: secrecy. Farrell was obliged to keep his contractual arrangement with Canada Post and CSIS to himself. "The contractor shall treat as confidential, during as well as after the rendering of services contracted for, any information of a character confidential to the affairs of the Corporation to which it becomes privy as a result of the performance of agreed services," the contract read. "No publicity shall be given to the contents of the Contract without the prior written approval of the Corporation." The key phrase in that haze of legalese was "the performance of agreed services." Farrell did nothing in his long and industrious career with CSIS without the approval, consent or direction of his superiors. On that score, at least, the annual contracts were a reflection of the truth.

Every week, Farrell and the other APIs filled out one-page invoices, listing the dates and hours worked, as well as the kilometres logged. The invoices also included CSIS warrant numbers and other expenses incurred by the investigators. Once completed, the invoice was reviewed and authorized by Lunau and faxed to none other than Farrell's former boss, Mike Thompson. After Thompson had signed off on the invoices, they were faxed to the Security and Investigation Services' head office at 785 Carling Avenue in Ottawa. (Later, it moved to 333 Preston Street.) Alan Whitson, national director for Security and Investigation Services, processed all of the expense claims. (Whitson had been one of Farrell's instructors during his federal investigator's training course in Ottawa.) The invoices were submitted to him as part of a fictitious expense account assigned to each of the APIs. Farrell's expense account code was 308870–830–000–1430. A cheque was then sent to each inspector to cover the "expenses" they accrued while working for the intelligence service. The money to cover the costs of the API program, Farrell says, was transferred into the Crown corporation's coffers by CSIS every month. There were APIs operating in every major city in the country under the cover provided by Canada Post.

CSIS and Canada Post did not make any of the standard employment deductions, such as pension, unemployment insurance and federal income taxes, from the so-called expense cheques. Lunau told Farrell that the earnings were "non-reportable income" and that the APIs were not supposed to pay tax on any of the money they received ostensibly from Canada Post for "professional services rendered." Lunau ordered the inspectors not to declare the money on their annual income tax returns in order to keep the arrangement secret, Farrell says, even from Canada's tax department. As far as Farrell knows, CSIS's band of APIs earned hundreds of thousands of dollars every year tax-free with the consent—indeed, at the direction—of Canada's spy service and Canada Post Corporation. That fact may now attract the attention of other less generous federal agencies like the Office of the Auditor General and this country's army of tax officials.

Using the one piece of helpful advice from Kenny Baker, Farrell kept meticulous records during his lengthy tenure with CSIS. He kept a copy of every invoice he submitted for his work and all the payment stubs issued by Canada Post. The records show that Farrell did not declare a single cent of the thousands of dollars he earned while working for CSIS. On March 23, 1991, for example, he completed an invoice for his first week of work with the intelligence service. Farrell began work each day at 6:30 a.m. and travelled to Port Credit to conduct a mail intercept for letters covered by warrant number CSIS 91–1. The new recruit worked a total of fifteen hours for the week March 19 to 23, inclusive. At $20 an hour, Farrell claimed $300 on the invoice. He logged 650 kilometres that week, which translated into a take of $175.50. He also claimed $3 in phone calls, for a grand total of $478.50. The following week, he worked 12 hours and claimed a total of $383.40. He even noted on the invoice that March 24, 1991, was a holiday, Good Friday.

And so it went, week after week for almost a decade. Farrell carefully completed his invoices and faxed them to Thompson for his review. Later, Farrell sent the invoices to Pat Bishop, a senior Canada

Post manager in Toronto, and Whitson. Lunau always received hard copies of Farrell's invoices. Canada Post sent Farrell's cheques to a post office box he set up at the Eglinton Square post office in Scarborough. Like the other APIs working on Operation Vulva, Farrell was thrilled that Lunau had instructed them not to pay any income tax. "Who was I to take issue with what this country's intelligence service had ordered me to do?" Farrell says.

Despite his willingness to run up his expenses, one investigator did balk at Lunau's order. Kenny Baker (who died in 1996) paid income tax on every cent he earned while working for CSIS. Baker's widow, Pat, says her husband worried that the secret payment scheme that CSIS and Canada Post had concocted would eventually be exposed, leaving him vulnerable to investigation and possible imprisonment for tax evasion. "We made sure of it [paying taxes]," Mrs. Baker said, as she reminisced in her north Toronto bungalow about her husband's career in the shadow world of intelligence. "The others [APIs] told him he was crazy for doing it," she adds, "but Kenny knew that some day the others would get caught. You pay [your taxes] as you go along."

She says that her husband was also concerned that if the scheme were exposed, CSIS would abandon him, insisting that they hadn't ordered anyone to avoid paying their taxes. Farrell also worried that he would be double-crossed if the program became public. But given the choice of not paying any income tax on a sizeable amount of cash and ponying up the money, the mercenary in Farrell chose the former option.

Lunau and CSIS were playing a shell game, concealing the APIs from the prying eyes of the service's oversight bodies. The bureaucratic and legal escape hatches CSIS plotted with the help of Canada Post to obfuscate its intimate relationship with Farrell and the other APIs could not rewrite history. From the moment Farrell shook hands with Lunau in the bullpen at Toronto headquarters in early 1991, he was CSIS's man.

For a time, Farrell believed he was living a charmed life. He woke up early and raced to Port Credit to intercept the target's mail. Then it was off to the gym for a quick game of squash, followed by a nap in his mom's solarium. All the while, his meter was running. In one two-week period in 1991 alone, Farrell claimed $1,844 in expenses, all of it tax-free. His lucrative runs to Port Credit padded his bank account, and he had more than enough time to resume his studies at SFU through correspondence courses, as well as to keep up shifts at the jail. He was determined to get his degree, and his paycheque from CSIS made it possible.

Farrell emerged as the cream of a rather mundane crop of about a dozen APIs in Toronto. The others had their own target lists and postal stations as far afield as London and Hamilton. Like Farrell, they dropped off their intercepts at the Canada Post administrative building and retrieved more letters. In time, Farrell learned that the other APIs also had their idiosyncrasies—some strengths, but mostly weaknesses. Like Canada Post's Security and Investigation Services, the API program was another white, middle-aged boys' club, and Farrell was the odd man out. He was serving with people who in some cases were thirty or forty years his senior and who were either at or approaching the end of their careers.

Many of the APIs had previously spent time with both the RCMP and CSIS before joining Operation Vulva. Brian Crump was a former intelligence officer and in semi-retirement before becoming an API. Bill McKeough was a former Mountie and a supervisor with CSIS's watcher service before joining Lunau's team. Harley Wittick spent time as a bank investigator and Toronto police officer prior to signing on to Operation Vulva. Wittick knew little, Farrell says, about CSIS or its mandate and worked on Operation Vulva for months without top-secret security clearance. For Farrell, Wittick's presence in the highly classified program was more evidence of the woefully inadequate security that marked the operation. Ken Pollit was another former police officer who worked for months on Operation Vulva without the requisite security clearance.

Many of Mike Thompson's friends were hired on as APIs. Along with Wittick and Farrell, Jim Troy was another of Thompson's mates who found work with Lunau and CSIS. Troy and Thompson had become close during their time together on the Toronto police force. In fact, Thompson hired Troy as a postal inspector before steering him to CSIS. Blaise Dobbin, a former letter sorter at the South Central postal plant, regularly played hockey with Thompson before becoming a postal inspector. Dobbin spent three years with Canada Post before taking a long stress leave. When he recovered, Thompson got Dobbin a less taxing job as an API.

Just as Thompson had harnessed all of Farrell's talents as divisional intelligence officer, Lunau recognized Farrell had skills that he could exploit. By the fall of 1991 Lunau began handing Farrell sensitive mail intercept files and unofficially appointed him to act as a kind of troubleshooter for the other APIs involved in Operation Vulva. The troubles never ceased.

Before becoming an API, Conrad Richter had been an officer with the RCMP Security Service and a veteran immigration officer. Richter enjoyed driving a conspicuous white Cadillac and was an inveterate talker—not ideal characteristics for work in a top-secret program. Lunau hired him anyway.

Using a fax machine at a postal station, Richter inadvertently sent a copy of his expense account invoice, which included a CSIS warrant number, to the Canadian Union of Postal Workers' headquarters in Toronto. In a panic, Richter frantically tried to reach Farrell, fearing his blunder might compromise the whole program. Farrell was in the middle of a squash game when his pager went off.

"What is it?" he barked, when he reached Richter by phone.

"I have, I mean, we have a problem," Richter said.

"What the fuck is it?" Farrell said.

"Well, John, I just sent my invoice to the union's executive office in Toronto. Jesus, I'm sorry, but I pushed the wrong button on the fax machine. Christ, what have I done?" Farrell says Richter sounded like he was close to tears.

Farrell needed to come up with a solution and fast. He thought for a moment and then told Richter to have the supervisor at the postal station call and explain the delicate problem. The supervisor called the union executive office and calmly said that a fax from the postal station had, regrettably, been sent in error.

"Could you just throw it in the garbage, please," the supervisor asked a union official with all the graciousness he could muster.

The union official complied, not realizing the dynamite she had in her hands. Farrell and Richter breathed a long sigh of relief.

Richter wasn't the only hire Lunau would later come to regret. Lunau recruited one ex-cop after bumping into him at an RCMP Veterans' Association meeting (he had worked with New Brunswick's highway patrol before it was amalgamated with the Mounties). "He would come in with one of those Bob and Doug McKenzie hats and fishing boots on. He didn't know what was going on," Farrell says. "His dream was to return home and live in a trailer." Every time Farrell asked the former highway patrolman to meet him to hand off intercepted mail, he got lost. Even when Farrell wrote out the address or sketched a detailed map that included precise directions, he still found a way to meander through the city aimlessly. The former patrolman seemed to have absolutely no internal compass to guide him.[1]

To Farrell, it seemed that Lunau was not running a top-secret undercover program but a benevolent association for friends, former police officers and veterans of the RCMP Security Service who needed to pick up some extra money to ease the financial pain, and perhaps even the boredom, of retirement.

The point of Operation Vulva was to intercept the mail so that a target wouldn't notice. This was supposed to be the *secret* service after all—any sign that letters had been tampered with effectively raised a red flag that said, "We're watching you."

Many of the APIs were less than diligent when it came to the handling of mail. Two of Farrell's colleagues, for example, often enjoyed

---

[1] After this man lost his job as an API in 1995, his wife repeatedly called Lunau on his private line at CSIS, pleading for a reprieve for her unemployed husband.

a large breakfast of bacon, eggs and coffee after they made their morning intercepts. (Their favourite hangouts were the Colony Restaurant, a greasy spoon at 2014 Lawrence Avenue East and the nearby Watts' Restaurant.) They often invited Farrell to join them and he always said no—he saw no need to cultivate friendships with the other APIs. One morning, however, he needed to meet them to retrieve an important piece of mail. When he arrived at Watts', the APIs were just finishing their morning feast. Coffee and ketchup stains had seeped through a manila envelope and onto some of the intercepted mail. The acrid and stubborn odour of cigarette smoke also permeated the letters.

The mail, stains and all, eventually made its way back into the hands of CSIS's targets, who no doubt wondered what strange culinary journey the letters had taken.

Other pieces of intercepted mail went on a peculiar trek at an API's home, a two-storey brick house in Mississauga, where Farrell occasionally had to drop off letters. The first time Farrell turned into the long driveway, he was startled by a huge dog that came bounding at his car. Farrell hurriedly rolled up his car's windows as the dog, salivating and barking, leapt up on his hood and began scratching at his door.

The dog was so big that Farrell thought he had mistakenly ventured into a game park. Moments later, the unapologetic API, with his ever-present baseball cap and a cigarette dangling from his mouth, emerged from his house to restrain his dog and greet Farrell. Farrell told the man that he didn't intend to get out of the car. Instead, he rolled down his window slightly and slipped the envelope of intercepted mail through the small opening. Relieved, he began pulling out of the driveway, but then he noticed the API offer the envelope to the dog as if it were a newspaper. The dog trotted into the house with the top-secret mail clenched between its teeth.

On a return visit to deliver more mail, Farrell thought he had caught a break when he spied the API working in his garden. He was wrong. The dog was lurking at the front door, waiting for his prey to come into view. Farrell had given the dog a nickname, Cujo, after the rabid St. Bernard featured in the Stephen King horror novel. Farrell parked a safe distance away and called the API on his cellphone. The man told Farrell he was being silly and urged him to park in the driveway. Against his better judgment, Farrell did so. As soon as he came to a stop, Cujo launched himself at Farrell's car. Farrell handed the mail intercepts to the API through the window and retreated. Again the man handed the envelope to his dog. This time, Cujo wouldn't let go. Farrell sat in his car and watched as the API and the dog engaged in an intense tug-of-war with CSIS's mail intercepts. Cujo's head jerked sharply from side to side as his master, using both hands, tried in vain to wrench the mail from his pet's steel-trap jaw. The struggle lasted over a minute before the API wrestled the mail free. The envelope was torn and dripping with slobber. Farrell didn't want to consider the fate of CSIS's precious mail; he was just thankful to get out of the driveway alive.

Evan Downie was a personable, well-liked commissionaire who manned the front desk at CSIS's Toronto headquarters. A native of Prince Edward Island and a former limousine driver, Downie had spent two years in the military before landing a job as a low-paid commissionaire. Downie enjoyed top-secret security clearance and, in time, Lunau got him hired on as a clerk with CSIS. Once Lunau asked Farrell to show Downie around the city. During their bar-hopping, Downie told Farrell that he was bored with his job and wanted to get more involved in SOS work. Farrell laughed. But Lunau had taken a liking to the young man—a relative of Canadian rock star Gord Downie—and before Farrell blinked, the security-guard-turned-clerk was handling CSIS's top-secret mail intercepts. "A clerk shouldn't be handling operational material ever. He had no training, no background in this sort of work. Absolutely nothing. It was like getting my mom to do this," Farrell says.

Farrell's bewilderment turned to shock when he learned that Downie, not an SOS officer, was sorting the letters of high-profile targets. The clerk even occasionally called Farrell to ask which API was handling a particular warrant for a mail intercept. Farrell asked Downie why Lunau wasn't sorting the mail.

"Well, he's out," Downie said. "I'm handling it for him."

Lunau, Farrell says, had engineered a make-work project for the bored ten-dollar-an-hour clerk. He warned Lunau that he was taking a big risk by allowing a clerk to have access to top-secret information about CSIS operations and the names and addresses of key targets. "I told Lunau that Downie shouldn't even be touching the mail and that he could make a lot of dough with that information if the right offer came along," Farrell says. His boss shrugged off his concerns, insisting that he had faith in Downie.

Farrell's fears were confirmed when he received a call at home late one evening from the wannabe spy.

"John, I got a problem. I need your help."

"What's up?"

"I'm fucking dead. I'm dead."

"What? What's going on?"

"I opened a letter," the clerk replied.

"What do you mean you opened a letter?"

"I opened one of the target's letters by mistake," Downie confessed. "I thought it was the manila envelope."

Farrell told Downie to meet him at the Boardwalk Cafe in Toronto's Beach district the next day and to bring the letter.

When Downie walked in, he looked like he hadn't slept the whole night. He handed the letter to Farrell, who immediately knew the mail couldn't be salvaged.

"John, what should I do?" Downie asked, as tears filled his eyes.

"You do whatever you've got to do, but I'm not taking it back like that," Farrell said.

As far as Farrell was concerned, the mangled letter was really Lunau's fault. He told Downie he was on his own. The clerk walked out of the restaurant, took the letter back to CSIS's headquarters and shredded it.

The worst was yet to come. Some of Farrell's former colleagues in the Security and Investigation Services were also making their way into Operation Vulva. Frank Pilotte made the jump. Then another senior postal inspector was hired on. His arrival was a particular shock to Farrell since his sudden departure from Canada Post was triggered by a criminal investigation by the Ontario Provincial Police.

Phil Cherry, one of Farrell's few friends among the postal inspectors at Canada Post, was suspected of allegedly conducting criminal background checks on the CPIC computer (which stores sensitive information about crimes and criminals) for a large private investigation firm. Worried, Cherry called Farrell for advice.

Any unauthorized use of the CPIC computer system can lead to criminal charges against both the provider and recipient of the sensitive information. Cherry vehemently denied the allegations and, with Farrell's support and encouragement, proclaimed his innocence to the OPP officer investigating the unauthorized CPIC searches.

At the time, Cherry claimed that someone was using his name and badge number to call the OPP to run checks on the CPIC system. Suspicion subsequently fell on a senior postal inspector, who later resigned from Canada Post. It turned out that he had set Cherry up to take the fall by giving the private investigators Cherry's name and badge number to use while making CPIC checks. Cherry was cleared. The former senior Canada Post postal inspector found a new home at CSIS, working as an auxiliary postal inspector.

After Cherry was exonerated, Mike Thompson abruptly left the Security and Investigation Services to become an API under Lunau's command. Farrell had abandoned Canada Post and agreed to join CSIS at Thompson's urging. Soon, his former boss at Canada Post would have a new, and unlikely, boss of his own: John Farrell.

5

CSIS AND THE MOB

In the early 1990s, the sometimes comical, often grave, lapses of security that Farrell routinely confronted as he became more involved in Operation Vulva seemed to infect Canada's spy service like a runaway virus. While the twenty-four-year-old recruit was dealing with the almost daily cock-ups that marred the intelligence service's supposedly top-secret mail intercept program, another colossal breach of security involving CSIS's Physical Surveillance Unit (PSU)—the "watcher" service—a batch of highly sensitive documents, and organized crime figures was playing itself out in Toronto.

The episode, successfully hushed up by senior intelligence officials until now, raises disturbing questions about how CSIS can safeguard the security of Canadians when it has so much difficulty safeguarding its own secrets.

The "watchers" are government-trained and -paid voyeurs who carefully track the movements, habits and contacts of the spy service's large quarry of targets: suspected terrorists and spies and their associates.

Watchers come in all shapes, sizes, ages, sexes and colours. They are expected to be discreet and meld into their physical surroundings with ease, using their bodies and wits as camouflage while they silently stalk their targets.

Watchers are an indispensable cog in the machinery of an intelligence service. Though none of them is a full-fledged intelligence officer, most aspire to make the grade. Many lack the requisite university education. Ordered about by intelligence officers like raw recruits in an army, they are told what to do, where to go and who to watch. They are the service's Rodney Dangerfields—they get no respect. They are privy to little about the operations they are assigned to, even though many are savvy veterans of the spy wars. Watchers are expected to keep their eyes open and their mouths shut.

Watchers turn to each other for support and friendship. Their ironclad bond is legendary at CSIS. In a sea of cliques at the service, the solidarity among watchers is forged by numbingly long hours of stillness, broken by a few tantalizing moments of action. They often spend years working together, usually in teams of four to six with a supervisor, and develop an almost telepathic ability to anticipate each other's movements, tendencies and techniques. That familiarity, however, can breed complacency and trouble. For instance, in early 1992, a high-profile counter-terrorism target, who was being tailed by a team of watchers just outside Toronto, turned the tables on his human shadows, jotting down the licence plate numbers, colour, make and models of their parked cars. He took the information to the Peel Regional Police and complained that he was being followed by a bunch of suspicious characters. The surveillance, not surprisingly, had to be temporarily called off.

Mistakes like that sometimes feed the intense rivalry that exists among watcher units across the country, particularly between units from Montreal, Ottawa, Toronto and Vancouver. Squabbles over money, a common complaint at the service, are often at the root of the disputes. Rank-and-file watchers grumble that supervisors rake in too much overtime and abuse the use of company cars. Despite the simmering frictions, the watchers' sense of brotherhood extends beyond work. They are renowned at CSIS for throwing wild parties where inhibitions, ranks and rivalries evaporate as spirits rise in a fountain of booze.

James Patrick Casey is a tall, curly-haired and lean veteran of the watcher service in Toronto. "He's a hell of a nice guy," says one intelligence officer who has worked with Casey. The watcher was at the centre of an incident inside CSIS that nearly snuffed out his career and raised the troubling spectre that a rogue employee was trading top-secret documents for drugs supplied by the Mob.

The Casey affair produced four undeniable facts: highly sensitive CSIS documents ended up in the hands of a lifelong criminal with strong ties to the Mafia in Ontario and Quebec; the trusted Mob associate made copies of the documents and approached at least one of CSIS's targets to sell the information; the theft triggered a frenzied damage assessment, involving every intelligence officer in Toronto, and effectively shut down CSIS's busiest and most important region for three days; a special anti-organized-crime team made up of members of the Metro Toronto Police, the Ontario Provincial Police and the RCMP rescued the prized documents and CSIS's reputation.

In the minds of many intelligence officers in Toronto who worked on the case, the watchers had lived up to their reputations as the service's rejects.

In late 1991, Casey was working on an undercover operation. As was his custom, he carefully tucked a stack of surveillance files into his unsecured briefcase before he hopped into one of CSIS's company cars and headed home to Loretto, Ontario, a tiny community north of Toronto. The files included the names, addresses and habits of high-profile CSIS targets that he and other PSU members were assigned to keep an intense eye on. When he pulled into the driveway of his house, he turned off the ignition, got out of the car and walked inside, leaving his briefcase containing the surveillance files in the car. When he woke the following morning, the briefcase and all its contents were gone, including Casey's CSIS identification badge, his airport security clearance, a leather gun-holster, a recording device called a "body pack" and as many as thirty active surveillance files. Vanished.

Casey realized instantly that he and the service were in very deep trouble. Did he call anyone? Not right away.

Barry Jesse Barnes is a tall, slim man of forty-three. With his neatly cropped beard, tanned skin, thinning white hair and polite, almost gracious demeanour, Barnes has the look of a maître d' at an upscale restaurant. But his charming manner conceals an unsavoury past. On his forehead, just above his left eye, sit two small craters connected by a faint scar—a permanent reminder of a brutal beating at the hands of a gang of kids angered over a double-cross. The blows came courtesy of a lead pipe.

Barnes has amassed over 150 criminal convictions and flitted in and out of Canada's most notorious maximum-security prisons. He has befriended some of this country's most feared and powerful Mafia bosses, peddled drugs, committed scores of robberies, escaped prison, stabbed a man in jail with a pair of barber's scissors and conspired to incinerate another inmate alive in his cell on the orders of a mobster.

Barnes was being groomed to become a Mafia hit man before opting to co-operate with police and go undercover to help combat the Mob from 1983 to the mid-1990s. A confidential police report on Barnes noted that "while incarcerated [Barnes] gained a good rapport with members of the Italian criminal element which has placed him in a good position to assist police."[1] But his help, which put Barnes at great risk, didn't prevent the cops from grilling him in 1992 as the prime suspect in the murder of a prominent Toronto mobster. The very different worlds of Barry Jesse Barnes and James Patrick Casey intersected when the missing briefcase and its highly sensitive contents ended up in Barnes's hands.

---

[1] The police report on Barnes was prepared on December 21, 1993, by Inspector J.E. McIlvenna and Sergeant Donald Kidder of the Combined Forces Special Enforcement Unit. Barnes's "confidential human source" file number was 0–2295.

Jesse Barnes was born on November 21, 1958, in Barrie, Ontario, a tornado-prone town at the southern edge of cottage country, about an hour's drive north of Toronto. An uninspired student, he dropped out of high school in grade nine and began to work the midnight shift at a local plastics factory. He was only sixteen and seemed destined for a life of work, marriage and children, when he was convicted of a break-and-enter of a friend's home in nearby Angus, Ontario. "It was one of the few crimes I was not guilty of," Barnes said in a series of interviews from the medium-security Beaver Creek Institution, on the outskirts of Gravenhurst, Ontario, where he was serving a six-year sentence for theft.

He vowed that if he was going to do time for crimes he did not commit, he might as well do the crimes. That curious logic launched a criminal career that Barnes, a very bright, articulate and literate man, can recall with uncanny precision.

Just seventeen, Barnes was sent to Kingston Penitentiary in 1976 to begin serving a six-year sentence for a series of thefts in Simcoe County, Ontario. At the time, Kingston was a holding centre where prisoners were processed before being shipped out to other notorious prisons, including Joyceville, Collins Bay and Millhaven. That year, Vincenzo "Vic" "The Egg" Cotroni, the Montreal godfather of New York's powerful Bonanno crime family, also briefly called Kingston Pen home. Cotroni, who liked to describe himself as a humble, illiterate pepperoni salesman, was serving time for an extortion conspiracy conviction. Earlier, he had been jailed for contempt of court after offering up "deliberately incomprehensible, rambling, [and] vague" testimony at the Quebec Police Commission inquiry into organized crime's ever-widening tentacles in that province.[2] The inquiry found that Cotroni and his heir apparent, Paolo "The Godfather" Violi, a fiercely cunning mobster, were the masterminds behind a mushrooming criminal empire in Montreal that was heavily involved in protection

---

[2] "Vincent Cotroni: Montreal meat packer called top crime figure," Canadian Press, 18 September 1984.

rackets, extortion, thefts, loansharking, drug trafficking, gambling and fraud.

Barnes and Cotroni had little in common. Cotroni was Mob royalty; Barnes was an inexperienced punk. Cotroni was fearless; Barnes was easily intimidated. At sixty-five, an ailing Cotroni was slowly beginning to recuse himself from criminal life, while Barnes was itching to kick-start his illicit career. Despite their profound differences in age, status, temperament and history, the two hit it off. Barnes and Cotroni and the other Italian mobsters at Kingston struck up what would become a lasting friendship. "I was scared. I must have been one of the youngest guys in the joint. I didn't know anybody. The Italian faction took me under their wing," Barnes says. "They just took a liking to me. I think they felt sorry for me."

Like a scene out of a gangster movie, the aging mobster beckoned the upstart Barnes over and, in broken, heavily accented English, offered him some advice. "Cotroni told me," Barnes says, "'Don't talk to the coppers, never put the finger on anybody, just do your time.'"

Barnes carried Cotroni's admonition with him when he was transferred to Collins Bay Institution, along with something infinitely more valuable for any aspiring crook. Cotroni wrote him a short letter of introduction in Sicilian for him to hand to Beneditto Zizzo, a feared gangster who was serving a life sentence for importing heroin into Canada. Zizzo's brother, Salvatore, was the undisputed Mob boss, or capo, of the crime family in Salemi, Sicily. Zizzo became a father figure to Barnes.

Zizzo introduced him to other Mob middleweights, including the hotheaded Dominic Racco, who was serving a ten-year sentence for the attempted murder of three Toronto youths who had foolishly called him a "wop." At the time, Racco was being groomed by his father, Mike, a Toronto Mafia don, to inherit his territory. Vespino Demarco, a heroin trafficker known as Wes or Uncle, was another member of the small Italian gang at Collins Bay.

Barnes was offered a place at the mobsters' large, corner table in the jail's dining hall. The message to the other inmates was clear: Barnes had influential friends and was not to be messed with. Racco helped Barnes get a job in the dining-room kitchen, where both were cleaners, and offered him work as a driver or bodyguard when he left jail. Barnes got to know Carmen Barillaro, a Niagara Falls mobster with an acumen for contract killings. A heroin trafficker, Barillaro was the crime lieutenant to Johnny "Pops the Enforcer" Papalia, who controlled the Mob in Ontario from his base in Hamilton. (Papalia was shot in the back of the head outside his vending-machine company in Hamilton in 1997. Just weeks after Papalia's execution, Barillaro was shot when he answered the door of his Niagara Falls home.)

Barnes was released from Collins Bay on October 4, 1978. His stint there had emboldened him but didn't make him a better crook. Less than two months later, on December 1, 1978, he was back in jail after another theft conviction for stealing stereo equipment and suits from stores in Toronto and selling them in Barrie. In April 1979, Barnes escaped and, predictably, returned to his hometown. He was on the run for a few weeks before being arrested and shipped, once again, to jail in May 1979.

This time Barnes ended up in Joyceville Institution, where he befriended a new batch of mobsters. He was determined to show his new friends that he was tough and ruthless enough to permanently join the crew.

Police records show that in Joyceville, Barnes, working in cahoots with a well-established organized crime figure, ran a bookmaking operation whose currency was cartons of cigarettes as well as money. Barnes also controlled a highly profitable drug ring inside the jail, trafficking in prescription drugs. As a result of his prison "business ventures," the records show, Barnes became responsible for collecting "outstanding debts."[3] According to the police, the wiry kid from Barrie became the muscle behind the illicit operations in the jail. Coincidentally, a rumour spread among the prisoners that Barnes was serving a fourteen-year sentence for attempted murder. It wasn't true, but Barnes wasn't eager to dispel the notion that he was a killer. "It was kind of funny," Barnes says. "Look at me, I'm just a little guy,

---

[3] Combined Forces Special Enforcement Unit, *Occurrence Report*, 0–2295: 4.

what harm could I do?" His new-found status as an enforcer, real or not, earned him the trust and respect of his Mob brothers-in-arms. It wouldn't be too long before their faith in him would be tested.

Victor Wolynck was an inmate at Joyceville who hit the jackpot—a treasured three-day, unescorted pass out of prison. Wolynck wanted to party on the outside, but he had no money. He and Barnes often hung out together, bumming smokes from each other. He knew Barnes was in tight with the Italians and so he approached him with an offer: if Barnes could arrange a four-hundred-dollar loan, he would return with drugs. Barnes went to his Mob friends, who were also running a loan-sharking operation inside the jail, and persuaded them to ante up. Wolynck took the money and thanked Barnes for his trouble.

Wolynck's three-day pass turned into an unofficial leave of absence of over a year. When he was eventually repatriated to Joyceville, Barnes's buddies were anxious to get their money back, with interest, of course. And Barnes was ordered to get Wolynck to make good on the loan.

At first, Wolynck promised he would pay the money back in weekly instalments, when his girlfriend visited the jail with cash. But he bluffed and stalled.

Barnes confronted him on the jail's range. "Look, Vic, you got to pay these guys. They're getting a little pissed off."

"What the fuck business is it of yours?"

"I'm the one who vouched for you to get the fucking money. So it's my problem," Barnes said.

Rumours ricocheted around the prison that Barnes and Wolynck were headed for a showdown. The pair bumped into each other again on the prison's range and concealed their mutual contempt behind disingenuous smiles, apologies and feigned favours. Barnes decided to settle the score at the movies.

That evening, as *Eye Witness*, a story about a blind man's devotion to his black Labrador retriever, began to flicker on the pull-down screen in the prison gym, Barnes sat down beside Wolynck. Barnes was carrying a pair of pilfered barber's scissors. Wolynck had a homemade knife or "shank" tucked up his sleeve. About ten minutes into the film,

Wolynck gingerly turned toward Barnes, pulling out the shank. Barnes struck first, plunging the scissors into Wolynck's back.

Surprisingly, Wolynck didn't thrash about in anguish. Barnes dragged him to the gym doors and pushed him out into the hall where he collapsed on the floor, the scissors still jutting out of his back. Illuminated by the hallway lights, the guards saw Wolynck and rushed to his aid. He survived. "Right away, in [the gangsters'] eyes," Barnes says, "I was a serious guy, who will do what he says he is going to do."

That was honour. The mobsters then asked Barnes if he was prepared to kill for money. He said yes. They were certain that one of their own had broken the ancient code of *omertà*, or silence, and turned police informant. They wanted him dead.

Barnes hatched a plan. First, he would arrange to have the emergency buzzer in the informant's cell disconnected. While the man slept, his cell would be doused with two cans of paint thinner. A match would be thrown in, lighting an inferno that would engulf him. But the informant won an unexpected reprieve. Just as he was about to execute his plan, Barnes was tossed into solitary confinement for stabbing Wolynck.

"He was a lucky man," Barnes says.

Barnes's improbable tale of a small-town hood venturing almost effortlessly into the dangerous world of godfathers, drug traffickers, contract killers, capos and *omertà*, could be dismissed as implausible save for one critical fact. When Barnes walked into an Ontario Provincial Police station in late 1983 and agreed to help investigate the Mob, the cops combed through his story carefully, searching in vain for any inconsistencies, exaggerations or fabrications. These were no ordinary police officers. They were members of an elite squad of experienced investigators from the RCMP, Metro Toronto Police and the OPP, called the Combined Forces Special Enforcement Unit (CFSEU), dedicated to combatting organized crime. Barnes's astonishing claims checked out. According to the unit, "All information supplied by Barnes to date has been confirmed through checks with other police forces, penitentiary security services and independent sources."[4] Barry Jesse Barnes was the real deal.

When Barnes went to the cops, he had recently been paroled. Back on the street, he committed another string of robberies. He also met with members of a high-profile Mob family in Toronto who wanted to resurrect the aborted hit against the informant. Despite his bravado and his stabbing of Wolynck, Barnes wasn't keen on becoming a Mafia hit man. He decided it was time to talk to the cops.

As his kid brother drove him back to Barrie one evening in late 1983, Barnes asked him to pull into an OPP station just off the Bradford exit of Highway 400. It was the impulsive act of a twenty-three-year-old in way over his head. Barnes walked to the counter, identified himself and asked to see Constable Doug Woolway. The OPP officer had been pestering Barnes's parents for his whereabouts.

"I'm Constable Woolway," the officer said. "I'm glad you're here. I was just typing a warrant for your arrest."

"For what?"

"Possession of stolen property."

As a parolee, Barnes knew instantly that he was likely headed right back to jail. This prospect, coupled with his growing reservations about becoming a hit man, prompted Barnes to blurt out an offer to the startled constable.

"You want to make a deal?" Barnes said. "I can give you conspiracy to commit murder."

In exchange, Barnes wanted the new charges dropped. Constable Woolway immediately picked up the phone and called the RCMP detachment in Newmarket. Within half an hour, a Mountie arrived. Barnes repeated the offer. The RCMP were prepared to co-operate.

On October 1, 1983, Barnes was spirited to the Town Inn Suites on Church Street in Toronto, where, for two days, he was grilled by a member of the OPP's intelligence unit and a CFSEU officer. Barnes was shown a gallery of photographs of the who's who of the Mob world and asked to identify them. He was also shown photos of himself in the company of top-flight mobsters whom he had befriended in jail.

---

[4] CFSEU, *Occurrence Report*, 0-2295: 1.

At the end of their marathon interrogation, the police concluded that Barnes "was as truthful as he could be" and recommended "that Barnes be debriefed as soon as possible after any involvement with our subjects."[5]

From that moment on, Barnes became a "confidential human source" for the CFSEU. "Barnes has shown a genuine concern to mend his ways and discontinue his previous involvement in criminal activities," two CFSEU commanders wrote in an April 1984 memo marked "secret." They added that "the purpose of recruiting this source is to gain evidence regarding a conspiracy to commit murder."[6]

Barnes sweetened the pot by agreeing to testify against his old comrades. In exchange, he wanted witness protection, a new identity, money to start a new life and a pledge that his role as an informant would never be revealed. Barnes says the cops agreed to the conditions.

The CFSEU wanted him back on the street, meeting his Mob friends. John Alexander, the deputy Crown attorney in Barrie, obliged them. Alexander did not oppose Barnes posting five hundred dollars bail, despite his lengthy criminal record. He was released and immediately went to work. His main handler was Sergeant Salvatore "Sam" LoStracco, a short, tough-talking Metro Toronto Police intelligence officer.

Months later the probe petered out and the police reneged on all their commitments to him. No witness protection program, no new identity. Barnes was even prosecuted for possession of stolen property, convicted and sent right back to jail. Strangely, he was relieved.[7]

---

[5] CFSEU, *Occurrence Report*, 0-2295: 2.

[6] CFSEU, *Occurrence Report*, 0-2295: 10.

[7] Barnes's relief turned to fear in March 1996, when his role as a police informant was disclosed by Crown attorneys during the murder trial of Graham Courts, who was accused of killing the mobster Dominic Racco. Ontario Superior Court Justice Stephen Glithero ordered that edited portions of Barnes's confidential source file be released to Courts's attorney, Jack Pinkofsky. Barnes was temporarily placed in protective custody. In 1997 the charges against Courts and his co-accused, Denis Monaghan, were stayed by Justice Glithero after he concluded that "virtually every item" of evidence that might have helped the defence had been withheld in a deliberate and abusive manner by the Crown.

"Nobody found out. Nobody knew what I had done. I was just thankful for that," he says. But in time, Barnes would be knocking on the cops' door again, looking for another deal. This time he had the goods, not just on mobsters but on Canada's spy service.

From 1984 to February 1991, Barnes flitted in and out of prison. In jail, Barnes renewed his friendship with mobsters, including Wes Demarco. Out of jail, Barnes stayed in regular touch with Sam LoStracco, keeping him abreast of Mob activity.

On January 22, 1992, Ignazio Drago was shot five times in the neck, chest and leg, and his body was dumped in an industrial mall in north Toronto. Drago's killer lured the Sicilian-born father of two from his home by posing as a police officer, telling him he was needed downtown for questioning. Drago, who counted key members of the Toronto underworld among his friends, was murdered because he was suspected of being a police informant, a rat.

When he heard about the shooting over the radio, Barnes called LoStracco. Later, he learned that he was the prime suspect in the killing. Homicide investigators with York Regional Police told Barnes that they had intercepted a telephone call that connected him to the murder of the fifty-three-year-old paving contractor.

"I was questioned, questioned, questioned," Barnes says.

He took a polygraph but failed. Police believed they had their killer. Barnes was followed closely for about two weeks. Spooked by the intense pressure, Barnes agreed to co-operate with the cops. In 1995, the police quietly closed their murder investigation. No one was ever charged. Barnes says he has no idea who killed Drago.

One afternoon in late 1991, Barnes was looking forward to enjoying an espresso and small talk with his friend Salvatore "Sam" Gallo at his small ceramic tile store in Scarborough. Gallo's shop, Tiles and Styles, was tucked away in a grimy industrial mall at 3447 Kennedy Road and was a regular haunt for Barnes, who did the occasional odd job for Gallo. A chubby, nerdy-looking man with stringy, grey hair, Sam was also a junkie. "He looked like Garth, the guy in the movie *Wayne's World*," Barnes says.

Sam's older brother, Mike, owned the business. The Gallos hovered around the fringes of the Mob in Toronto. Mike was particularly close to Wes Demarco, and sold drugs for him. Barnes had known the brothers since 1987, when he was introduced to them at a party in Barrie.

When he walked into the tile store that winter afternoon, Sam was leaning on a small counter near the espresso machine. Beside him was someone Barnes didn't know, a lean man in his early forties, with greying brown hair. He was about six feet tall, wearing beige cotton pants, a pullover and a brown windbreaker. Gallo pulled Barnes aside and whispered to him that the man was with CSIS.

"CSIS?"

"The Canadian Security Intelligence Service. Spies, all that bullshit," Sam replied.

"What the fuck does he want?" Barnes said.

"He's a junkie. He wants some junk."

"Stop playing with me, Sam."

"No, no," Sam insisted. "He's a junkie."

Barnes didn't believe Gallo. In all the years he had been around heroin addicts and dealers, Barnes knew very few professionals who were hooked on the drug. Heroin was not a yuppie pastime. A CSIS officer using smack—it was impossible, he thought. Together, the three sipped espressos and chatted. Sam eventually handed the man a gram of heroin, with a street value of four hundred dollars. The man appeared to know Sam as well as a regular customer would.

The man then asked Barnes if he was interested in making a quick buck. Barnes's ears perked up. Sam's customer asked him to retrieve a briefcase sitting on the back seat of his car. Barnes dutifully walked out to the parking lot, opened the back door of the late model Buick LeSabre, reached in and grabbed a brown, slightly worn leather attaché case with two flip latches. The trio retreated into a small anteroom in the tile store and opened James Casey's briefcase. The man explained that the briefcase belonged to a fellow CSIS officer and that it contained sensitive surveillance files about CSIS targets. One of the targets lived in Etobicoke. Handwritten notes on the file made reference to the target's leisurely canoe trips down Toronto's Humber River. Sam's customer suggested that copies of the documents be made. The targets could then be contacted and offered the files in exchange for a tidy sum of cash. The other option was to use the information to blackmail them.

Barnes and Gallo liked the idea. The briefcase also contained a brown leather shoulder holster, a body pack and several hockey tickets. What really caught Barnes's eye, though, was a wallet folder containing Casey's CSIS identification photo and his airport security clearance, which permitted the bearer to enter restricted areas at airports. There was also a turquoise-coloured CSIS handbook detailing the rules and regulations governing the conduct of the service's employees and stamped with the CSIS insignia. Barnes briefly flipped through the eighty-page handbook, which suggested among other things that CSIS employees should avoid the media at all costs and refrain from discussing their secret work with the public.

The man said that Barnes and Gallo could have the material for a day, and then he would have to return it to CSIS. He promised to provide more surveillance files in the future. Handling stolen secret documents was virgin territory for Barnes. He'd spent a lifetime trying to sell hot suits, appliances and drugs. But he was willing to try anything if there was a dollar to be made.

They hoped to sell the information for $5,000 per target. With thirty surveillance files, they were looking at a possible haul of $150,000. It was wishful thinking, but even thieves can dare to dream. They intended to split the money three ways.

They decided that Barnes would take the briefcase, photocopy the documents and then return them all to Gallo the following day. Gallo would meet the man and return the briefcase and all its contents. The man was insistent: he needed the briefcase back the following day.

Barnes took the briefcase and climbed into his silver four-door 1976 Cadillac Seville. At the time, he was living in Port Sydney, a small lakeside community just south of Huntsville, Ontario. On his slow drive home, Barnes decided to drop in to see Tim Woodward, an old friend who owned a garage in town. Barnes proudly showed the surveillance files to Woodward and two other mechanics. He knew they would get a good chuckle out of his new-found cache.

"Timmy, I'm going into the spy business," Barnes said, flashing a broad smile, along with the secret documents and gun holster.

"You're fucking retarded," Woodward replied.

Leaving Woodward's garage, Barnes headed north on Highway 400. He took the Dunlop Street exit at Barrie and turned into an industrial plaza. Right beside the Mack truck dealership was a Kwik Copy outlet. He went in and made photocopies of all the CSIS surveillance files, paid the bill and then headed home.

Once there, he tucked the copies of the surveillance files into a box where he kept some of his personal belongings. He then took the briefcase, the original documents and other contents and went to visit Demarco, his long-time partner in crime, in Novar, a small town just north of Huntsville.

Demarco agreed that the CSIS files could fetch a good chunk of change. But he wasn't eager to hide the files at his house. He and Barnes drove out to the home of one of Demarco's friends on the outskirts of Novar. The house was more like a shack, sitting on a small, grassy patch of land—Demarco's friend was in the midst of renovating. Barnes hid Casey's briefcase behind some fresh drywall. The pair drove away, pondering the fate of CSIS's well-travelled files. Eventually, they decided to cut the Gallo brothers out of the deal and forget about returning the briefcase.

Jean-Luc Marchessault remembers the mixture of fear and determination that gripped CSIS's Toronto office when word hit of the theft of James Casey's briefcase and the top-secret surveillance files.

"I remember it as one of the few times the office actually pulled together," Marchessault says.

At the time, Marchessault was a keen, young intelligence officer, who, along with every other CSIS officer in Toronto, was enlisted to assess the damage Casey's monstrous security blunder might have caused the service and its operations.

Resources normally devoted to counter-intelligence and counter-terrorism operations were diverted to try to determine the extent of the damage. The security breach was particularly egregious since the material lost included the names, addresses and private habits of some of CSIS's prime targets. Existing covert operations were jeopardized. The likelihood of a potentially catastrophic domino effect that could compromise other operations loomed depressingly large. Intelligence officers were busy cross-referencing key information about the missing files with other operations to see how much of the region's covert business might be imperilled. "Every available body was working on the damage assessment. The loss of those documents represented an enormous breach of security," Marchessault says.

Amid concerns about the risk the security fiasco posed to CSIS's operations, the service's spymasters were seized with another, perhaps equally pressing, worry. If word got out, how badly would it damage CSIS's reputation with the public and its sister intelligence agencies? How many heads would roll?

There were other uncertainties. Why did Casey leave such sensitive material in his car? Who stole the briefcase? Did a foreign intelligence agency or hostile government have a hand in the theft, or was it a simple smash and grab? Was it a theft at all? Where were the documents? How and when would they resurface?

No one at CSIS imagined a streetwise criminal like Barnes had some of those answers.

After a day or two with the documents, Barnes was beginning to have second thoughts. When he stole a television or drugs, he was on familiar terrain. He may not have been the most polished or successful thief and drug dealer, but he knew his way around. Terrorists and espionage represented an alien world and an undue risk.

Still, he planned to doctor the CSIS ID to extort money directly out of the targets named in Casey's files. "I was going to present myself as a CSIS guy. I was going to approach these guys and say, 'We need to talk.'"

In his wallet, Barnes routinely carried stolen RCMP identification that he had altered to feature his own mug. Barnes often used it to get out of jams or to rip off other drug dealers. "I would say, 'You're busted,' and take all their drugs and their money," Barnes says. "Then,

I would say, 'I'm giving you a break, see you later.' "

Using Casey's pilfered ID, he would be able to adopt the persona of a government agent. It was too much temptation to resist. Using a razor blade and a steady hand, Barnes sliced into the ID's laminate skin and removed Casey's picture. He then gingerly inserted a small head-and-shoulders shot of himself, using an iron to reseal the laminate. Jesse Barnes had instantly become a card-carrying member of Canada's secret service.

By now, he had had the briefcase for over a week. While CSIS was undertaking its harried damage assessment, Barnes was weighing the pros and cons of his extraordinary find. Instead of selling the surveillance files, Barnes decided to make an investment of sorts. He picked up the phone and called another old Italian friend, Sam LoStracco.

LoStracco despises the Mafia. The small, cocky cop speaks in rat-a-tat clipped tones, his imperfect English laced with a heavy Italian accent. He was a valued asset in CFSEU's war on the Mob, and his battle was personal. To him, the Mafia is a blight on the reputation of every Canadian of Italian descent trying to build a better life for his family. As far as he is concerned, the Mob aren't goodfellas with a code of honour to be immortalized in film, but ruthless thugs and parasites that need to be eradicated.

One of LoStracco's proudest moments in his adopted homeland came in 1987, when along with the future Toronto police chief Julian Fantino and other police officers of Italian descent, he was honoured with life membership in the famed Italian police force, the *carabinieri*.

Even though Barnes thought LoStracco was a ball-breaker who made promises he couldn't keep, he had an inkling his old handler might know what to do. He got in touch with LoStracco from a phone booth at a Toronto hotel where the pair would often meet clandestinely. He spoke cryptically.

"Sam, suppose somebody has something that they didn't want anymore?"

LoStracco insisted that Barnes be a touch more specific, and Barnes told him that he had access to a briefcase. LoStracco immediately asked if the case belonged to a cop, judge or lawyer.

"No," Barnes said. "It belongs to CSIS."

"You fucking asshole. You're not bullshitting me, are you?"

"No, I'm not," Barnes replied.

LoStracco said he would make a few phone calls and told Barnes to call back in an hour. LoStracco confirmed that CSIS had lost an important briefcase. When Barnes called back, he arranged a meeting in the cafeteria of the York Finch General Hospital, in north Toronto. (The hospital is close to RCMP offices.)

"Be there in an hour," LoStracco said.

Barnes arrived first. LoStracco walked in a few minutes later. He wasn't alone. George Capra, an RCMP officer whom Barnes had never met, was with him.

"Let's cut the fucking bullshit," LoStracco said. "Where is it and how did you get it?"

Barnes told the cops the whole story, from the meeting in Sam Gallo's tile store with the heroin addict who said he was from CSIS, to stashing the case behind some drywall in a shack in Novar. Barnes left out one important detail, though: he didn't tell LoStracco that he had made duplicates of the documents.

At first, LoStracco didn't believe him. "No fucking way."

LoStracco only became convinced that Barnes was telling the truth when Barnes volunteered the name of the missing briefcase's owner: James Patrick Casey.

"You fucker," LoStracco said. "We have to get that fucking brief-case back."

LoStracco retreated to make phone calls. In the meantime, Capra, a slightly overweight constable in his early fifties, asked Barnes a few questions. LoStracco returned and ordered Barnes to get the briefcase back. Right now.

Barnes hopped into his Caddy. LoStracco and Capra followed behind closely in an unmarked cruiser. It was late afternoon. When the trio reached Novar, they pulled into a gas station to discuss their next move. Barnes didn't want the Mob-connected Demarco to find out that he was co-operating with police. So, as Barnes approached the house where the briefcase was hidden, LoStracco drove right by and waited at a nearby gas station. But Demarco's friend wasn't home. Barnes and company decided to head to the posh Deerhurst Resort for a drink. Barnes and LoStracco had cognacs while Capra ordered a beer.

Barnes called back. Still no luck. LoStracco was getting impatient, Barnes was frustrated and Capra was hungry. They had dinner at The Sportsman restaurant in Huntsville. Capra and LoStracco flirted with the waitress. Typical cops, Barnes thought.

After dinner, Barnes went back to the shack, weaving his way through the back roads. Demarco's friend still wasn't home. Barnes's little odyssey was turning into a not-so-entertaining road movie. LoStracco and Capra decided to head back to Toronto. But LoStracco was adamant: Barnes had to get the briefcase back that night.

Finally, at about midnight, Demarco's friend arrived home.

Barnes reached behind the drywall, pulled out the briefcase and checked to make sure that its contents were still intact. He jumped into the car and made a beeline for Toronto.

Just outside Schomberg, Barnes heard the all too familiar wail of a siren, and the blinding glare of headlights streamed into his car. A York Regional policeman pulled him over. It turned out that his car had stolen plates and he was driving under suspension. The officer took an immediate interest in the briefcase.

"What's in the case?" he asked.

It was half past two in the morning and Barnes's patience was wearing thin.

"Please don't open it," he pleaded. "If there's a problem, please call these two officers." Barnes handed the policeman LoStracco's and Capra's numbers.

"I don't have to call anyone," the cop replied.

And with that, an exhausted Barnes and the jinxed briefcase were hauled to a police station in Newmarket.

The station supervisor ordered Barnes to open the briefcase. He refused. "Call these fucking guys," Barnes pleaded. "Call them!"

The supervisor called LoStracco.

"Take him back to his car," the supervisor told his patrolman when he got off the phone. "Don't let me pinch you again, Barnes. Get the fuck out of here."

Barnes snatched the briefcase and headed for the home of his god-parents, Laura and Anistasio Scaini, for a few hours of sleep. When he awoke, he called LoStracco, anxious to rid himself of the briefcase. They agreed to meet again in the York Region hospital's cafeteria.

Barnes had taken a seat in the near-deserted cafeteria and was enjoying a rejuvenating cup of coffee when LoStracco and Capra sidled up beside him.

"Go into the washroom," LoStracco whispered.

"What?" Barnes said, slightly mystified.

"Go into the fucking washroom. Now."

Barnes went to the washroom. Alone, he waited for the next move to unfold in the surreal drama. LoStracco came in, checked all the stalls and slipped Barnes a motel room key. Now Barnes was convinced he was starring in a very bad spy flick. An unusually furtive LoStracco told Barnes that he and Capra were being followed by CSIS. The watchers, it seems, were on the job.

Still whispering, LoStracco told Barnes that the key was for a room at the Journeys End motel a few miles from the hospital. "Be very careful. We are under surveillance. Dip and dodge. But however you get there, make sure nobody sees you. We'll leave separately and meet you there later."

Barnes casually walked to his car, retrieved the briefcase and mean-dered for a few blocks on foot before hailing a taxi to drop him off at the motel. He used the key to open a small, Spartan room on the second floor. He waited, his only companion the prized briefcase. He worried that LoStracco would betray him and that he would be arrested. "I didn't know whether to stay or get the fuck out of Dodge," he says.

An hour later, he heard three firm, evenly spaced knocks on the door. The veteran cops had taken a circuitous route to the motel, try-ing to evade CSIS. They pushed their way into the room and drew the blinds. They pressed their ears against the hotel door whenever some-one or something stirred in the hall. These were two nervous rabbits,

Barnes thought, calmly watching the pair while perched in a chair.

"We got heat all over us. CSIS is everywhere," LoStracco said.

Barnes handed over the briefcase. LoStracco opened it like a child ripping into a gift on Christmas morning. He eagerly flipped through the surveillance files, shaking his head in amazement. LoStracco laughed when he came upon Casey's doctored ID. "George, look at this shit," LoStracco said, showing his partner Barnes's beaming face.

Barnes repeated the story of his find. LoStracco remained skeptical, but he couldn't interview the Gallo brothers or Demarco because that would mean burning Barnes. LoStracco handed Barnes about $1,300 for being a good boy scout and returning the briefcase. Barnes hoped he had scored some brownie points with LoStracco and the Mob-fighting task force. Instead, LoStracco lectured him about driving with stolen plates and no licence. The following morning, Barnes met again with LoStracco and Capra at the Journeys End. For two hours, the trio went over the story one last time.

"Barry, this is serious shit. You start fucking with these people, they don't like it," LoStracco told him. He added that CSIS was concerned about whether Casey had been targeted. He also said that Casey hadn't alerted CSIS to the loss of the documents for three days. "This guy never reported it for three fucking days. Can you believe it?"

LoStracco wasn't eager to tell CSIS that one of its own may have been peddling secret documents for dope. He pressed Barnes for the name of the man who gave Gallo the case. Barnes drew a blank. So they decided to concoct a more palatable cover story. LoStracco would tell CSIS that Barnes happened upon the briefcase in a car he was jockeying to Barrie for a used-car dealer who had bought the vehicle at auction in Toronto. The story was implausible, but LoStracco considered the alternative and shuddered.

LoStracco handed Barnes another $1,200, bringing his two-day take to $2,500. It was a lot less than the $150,000 he had originally envisioned, but Barnes was content to rid himself of the briefcase and the attendant grief. In any event, he had copies of the documents stashed at his home in Port Sydney. LoStracco made him sign a receipt for the money. The security service wanted a record that it paid a close associate of the Mob $2,500 for returning their cherished briefcase and documents. "This is their money," LoStracco told Barnes. "I tried for more, but this is all I could get out of them."

LoStracco then issued a warning: if Barnes breathed a word of the find, he would be charged under the Official Secrets Act.

"Don't fuck around, Barry. You don't know what you have stepped into here," LoStracco said.

Barnes shrugged. He was eager to step right out of the world of spies and secret files and right back into the warm, welcoming world of petty crime and hoods.

Meanwhile, James Casey was fighting for his job. His colleagues in the tight-knit watcher service came to his defence. Other CSIS intelligence officers had been hounded out of the service for committing relatively minor transgressions, but Casey survived. He still works for the service, and when I visited his new split-level, red brick home in Loretto, he was reluctant to discuss the incident that thrust him into the unwelcome spotlight. "I don't want to talk to you. No. Goodbye," he said before slamming his door.

Sam LoStracco no longer works for CFSEU. The veteran cop is back working a regular shift out of 32 Division in north Toronto. Clad in a dark flak jacket and the force's new jet-black uniform, LoStracco looked every inch a tough, intimidating cop. At first, he was reluctant to talk to a reporter. "I've been around the block and been burned before," he said.

But his eyes lit up when I mentioned Barnes and CSIS. Leaning on the police station's large, antiseptically clean front counter, he looked around to make sure no one was in earshot before speaking.

"It was a very sensitive case," he said.

LoStracco insisted the case was so sensitive that he required the approval of his police chief, Julian Fantino, before he uttered a word. But then, he called his station chief over to us and made a public confession. "Chief," he said, "a few years ago I was involved in a very sensitive case while I was working with the RCMP. I retrieved a briefcase containing some very sensitive CSIS documents. This gentleman wants to talk to me about it."

A few phone calls later, LoStracco's reserve dissolved and he began to answer questions. The case, he said, was in fact handled by the joint forces unit. The RCMP took the lead. He confirmed that Barnes contacted him about his amazing find. He also confirmed that Barnes was in possession of a CSIS briefcase containing sensitive surveillance files for which he was paid money to return.

"The majority of events [as you describe them] are correct," LoStracco said. "It was a very touchy situation in relation to the safety of the Canadian people."

In April 1995, Barnes was back home—that is, in jail. He was charged with theft and arson after trying to break into a safe in a municipal office using an acetylene torch. Unfortunately, he left the acetylene torch behind and it triggered a minor explosion. A few weeks after the break-in, Barnes was nabbed with his then common-law wife while trying to pull off another heist. In exchange for his companion's freedom, Barnes admitted to the earlier robbery. Clearly, Barnes's luck is not of the Irish.

At the Walkerton Jail, Barnes had an idea. He thought that he might be able to persuade CSIS to make a deal. He would hand over the copied surveillance documents he had kept hidden from LoStracco if the service would help knock down the new criminal charges he was facing. Barnes had his common-law wife call CSIS in Toronto. Angela Jones, a young intelligence officer with CSIS's internal security branch, called Barnes at the jail at 11:55 a.m. on April 24, 1995, leaving him a message to call her back. When he did, Jones told Barnes she was prepared to meet him but was in no position to make a deal.

It was the first time since the loss of the documents more than three years earlier that anyone at CSIS had contacted Barnes. Though the service had been convulsed by the loss of Casey's documents, no one at CSIS had bothered to question Barnes about how the documents had fallen into his hands. Barnes had not been asked a single question about the real possibility that a CSIS officer was trading secret documents for drugs. No one had been in touch to ask whether he had copied the documents.

Barnes was prepared to tell Jones the whole story. But when the CSIS officer saw him in jail, she seemed in no mood to talk or deal.

"You don't know what really happened," Barnes told Jones. "What LoStracco told you about the briefcase being found in a car I was driving is shit."

Jones didn't even bother taking notes. Barnes repeated his offer. Jones promised to get back to him. She never did. On May 29, 1995, Barnes wrote the solicitor general of Canada, offering the same deal: he would tell all about the CSIS documents in exchange for some special consideration.

On August 4, 1995, Barnes received a curt letter from Tom Bradley, CSIS's director general. Bradley confirmed that a CSIS "representative" had been dispatched to meet him and had listened to his demands. "The Service's position was made clear to you at that time," Bradley wrote. "CSIS's position has not changed in the interim and I consider the matter closed."[8]

---

[8] Barnes was released from jail in July 2002 and is now living in Orillia, Ontario.

6

FRIENDS, NEO-NAZIS AND ENEMIES

D on Lunau was a refugee from the discredited days of the RCMP
Security Service. And like anyone with a long history at the service, he was a political animal. For an intelligence officer to stand out
in CSIS's bureaucratic labyrinth, he needed to be well-liked, get results
and perhaps most importantly, impress the right people. In Farrell,
Lunau had found a capable deputy who could help him achieve all
that and more. Their relationship was like a love affair: Farrell was
potentially dangerous to him, but Lunau could not resist his allure.

By early 1992, the pair were inseparable. They called each other
every day or met at bars or restaurants across the city to discuss their
clandestine work. Farrell was often the first person Lunau called in the
morning and the last person he called at night. Lunau would check in
with Farrell as he slowly made his way to the office through rush-hour
traffic in his blue Astro Van.

Lunau's confidence in Farrell became so complete that later that
year he put him in charge of the day-to-day mechanics of Operation
Vulva. Farrell was determined not to disappoint his boss.

It became Farrell's job to ensure that the letters—Lunau's verbal code for them was "apple pies"—of targets living throughout southern Ontario were intercepted, delivered to CSIS and then returned to the APIs to be put back in the mail stream. Farrell also checked all the APIs' invoices before they were faxed to Ottawa. He was organized and thorough. When an API didn't share his level of commitment to the job, he didn't hesitate to crack the whip.

Farrell's ascendancy within Operation Vulva was not surprising. As a new recruit, he had suggested a number of ways to tighten security surrounding the program. For instance, he thought it was unnecessary, and even dangerous, to attach the label "CSIS" to the warrant numbers on the API invoices. What if the invoices ended up in the wrong hands, notably in the mitts of the union leadership? Lunau eventually agreed. By the summer of 1993, on Lunau's instructions, "CSIS" disappeared from the invoices.

Farrell was also concerned that when the APIs dropped off their mail intercepts at the CSIS safe house, they were privy to the names and addresses of other targets—an unnecessary breach of security. To lessen the chances of a mix-up, Farrell purchased plastic folders for each of the APIs. He wrote out their names on large stickers and stuck them on their folders. The APIs dropped their intercepted mail into the folders and then deposited them inside the secure briefcase, without having to sift through all the target mail. It was pretty rudimentary stuff, but the measures hadn't even been considered before Farrell's arrival.

But Lunau continued to use manila envelopes emblazoned with the CSIS logo to return the intercepted mail to the auxiliary postal inspectors. The APIs routinely took the envelopes to postal stations where they opened them, removed the target letters and dumped them back into the mail stream. The APIs often tossed the envelopes, stamped with the hard-to-miss CSIS logo, into a postal station trash bin for anyone to spot and retrieve. If the unions wanted evidence that CSIS was alive, well and operating inside postal stations across Ontario, Lunau had just delivered it to them on a platter.

Farrell emerged as Lunau's right-hand man on the mail intercept program just as CSIS's campaign against virulent neo-Nazis was gathering momentum. In 1992, the service began to devote resources to keeping track of white supremacists who might pose a threat to the security and safety of Canadians. Later that same year, the service pointed to a precipitous rise in hate literature and racist hotlines as evidence of the ominous potential for widespread racially motivated violence in this country.[1]

Intelligence provided by an undercover source working for CSIS inside the Heritage Front, a neo-Nazi group in Canada, also helped persuade the service that white supremacists were mobilizing to use violence to achieve their objectives. The white supremacists' political aim was to foment racial discord and promote the creation of an Aryan homeland. There was proof that such groups were using new technologies to form links with hate groups in the United States and Europe for financing and direction, for collecting information on their enemies and for cementing ties with violent neo-Nazi skinheads. By early 1993, CSIS concluded that the Heritage Front, led by Wolfgang Droege, a labourer and devout Holocaust denier, had emerged as "the most prominent white supremacist organization in the country."[2] As a result, the service widened its target list to include not only the heads of neo-Nazi organizations in Canada but all "racists, fascists and anti-Semites."[3]

It was a potentially lethal business: hate groups, skinheads and racially motivated violence. Information gleaned from the mail intercept program was meant to be a critical component of the service's efforts to keep Canada's neo-Nazis in check.

But the vital, covert business of thwarting white supremacists in Canada was compromised by the unbelievably shoddy practices of Lunau's hand-picked stable of APIs. And, according to Farrell, in its pursuit of the white supremacists CSIS did what it explicitly and repeatedly pledged to Canadians that it would not do: break the law.

---

[1] Security Intelligence Review Committee, "The Heritage Front Affair: Report to the Solicitor General of Canada," 9 December 1994, Chapter 1, p. 3.
[2] ibid, p. 5.
[3] ibid, p. 2.

The early 1990s were heady times for neo-Nazis in North America. Louisiana was home to America's fastest rising political star, David Duke, a tall, blue-eyed, blond former grand wizard of the Knights of the Ku Klux Klan (KKK), who nearly rode his sanitized message of hate into the governor's mansion in Baton Rouge in 1991. His appeal resonated with white voters in the mercurial southern state, who had also voted overwhelmingly for Duke in his unsuccessful bid for a U.S. Senate seat in 1990. Duke's success at the polls also raised the hopes and aspirations of his admirers north of the forty-ninth parallel, who saw the charismatic racist as the political standard–bearer, if not the saviour, of the white race.

Wolfgang Droege was among Duke's followers in Canada. Portly and balding, the white supremacist had travelled to New Orleans in the mid-1970s to attend an international gathering of racists organized by the then Klan leader. At that rally, Duke had exhorted the faithful to unite in order to save the white race from extinction. For Droege, an unabashed admirer of Hitler who had yearned for a white homeland since his boyhood days in Bavaria, Duke's evangelical call was an uplifting, unforgettable rallying cry. He reciprocated by inviting Duke to Toronto in 1977.

The visit caused a media stir and, according to Droege, a flood of requests for Canadian memberships in the Klan. Following his first visit, Duke travelled to British Columbia in 1979 and 1980 to promote a scheme to have the federal government pay for the repatriation of blacks "back to their own countries." The lunacy of Duke's message did not, however, prevent the telegenic racist from receiving scores of invitations to appear on television and radio programs. By late 1980, Duke's followers in Canada, emboldened by the success of his rhetoric of hate, launched the Canadian Knights of the Ku Klux Klan in Toronto, with Droege as the main organizer. Soon, ominous reports began to emerge of cross-burnings in British Columbia and Ontario, as well as of synagogues and cemeteries being vandalized and desecrated.

Taking their cue from Duke, Droege and the Canadian KKK leadership targeted disenchanted white teenagers with an appeal for "white pride" and "racial purity." Not content simply to promote their message of white supremacy in Toronto schoolyards, Droege and other KKK members tried exporting their dreams for an Aryan homeland to the tiny Caribbean island of Dominica. In 1981, Droege was among a group of ten Canadian and American mercenaries arrested by the FBI during a badly botched attempt to invade and overthrow the black government of the impoverished island. The plan went awry when a boat captain tipped off police about the attempted invasion. Droege and his bungling co-conspirators had planned to use the island as a power base to fund white supremacist activities throughout the world. Instead, Droege, along with his co-conspirators, was arrested and sentenced to three years in prison in the United States.

In 1985, Droege was arrested in Alabama as an illegal alien and charged with possession of cocaine and a deadly weapon. He was sentenced to 13 years, paroled in 1989 and deported to Canada. Undaunted, Droege looked once again to his mentor, Duke, for inspiration and guidance. The result: Droege became the brains behind the Heritage Front. Droege and his followers abandoned cross-burnings and the KKK and instead drew up pseudo-political manifestos that parroted the toned-down, anti-immigrant rhetoric developed by Duke. Unlike Duke, the Heritage Front failed to attract meaningful political support with its "white and proud" message. But it did attract the interest of violent neo-Nazi skinheads, the Toronto-based Holocaust denier Ernst Zundel, and CSIS.

As part of its probe into white-supremacist activity in Canada, CSIS routinely intercepted mail destined for Droege's Toronto home as well as for a post office box the Heritage Front leader kept at a small postal station at 2 Laird Drive in Leaside. Droege boasted that there were as many as three hundred active sympathizers on the Heritage Front's mailing list, including some Toronto police officers. (In 1993, Constable Bradley Coulbeck was charged with discreditable conduct by the Toronto force after allegations surfaced that he was on the Heritage Front mailing list, that he bought and distributed the group's racist literature and that he had attended a meeting of the KKK in the United States. He left the force in 1997.) The mail intercepts were designed to unearth as much information as possible about the white power group's membership, connections to like-minded organizations overseas and its future domestic and international plans.

Lunau instructed Farrell to personally intercept mail destined for Droege's home address at 2 North Drive, Apartment 207, in Scarborough. CSIS also had the necessary federal warrants in hand to tap Droege's telephone line and, if necessary, break into his apartment. But the intelligence service did not obtain a federal warrant or the solicitor general's approval, Farrell says, to intercept the mail of Max French, a Heritage Front member and a close associate of Droege's who lived on the third floor of the same apartment complex.

The spy service was certain that Droege was using French's apartment to make phone calls to other white supremacists in Canada and overseas. CSIS needed to obtain French's phone bills to find out where and to whom calls were being made. Lunau also wanted to avoid tipping Droege off that his mail was being intercepted. "If Droege's friend in the same building got his phone bill and Droege didn't, that would have raised suspicion," Farrell says. So Lunau ordered Farrell to intercept the friend's mail without either a federal warrant or the solicitor general's approval, which is required by law.

Lunau gave Farrell this order at a face-to-face meeting in the underground parking lot at CSIS's Front Street headquarters. (After his first interview, Farrell never met Lunau inside headquarters. And one of his boss's preferred rendezvous spots was this well-lit and spacious parking lot, which Farrell thought was another peculiar choice. There was too much traffic there to afford them any real privacy, and scores of office workers often used the parking lot's back entrance as a convenient spot to smoke and gossip. Farrell worried that an eagle-eyed counter-intelligence officer from a hostile spy service could easily have identified them as CSIS operatives, and he feared being tailed. He protested mildly, but Lunau prevailed.) It was Lunau's decision to intercept French's mail, Farrell stresses. He never acted unilaterally, and there was no incentive or motive for him to do so. Farrell showed initiative, imagination and creativity in his covert work, but the theft of mail was a step he would not have contemplated without Lunau's approval. As a former postal inspector, he was acutely aware of the serious risks in pilfering someone's mail without the necessary federal warrant. If caught, Farrell knew he could probably kiss his pardon goodbye and say hello to a small, cold jail cell. Surprisingly, Farrell says, there was little discussion in the parking lot about the grave consequences if word of the illegal intercept leaked: "He [Lunau] was very matter of fact. He told me to intercept the mail, knowing that there was no federal warrant."

Lunau should have known the consequences of breaking the rules. In 1987, CSIS's first director, Ted D'Arcy Finn, resigned in disgrace after the service submitted an inaccurate and misleading affidavit, based in part on information supplied by an unreliable informant, to the federal court in order to obtain a wiretap in a terrorism investigation. Finn had been pushed out even though there was no evidence that the CSIS officers responsible for preparing the error-riddled affidavit had acted with criminal intent. Finn had been forced to take the fall by a Conservative government already ensnared by a string of scandals. The intelligence officers who authored the ill-fated affidavit enjoyed a better fate than their former director: none lost his job, and later a few were promoted. Even the unreliable informant's career was resurrected on one condition: he stop telling lies.

Since Farrell was not a bona fide intelligence officer and was, on paper, a contractor with Canada Post, how would CSIS's oversight bodies ever learn of Lunau's instructions? Farrell was, in effect, Lunau's secret weapon, comfortably beyond the reach of SIRC and the inspector general.

By the spring of 1993, Farrell was handling several mail intercepts linked to white supremacists in Toronto; among these were a post office box number close to CSIS's Front Street headquarters, and a home on Donlands Avenue in the city's east end (both with the proper warrants). Farrell's records show that two female white supremacists connected to the Heritage Front were living at the Donlands address. The inner-city intercepts meant slightly less money for Farrell, but he made up the mileage shortfall by working longer days. Then came an unexpected but welcome surprise: Lunau began topping up Farrell's expense cheques with cash bonuses, expensive gifts, and tickets to sporting events.

A sports fiend, Lunau often invited Farrell to join him for an afternoon of lukewarm beer, overpriced hot dogs and decent baseball at the SkyDome. Farrell had no interest in professional sports, but he went along. CSIS's expensive seats were right behind home plate. At the games, Farrell was surprised to see his boss fidgeting like a nervous schoolboy. Lunau was worried that the huge video screen at the stadium— the JumboTron—would pluck his face out of the crowd and plaster it up like an advertisement for hooky-playing spies. (Farrell kept the ticket stubs for one game they attended, the Jays' June 10, 1997 tilt against the Seattle Mariners. The Jays won eight to three.)

The money and gifts, Farrell says, were Lunau's way of showing his gratitude for a job well done. Lunau would reach into his small, leather fanny pack and pull out a wad of cash for Farrell. Each time, Farrell had to sign a receipt for the money. "He always had a receipt book handy," Farrell says. "He would hand me the money and I would sign for it."

While Farrell was busy attending baseball games with Lunau and intercepting Droege's home mail, Frank Pilotte was given the important job of seizing letters destined for the Heritage Front leader's post office box. It was a tricky assignment. The service had information that at least two Heritage Front sympathizers were working at the postal station and providing Droege with warnings about anyone who asked about his mail.

Droege and the Heritage Front were beginning to attract the kind of media attention they thirsted after. The Heritage Front leader and four other members of the group made headlines when they were expelled from the fledgling Reform Party. Despite the expulsions, Droege confidently assured the press that other Heritage Front members had infiltrated the Western-based, right-wing party. More stories about the alarming rise of the Heritage Front followed after Tom Metzger, a one-time grand dragon of the KKK (who later founded a virulent anti-Semitic group called the White Aryan Resistance), was arrested with his son after attending a rally in Toronto organized by Droege. While he was in Toronto, three local synagogues were spray-painted with anti-Semitic slogans. Metzger and his son were later deported.

Then, in an undeniable coup for the Heritage Front, newspapers and television screens were filled with unsettling images of its members clashing with hundreds of anti-racism activists at Nathan Phillips Square in front of Toronto's city hall. Police on horseback rushed into the crowd smashing the anti-racist protestors over the head with riding crops and batons. A few months after the melee, the home of Gary Schipper, who operated the Heritage Front hotline, was trashed by over three-hundred anti-racism activists. Hours later, Droege was arrested and charged with possession of a dangerous weapon and aggravated assault when a large brawl erupted between Heritage Front members and anti-racism activists. Enraged by the attack on Schipper's home, Heritage Front members used baseball bats, rocks, pipes and bottles to pummel activists outside a downtown nightclub.

As the Heritage Front's notoriety grew, so too did the number of hate crimes in the city. A Tamil immigrant was left partially paralyzed after a vicious beating at the hands of a nineteen-year-old skinhead. Three Sikh students were badly beaten after a high school dance in the city's suburbs. The police were sure that such incidents were not a statistical blip but a disturbing harbinger of things to come.

On September 14, 1993, Lunau moved the API safe house from Canada Post's administrative offices at 1200 Markham Road to a "super" postal facility at 280 Progress Avenue in Scarborough. The massive facility housed several postal stations that had been amalgamated. Canada Post had shut down its satellite Security and Investigation Services branch at the administrative office and moved its postal inspectors to Progress Avenue, and Lunau decided to follow. The move puzzled Farrell. He couldn't fathom why his boss would move the safe house to a building teeming with postal workers who were bound to get curious over the comings and goings of the APIs.

If Lunau wanted privacy, he definitely picked the wrong spot. The rear entrance from the large parking lot was just steps from the newly minted CSIS safe house. Scores of postal workers loitered at the entrance chatting or having a cigarette. There was even a park bench just outside the safe house's window where postal workers lingered and could easily note the arrival and departure of strangers. But Lunau was unperturbed. For Farrell, the move reflected his boss's arrogance: Lunau believed that he could set up shop right in the lion's den, confident that the operation wouldn't be detected.

The new safe house (really a room with a high-security lock on the door) was almost a carbon of the old one, sparsely furnished with a desk, phone and secure briefcase. Directly across the hall was the office where Canada Post's postal inspectors did business at the plant. Apart from using the Progress Avenue plant as a secret rendezvous point to exchange mail, Richter, Wittick and Farrell were also regularly intercepting targets' mail at the facility.

It was on one of Farrell's regular afternoon visits to the new safe house that disaster hit. He opened the secure briefcase, looking for Droege's home mail, which intelligence officers had read, copied and analyzed and which now had to be slipped back into the mail stream. Three of Droege's letters were missing. Perhaps Lunau had failed to drop them off or the service had kept the mail for longer than the warrants allowed. A little unnerved, he reached Lunau at CSIS's Toronto headquarters.

"Hey, Donnie, where are my intercepts?" Farrell asked.

Lunau cupped his hand over the phone and asked another SOS officer about the whereabouts of Droege's mail.

"Yep, John, they're up there," Lunau said.

"Well, I'm telling you right now that they're not here."

Lunau was stunned. He asked Farrell to check the attaché case again. Still no letters.

"I'll get back to you," Lunau barked.

Farrell waited impatiently while his boss spent the rest of the day trying to solve the mystery of the missing letters.

It turned out that Frank Pilotte had taken Droege's home mail from the briefcase and deposited it in the Heritage Front post office box at the Laird Drive postal station. Even at error-prone Canada Post, the chances of mail destined for a home address showing up at a post office box were infinitesimal, because Canada Post sorts mail by postal code, not by name. Droege didn't need any sympathizers inside the postal station to alert him to the fact that his mail was being intercepted: Frank Pilotte and CSIS had just done it for him.

Farrell says he had repeatedly warned Lunau that security surrounding Operation Vulva needed to be tightened. In fact, shortly before the mishap, Farrell had urged Lunau to distribute secure briefcases to each of the APIs to use when they were handling intercepted mail. Lunau had brushed him off, saying it wasn't necessary.

Pilotte escaped punishment. Lunau took him aside and scolded him.

A few days later, Lunau told Farrell that a review of the wiretaps of Droege's home phone revealed that the white supremacist had figured it out. Farrell believed Pilotte's grievous mistake could not be dismissed as a silly little mix-up. The leader of the country's most active and violent white supremacist group now knew beyond any doubt that he was being watched.[4]

Farrell later learned that letter carriers at the postal station who dealt with Heritage Front mail were well aware that Pilotte was working for CSIS. Pilotte would arrive early at the postal station to intercept the mail. But rather than sifting through the mail bag to pluck out Droege's mail, he actually sorted all the letters in the bag. The longer he stayed at the postal station, the more money he earned. He might as well have been wearing a large, illuminated CSIS button on his lapel. Contacted recently to comment on his work as an API, Pilotte said he had never been part of CSIS's mail-intercept program. "I don't know what the hell you're talking about," he said, laughing. As for the mail mix-up, Pilotte said: "This whole conversation is crazy."

---

[4] In an interview, Droege confirmed that he once picked up mail from his post office box in Leaside that was addressed to his home in Scarborough. "I knew right then that the authorities were tampering with my mail," he said. He added that occasionally some of his correspondence, which had been sealed with Scotch Tape, was simply sliced open. He complained to Canada Post and was given the brush-off. "It really was amateur hour," he said.

Ernst Zundel was another prime target of CSIS's allegedly covert campaign against white supremacists. For years, the balding, German-born immigrant ran what amounted to an anti-Semitic propaganda factory from his Victorian home in downtown Toronto. Working out of his ramshackle basement, Zundel churned out pamphlets on his printing press, held meetings and gave lectures, all with a common theme: the Holocaust was a hoax.

The man who once described Hitler as his idol distributed his message to fellow travellers around the globe in an infamous booklet entitled *Did Six Million Really Die?* In it, Zundel claimed the Holocaust was a Jewish-inspired fraud. Canada Post temporarily stopped delivering Zundel's mail in 1981 because he was using the postal service to spread hatred. In 1985, Zundel was sentenced to fifteen months in jail after being found guilty of wilfully causing harm to Canada's racial and social harmony. Three years later, his conviction was upheld on appeal. But in 1992, Zundel won an unexpected victory when the Supreme Court of Canada overturned his conviction on a charge of knowingly spreading false information about the Holocaust. The decision, not surprisingly, thrilled and emboldened the Holocaust denier and his supporters, including the nascent Heritage Front.

After winning his legal reprieve, Zundel often made public appearances wearing a hard hat and carrying a large wooden cross. To his followers, he was a courageous martyr in the fight to protect freedom of speech. His opponents thought differently. In late 1993, they descended on his home, hurling paint canisters and eggs. Zundel had prepared for the onslaught by wrapping his home in plastic. Riot police beat back the demonstrators. The ugly skirmish helped Zundel and his admirers get the media attention they longed for. But CSIS was also training a close eye on Zundel.

The service was busy intercepting mail destined for Zundel's home from a postal station at 1 Yonge Street. Farrell says Zundel was also watched by the service. The APIs were called when Hitler's admirer was seen posting mail. A Canada Post driver would then be summoned to open the mailbox and allow an API to retrieve the mail. Who was this API? Frank Pilotte, though Farrell was often enlisted to help. Letters and packages for Zundel arrived from all over the world. On some days he received as many as twenty pieces of registered mail. CSIS was keen to establish a list of Zundel's worldwide supporters by noting the return addresses attached to each piece of correspondence. To Farrell's surprise, Zundel often received letters of encouragement and support from doctors, lawyers, university professors and other professionals, as well as prison inmates.

Farrell noticed that Pilotte took a particular interest in Zundel's mail. Just how much interest became apparent early one morning when the two APIs met behind a large grocery store on Danforth Avenue. Pilotte drove up in his white Buick, while Farrell arrived in his Geo Metro, a car he liked because it saved him money on gas. Pilotte had just returned from the postal station carrying a batch of Zundel's letters. As he flipped through the mail, Pilotte noticed that one letter was partially open. Curious, he decided to unseal it. Farrell urged him not to, warning him that the letter might be booby-trapped and that he was only inviting more trouble from Lunau. Pilotte opened the letter. Inside, he found a short note addressed to "Dear Ernst" urging the Holocaust denier to continue his campaign "to tell the truth." To help in that effort, the letter also contained a ten-dollar American bill, which the API slipped back into the envelope.

"It was amateurish," Farrell says. "It was none of the API's business what was in the mail."

Farrell didn't want to get embroiled in Pilotte's escapades, but as the program's troubleshooter, he had little choice. He told Lunau, who once again went easy on Pilotte.

Then Farrell caught a break on the Zundel beat during one of his routine visits to Canada Post's station at 1 Yonge Street. Dishevelled and unshaven, he arrived at 6:30 a.m. and walked up to the station's second floor offices. He lumbered through a door leading to a restricted area that housed bag after bag of registered mail. On his way in, he waved to Patrick Hilberg, the registration clerk who often handled Zundel's registered mail, and George Fyfe, the station's supervisor. Farrell had befriended them because he knew the pair could make his job a whole lot easier. They didn't know he was working for CSIS; they assumed he was still a postal inspector.

Farrell began rifling through the mail bags, searching for Zundel's registered mail. He often had to flick through a thousand pieces before plucking out Zundel's letters and packages. The mail, marked priority post, arrived from Australia, Germany, Austria, France and Switzerland. It was imperative that Farrell get his hands on the mail before Hilberg, because once the clerk documented its arrival, the clock began ticking on how long the service could hold on to the letters and packages. The sooner Farrell dumped Zundel's letters back into the mail stream, the less likely Zundel would complain about how tardy the postal service was.

Farrell reached into the mail bag and pulled out a small box. Later he learned that he had just laid his hands on the Heritage Front's complete membership list and the names and addresses of every individual in Canada and overseas who received Zundel's anti-Semitic literature.

It was an extraordinary stroke of luck. Rarely did that kind of information fall so conveniently into the laps of spy services. Finally, Farrell thought, Operation Vulva had paid dividends.

Handling Zundel's mail was a risky business. Violence gravitated to the Holocaust denier. A pipe bomb once exploded behind his Carlton Street home, causing extensive damage. Farrell was always concerned when he intercepted Zundel's mail. He knew the self-promoting propagandist had enemies and that one day one of them might use the mail to deliver an unmistakable and violent message to his front door. Farrell liked his hands and wanted to keep them.

Lunau warned the APIs to be especially careful when handling any mail addressed to Zundel from a post office box from Vancouver. He refused to explain why the Vancouver address was on a watch list, but it was clear that he was worried that mail from that address might be used to conceal a bomb.

Farrell's own nervousness peaked when Lunau ordered him to temporarily stop intercepting parcels destined for Zundel's home. "I got a call from Lunau and he said, 'Stop checking the parcels. Just check the registered letters,'" Farrell recalls. Lunau wasn't kidding. Farrell could hear the urgency in his voice.

In May 1995, a package arrived at Zundel's door apparently from a Vancouver post office box. Zundel let the package sit unopened in his home for nearly a week before claiming to notice that "it made a funny noise" when he shook it. He drove the suspicious package, cushioned by a bag of bird seed in the trunk of his car, to a local police station, where bomb experts discovered that it contained a powerful pipe bomb filled with large nails. Police cordoned off a block around the 51 Division police station in downtown Toronto. A remote-controlled robot gingerly placed the package in a blast-proof hopper. Later, the pipe bomb was detonated at a nearby spit, leaving behind a large crater. Zundel said the parcel, camouflaged to look like a book, bore an outdated return address for the post office box of his friend Tony MacAleer, a B.C.-based white supremacist. Police said the bomb was packed with enough explosives to seriously maim or kill anyone within ninety metres of the blast.

Zundel was certain that Jewish groups were behind a plot to kill him. Initially, police investigated a phone call to the *Toronto Sun* by someone claiming responsibility in the name of an unknown organization called Jewish Armed Resistance. But the police weren't convinced that the Holocaust denier was telling the truth about the circumstances leading up to the discovery of the mail bomb. Why had Zundel waited five days before alerting them to the suspicious package? By late summer, however, that skepticism evaporated. Several police forces launched a joint probe after mail bombs were sent to five different targets: Zundel; another B.C.-based white supremacist, Charles Scott; the Mackenzie Institute, a Toronto-based terrorism and security-policy think-tank; Kay Gardner, a Toronto city councillor; and Alta Genetics Inc., a Calgary cattle-breeding centre. The Mounties believed that four of the bombs originated in Vancouver.

The mystery surrounding the mail bombs was solved when a shadowy group of anarchists, called the Militant Direct Action Task Force, sent "communiqués" to several media outlets claiming responsibility for all the potentially lethal letters, save the one to Kay Gardner. In its letters, which provided compelling evidence that the group was behind the mail bombs, the anarchists responded to media reports about the grave dangers to postal workers who had unwittingly handled the mail bombs. "We have tested our devices and found that only extremely rough handling (or opening them) would cause them to detonate. All packages have been marked PERSONAL to keep unauthorized people from opening them," the group wrote.

Farrell is convinced that the package containing the pipe bomb delivered to Zundel's home was intercepted by either himself or Pilotte. This raises the possibility that the intelligence service was aware of the package's potentially lethal cargo before Zundel received it. Farrell says Lunau's warning to temporarily stop intercepting packages addressed to Zundel's home came only after police had detonated the first pipe bomb. What CSIS might have done to alert either Canada Post, Toronto police or Zundel himself remains a mystery. But what is clear is that the rash of letter bombs prompted police to issue an extraordinary warning to Canadians to be extremely cautious when receiving unexpected packages or letters.

Regrettably, Farrell says, Canada's spy service failed to heed the warning and, as a result, unnecessarily put the lives of Canadians at risk. That's because when CSIS resumed the interception of Zundel's mail, it continued to ship hard-to-open packages by passenger plane to Ottawa for inspection, even though a pipe bomb had already been discovered. "My concern was that there could always be a bomb in Zundel's mail," Farrell says. "And how are we sending that stuff up to Ottawa? It was being shipped by Air Canada. So what do you think was likely to happen if a bomb went off while we were transporting his mail by commercial jet?"

Farrell repeatedly raised this issue with Lunau. "I was concerned about my own safety and the crew and passengers on the plane. I told Donnie many times that I didn't think it was wise to send Zundel's packages up to Ottawa by plane. But he didn't seem that concerned. I would say, 'Don, for the record, we shouldn't be doing this.' Lunau would say, 'Okay. Noted.'"

Farrell rang the alarm, but no one at CSIS bothered to listen.

In spite of its bungling of the Droege and Zundel files, CSIS still had an ace in the hole in its covert war against white supremacists. His name was Grant Bristow. The tall, bearded, slightly overweight former security guard was the service's dream come true: an unimpeachable deep throat who, from 1989 to 1994, provided intelligence about the rising threat posed by the Heritage Front to Canada's social and racial fabric. But CSIS's dream would soon turn into a nightmare. Bristow wasn't just the service's mole inside the Heritage Front; he was allegedly one of the white supremacist group's founding fathers.

On August 14, 1994, the *Toronto Sun*'s leading investigative reporter Bill Dunphy revealed that Bristow was believed to be the principle architect of the hate group as well as a paid CSIS informant. The intelligence service was once again thrust into the uncomfortable spotlight. The allegations that CSIS, through its undercover source, had had an indirect hand in creating and funding a white supremacist group that systematically threatened Canadians, pushed SIRC to investigate.

SIRC launched its probe the day after the tabloid newspaper published its exposé. Four months later, on December 15, 1994, the review committee issued its report, based on a "thorough cross-checking of sensitive information, source reports, CSIS files and interviews."[5] Its conclusion: CSIS had done the right thing.

Rather than scolding the intelligence service and Bristow, the committee found that Canadians owed Bristow (never identified by name in the report) a debt of gratitude for risking his life to spy on the Heritage Front. SIRC found that while Bristow "was part of the inner leadership of the Heritage Front," he "did not initiate programs, though he would suggest alternatives or refinements." In other words, Bristow may have been part of the Heritage Front's inner circle but, somehow, he only played a small role in its genesis and growth. SIRC also dismissed allegations that Bristow helped fund the white supremacist group and recruited members, since the bulk of the eighty thousand dollars that Bristow earned from CSIS was paid out in one year. "The cost of living and supporting a family make a mockery of the allegations that CSIS supported the

---

[5] Security Intelligence Review Committee, "The Heritage Front Affair: Report to the Solicitor General of Canada," Foreword.

extremist group in any way," the committee concluded.[6]

However, SIRC did find that Bristow was occasionally "over-zealous" in his covert work. That zeal—for instance, helping draw up a "hit list" of twenty-two prominent Canadians, mostly Jews, and placing threatening phone calls to anti-racists—was regrettable, but ultimately pardonable, the review body said, because Bristow was instrumental in providing CSIS with information that blunted the growth of right-wing extremism in Canada. SIRC also acknowledged that Bristow's enthusiastic involvement in the so-called IT campaign, the Heritage Front's systematic harassment of anti-racists, "tested the limits of what we believe Canadian society considers to be acceptable and appropriate behaviour from someone acting on behalf of the government." These actions were disturbing but not illegal. To prevent a government-funded repeat of Bristow's troubling zealotry, the watchdog recommended that CSIS put a tighter leash on its active sources.

The committee saved its most scathing criticism not for this country's spies but for its reporters. SIRC singled out journalists with the CBC's investigative program *the fifth estate* for broadcasting information given to them by violent white supremacists without "any serious attempt, that we could determine, to corroborate the statements." The CBC was also blasted for reporting that CSIS had spied on postal workers and CUPW. "We concluded that the allegations were completely without foundation," the committee wrote. "We have conducted detailed reviews of all CSIS activities and all of its targets for ten years. We were aware, therefore, that the CBC's story that CSIS was spying on, or had spied on, the postal workers was not true." SIRC appeared to relish reporting that CBC News had, in the end, retracted its reports that CSIS spied on postal workers.

Not surprisingly, CSIS Director Ward Elcock described the committee's report as a complete vindication of the service's long association with Bristow. In a statement, Elcock defended CSIS's actions, insisting the service "made a substantial contribution to the public

---

[6] ibid, section 13.3, p. 3.

safety of Canadians" by using a mole to act as its eyes and ears inside the Heritage Front. Elcock added that the SIRC report made it clear that the service did not help create or finance the Heritage Front. He also stressed that the agency's actions were lawful and warranted in the face of the threat posed by white supremacists, who preyed on vulnerable people and "instilled fear among Canadians."

Elcock also issued a carefully worded denial that CSIS "has not and is not investigating the Canadian Union of Postal Workers."[7] Elcock, a career civil servant who was appointed CSIS director in May 1994, did not deny that the service had spied on individual postal workers as opposed to the union.

SIRC had collected and reviewed all the evidence and found that the service had not spied on the union and that the media had acted irresponsibly by whipping up fears based on unsubstantiated information. A success story: case closed.

CSIS may have expected that SIRC's favourable report would quell the uproar over the Grant Bristow affair. It didn't. Both the report and the intelligence service came under withering assault from civil libertarians, parliamentarians and lawyers. Alan Borovoy, general counsel for the Canadian Civil Liberties Association, blasted the report, saying it raised as many questions as it answered. Chief among them: Why hadn't CSIS been aware that Bristow was the chief architect of death threats against anti-racist leaders?

Preston Manning, leader of the Reform Party, slammed the report as "a mockery of natural justice," after SIRC dismissed allegations that CSIS or the former Conservative government of Brian Mulroney had ordered Bristow to launch a dirty tricks campaign against his party. In a stinging letter to Prime Minister Jean Chrétien, Manning called on the whole oversight committee to resign. "I submit this report is a whitewash, a cover-up and a disgrace . . . [it] disgraces those who prepared it and it will disgrace any government that accepts it."

---

[7] Rosemary Spears and Derek Ferguson, "CSIS denies snooping on postal workers," Toronto Star, 10 September, 1994, p. A15.

Manning also heaped scorn on SIRC's curious decision to devote a section of its report to a fruitless CSIS investigation into allegations that South Africa's apartheid government offered Manning forty-five thousand dollars in campaign money in 1988. The Reform leader called the allegations "nonsense." Manning went on to angrily attack the review committee's objectivity, charging that it was stacked with "political partisans" who owed their allegiance to the former Tory government.

Barbara Jackman, a prominent human rights activist and immigration lawyer, also charged that the committee was dominated by Tories who were unlikely to criticize their own. Three of the five committee members who authored the report had strong links to the Tories. The committee's chairman, Jacques Courtois, a former president of the Montreal Canadiens, was a key fundraiser for Brian Mulroney. George Vari was a close friend of the former prime minister and, along with his wife, Helen, had made very generous donations to the federal Progressive Conservative Party. Lawyer Edwin Goodman was also a long-time supporter of the PC party. The remaining members of the committee were Rosemary Brown, a former NDP member of Parliament from British Columbia, and Michel Robert, a former Liberal Party president. Robert rushed to the report's defence, insisting that the committee had seen no evidence to support Manning's "conspiracy theory." More tellingly, Barbara Jackman criticized the report as a reflection of the committee's "natural tendency. . . to accept the CSIS version of things."

There was, in fact, much that SIRC wittingly or unwittingly kept out of its report exonerating CSIS. The committee, for instance, failed to point out that most of the APIs who worked on Operation Vulva in Toronto were former postal inspectors who had helped gather intelligence on union leaders. Mike Thompson, Frank Pilotte and John Farrell had all made the jump and were working for CSIS when the Bristow affair exploded on the front pages and on television screens. Canada Post and the spy service were joined together by an invisible cord. The service was so worried that its intimate relationship with Canada Post would be exposed that it briefly shut down Operation

Vulva. And despite Elcock's denials, CSIS had spied on postal workers. The operative who was ordered to do it was John Farrell.

The white-hot cinders from the Grant Bristow affair hadn't been extinguished when Lunau called Farrell at home on March 28, 1995.[8] His tone was terse and serious.

"John, we have a problem."

"What's up, Donnie?"

Lunau said he didn't want to discuss it over the phone and summoned Farrell to an urgent meeting at CSIS's safe house in the postal station at 280 Progress Avenue. Farrell was by then living in a tiny house at 24 Kenworthy Avenue in Scarborough with a couple of roommates. He shaved, threw on a jacket and baseball cap and raced to the safe house. Pilotte or another API must have screwed up again, Farrell thought, and the fireman was being called in to douse the flames.

Lunau got right to the point: he was immediately pulling the plug on Operation Vulva. "We've got to stop all the intercepts right away," Lunau said. "I want you to notify everyone to stop going in to pick up their intercepts. I want you to make sure that we get everything back into the mail stream. You got it?" They were to shut down the safe house. Lunau told Farrell that the order had come directly from Keith McDonald, the national director of SOS in Ottawa.

CSIS was intercepting the mail of at least seventeen high-profile targets in the Toronto area. Farrell wondered how long the stop order would last. Were the APIs about to lose their jobs? He didn't often ask Lunau questions, but he demanded to know why the program was being shut down. Lunau looked taken aback and asked the young man if he had bothered to glance at a newspaper over the past year. Farrell admitted to his boss that he didn't read newspapers or watch much

---

[8] A month earlier, a videotape emerged showing Bristow at Heritage Front rallies exhorting followers on. The images reignited debate about Bristow's true role in the Heritage Front. The *Toronto Star* wrote a scathing editorial calling into question the need for the service in the aftermath of the Bristow affair, and in April, one of the *Star*'s reporters tracked Bristow down in Edmonton.

television; he had been blissfully unaware of the controversy engulfing the service. Lunau also told Farrell that a postal worker was leaking information to the press about the Bristow affair. If word got out that CSIS enjoyed a long and largely undisturbed presence at the postal plants and stations across the country, the future of the program would be threatened. And Lunau was worried, Farrell says, about the way that allegations that the service was spying on postal workers still persisted, aided by the fact that Bristow had worked as a so-called loss prevention officer at the Gateway plant for the shipping firm Kuehne & Nagel.

Farrell stopped asking questions and got to work. Lunau wanted him to co-ordinate the temporary halt without attracting the attention of the press, the unions and perhaps, most important of all, SIRC.

Invoice number 211 offers up confirmation of Lunau's unprecedented order to Farrell. Marked confidential, Farrell's "API Contracted Service Invoice" was submitted as part of his weekly tally of expenses incurred while conducting mail intercepts. For the week ending March 31, 1995, Farrell faxed an invoice to Canada Post claiming expenses totalling $795.34. A copy of the invoice shows that Farrell worked 23 hours and logged 507 kilometres. Farrell often jotted notes about the week's work on the invoices in his clean, legible handwriting. On the back of invoice 211, Farrell carefully wrote, "Notified on Tuesday [of] possible media leak. Advised not to intercept until further notice, worked many hours meeting many people and putting items back."

Farrell zigzagged across the city, meeting with shocked APIs at their homes and at key intersections to pass on Lunau's order and to hand back the mail intercepts. Farrell made notes about his mad dash on the back of another of his invoices:

4:15 a.m.: left house.
5:15 a.m.: met Doug [Lamb] at Highway 10 and 401.
6:00 a.m.: met Con [Richter] at Highway 401 and Kennedy.
6:30 a.m.: met Don (YoYo) Yiomen at Keele and 401.
7:00 a.m.: met M.T. [Mike Thompson] at House.
7:30 a.m.: met Kenny Baker at 401 and Kennedy.

8:15 a.m.: met Con at Yonge and Eglinton.
10:05 a.m.: met Kenny Baker at Bayview and 401.
11:39 a.m.: Stuff ready for Don L. [Lunau] Head to HQ.
12:30 a.m.: arrive home.

But not before he earned himself a speeding ticket.

The APIs worried that the CSIS gravy train was about to come to a total halt. Farrell didn't worry, since on top of the generous cash bonuses and expensive gifts, Lunau had begun paying Farrell for five and a half hours and one hundred kilometres a day even if he didn't work the hours or chalk up the kilometres. It was a sweetheart deal and tangible recognition of Farrell's status as a kind of Robin to Lunau's Batman. (Farrell's invoices show that Lunau and CSIS had begun paying out on the private arrangement in March 1994.)

Pilotte, Richter and the other APIs wanted to know why Operation Vulva had been shut down cold turkey. Farrell calmly told them to follow Lunau's order and not ask any questions.

But just as suddenly as the storm blew in, it passed. Lunau called Farrell four days after the stop-work order and gave him the green light to resume the mail intercepts. Pilotte and the other APIs were relieved, but it was relief mixed with uncertainty. Would they abruptly be thrown out of work again? Why had they been left in the dark? Were their days as APIs numbered?

While the APIs fretted about their futures, Farrell was busy plugging a possible leak. Lunau was a very close friend of Al Treddenick, Bristow's handler at CSIS. Like Lunau, Treddenick had been with the RCMP Security Service before joining the civilian service. They suspected that a postal worker was leaking dirt about Bristow and his apparent relationship with Jim Troy, an API who was once a Toronto cop and the former plant protection officer at the Gateway plant (the same job that Farrell had held briefly at South Central). Word was that Troy and Bristow had struck up a friendship while working at the plant. The suspicious postal worker had also discovered that Troy was now working for the intelligence service, intercepting mail at a small postal station in Toronto's west end. Lunau desperately wanted to find out who the troublesome postal worker was and who he was feeding information to.

The postal worker, Lunau told Farrell, was making furtive calls to his media contact from a small room at a postal station at 19 Toryork Drive, the same postal station where Troy was assigned to conduct mail intercepts. Farrell met Troy at a nearby McDonald's restaurant to tell him that he was briefly taking over his duties, and Troy handed Farrell a batch of letters that had to be returned to the mail stream.

Lunau and Farrell discussed various ways to expose the pesky mole and his media ally before settling on a simple, though illegal, plan. First, Farrell photocopied a list of all the employees working out of the postal station and handed it to Lunau. His next step was to visit one of his contacts, Ursula Lebana, the co-owner of Spytech, a popular shop in Toronto that stocks a range of devices for spying on neighbours, friends, spouses, co-workers, nannies, babysitters or any other potential target. (Lebana knew nothing about Farrell's relationship with CSIS, since he only identified himself to her as an investigator.) Farrell told Lebana he had a special job that required an equally special listening device. The bug had to be small, effective and cheap. Lebana put Farrell on to a Russian contact who, she said, might be able to provide him with the perfect gadget. Shortly after his helpful meeting with the charming store owner, Farrell met with the Russian technician. Lunau had given Farrell more than five hundred dollars to purchase the bug. The Russian handed over a small, battery-operated listening device disguised to look like a phone jack. Sale price: $250 cash. The Russian didn't want to know Farrell's name, what he did for a living or what he planned to do with the device. He just wanted the money, and Farrell was happy to oblige him.

The simple device, with its concealed microphone and a slim red wire that acted as the antenna, was easy to install. Using a nine-volt battery, the bug was able to transmit conversations over a fairly wide range via a radio frequency. All Farrell had to do was set his car radio to a specific frequency on the FM band to pick up the live transmission, and press record on his tape machine to make an instant recording of a conversation between the postal worker and his media pal.

The day after Farrell bought the bug, Lunau ordered him to put it to use. To Farrell's knowledge, Lunau and the service had not obtained the necessary federal warrant or the solicitor general's consent either to target the postal worker or to tape him on the phone.

Farrell drove out to the postal station on Toryork Drive and parked directly in front of the one-storey, brick building, well within the bug's range. He slipped into the room where the postal worker made his calls and, using some duct tape, attached the device to the base of a wall behind a desk. He then retreated to his car. Farrell tuned the radio to the proper frequency and waited. He lucked out. Only a few minutes passed before he snapped back in his seat as the first crackle of noise came over his radio. Farrell listened intently as someone opened the door, walked into the room and began dialling. A burst of adrenalin raced through Farrell as he overheard the postie tell his contact about Farrell's own movements.

"The guy [Farrell] just left," the postal worker said. "He was in and fucking out. Something's up."

Clearly suspicious, the postal worker kept the conversation short. Farrell waited a few minutes before returning to the postal station to retrieve the bug, and unexpectedly bumped into the station's supervisor. His heart jumped. Looking for an excuse, Farrell said he had left his favourite pen behind in the room. Back inside, he pressed the redial button on the phone. "A guy from a radio station picked up. I jotted down the phone number, and I passed it along to Lunau with the postie's name, mail run and SIN number as well as the tape recording of his telephone call."

SIRC's report on the Grant Bristow affair was emphatic: CSIS never spied on postal workers.

"They don't know shit," Farrell says.

When the controversy swirling around CSIS inevitably died down and the media's attention was consumed by other matters, the APIs bugged out of their safe house on Progress Avenue again. This time the move was permanent.

Lunau's decision to abandon the safe house was triggered by yet another in a seemingly endless string of mind-boggling security lapses.

The architect of this security breach was not an API but Richard Garland, a member of the service's watcher unit who was briefly seconded to work as administrative assistant on Operation Vulva. His job was to answer phones and hand-deliver the mail intercepts to Farrell at the entrance of CSIS's Front Street headquarters. The APIs dubbed Garland "delivery boy."

It may have been pedestrian work, but Garland had top-secret security clearance. He also had access to the names, addresses and pager and phone numbers of all the APIs and key members of the SOS unit, as well as the names and addresses of some of the service's high-profile targets. With his blond hair, megawatt smile and ever-present tan, Garland looked more like a beach boy than a spy. He also had a reputation for having loose lips. And those lips often got him into trouble. A self-described ladies' man, Garland was an inveterate barfly who tried to impress young, attractive women by sharing intimate details about his covert work for the intelligence service.

"Richard had a very big mouth," says Farrell.

Garland shared a house in Oakville with his girlfriend. CSIS employees are supposed to guard their secret work jealously—even from their family, friends and lovers. But, like most CSIS employees, Garland had a difficult time not sharing secrets with the person he was sharing a bed with. Unfortunately, his relationship with his girlfriend, who had close ties to the Mounties, began to fray terribly. And when it came, the separation was not amicable. The former lovers traded charges about alleged stalking that threatened to end up in court. Then a bombshell dropped on the service. CSIS learned that Garland's girlfriend often searched her boyfriend's briefcase while he was asleep, eagerly digesting highly classified information about the service's mail intercept operation. She had also made copies of the lists of the names and numbers of the APIs and SOS members. Most disturbing of all, she had kept some of the mail intercepts. (Garland, Farrell later learned, had been authorized to take some of the mail intercepts home.)

One day, Farrell was busy with a mail intercept at the safe house.

Only APIs and select intelligence officers connected to Operation Vulva were supposed to have access to the secure phone number for the room. The phone rang, and when Farrell picked it up, Garland's ex-girlfriend was at the other end of the line, demanding to know Garland's whereabouts. Farrell immediately called Lunau.

Lunau angrily confronted Garland, and an internal security probe was ordered to look into the affair. But the damage had been done. The safe house's cover had been blown. Highly classified information about Operation Vulva had fallen into the hands of an unpredictable and angry woman who was threatening to reveal all to the RCMP. The SOS boss had no alternative but to pull the plug permanently on CSIS's secret safe house. Garland avoided being suspended. Two years later, he became a supervisor in the watcher service.

Farrell wrote Lunau a three-page proposal, offering up calculations that showed how the service could save as much as $360,000 a year on mileage and other costs if it allowed him to deliver and pick up all the intercepted mail from the APIs, rather than have the APIs drop off the letters at the safe house. Farrell also pointed out that he could safely store the mail intercepts in a government safe he had at home. Lunau agreed and handed the job to Farrell. The other APIs were upset, but Lunau was the boss and they had little choice but to agree to the new procedure. To this day, the former safe house at 280 Progress Avenue sits empty, save for a telephone on the floor.

While Farrell was busy keeping watch over Droege, Zundel, Pilotte and Garland on behalf of CSIS, he was still working at the York Detention Centre. The money was good, and he could easily fit his shifts into his more demanding schedule for CSIS. But in early 1993, after four years at the prison, Farrell decided that he could not turn a blind eye to what was going on at the jail. He and his friend and fellow guard, Findlay Wihlidal, decided to blow the whistle on rampant nepotism and sexual abuse.

Their decision would thrust them into the spotlight and precipitate a long and withering battle with the provincial government—a fight they eventually won. Farrell's second stint as a whistle-blower taught him an important lesson that stood him in good stead when he butted heads with CSIS years later. Farrell understood that bureaucracies shook violently when a hidden world of favouritism, incompetence and criminality was suddenly the fodder for headlines like "Scandal," "Cover-up," "Probe," and "Charged." Farrell blew the whistle at the jail, drawing media attention to himself, with the full knowledge and approval of his CSIS boss, Don Lunau, who seemed to admire the young man's courage.

Findlay Wihlidal was a former nursing assistant and youth worker with the Children's Aid Society. Although he was eleven years older than Farrell, they were brothers-in-arms at the jail. Both men were athletic, outgoing and perpetually horny. The pair spent many hours trolling Toronto's bars in search of sex, and they often found it. Farrell and Wihlidal also shared a disdain for unfairness, particularly when they were its victims.

Like Farrell, Wihlidal worked part-time at the centre. But unlike his friend, Wihlidal didn't pad his take-home pay by secretly toiling for CSIS. Farrell never told his buddy about his tax-free, covert work. He also didn't tell a string of girlfriends, family or friends that he was the right-hand man of one of CSIS's most senior officers. (Only Farrell's faithful dog, Heidi, was aware of his highly classified work. Farrell let Heidi tag along during his mail intercepts, confident that, unlike his colleagues, she wouldn't betray their secrets to anyone.)

Wihlidal was anxious to get hired on full-time at the jail, but he confronted an impenetrable wall. His applications were repeatedly rejected; senior officials at the jail routinely gave their relatives and neighbours full-time contracts instead. For instance, Farrell documented how a manager hired his out-of-work neighbour and another laid-off friend. The pair were first hired on as part-timers to get their feet wet and were then handed lucrative forty-hour contracts ahead of more qualified candidates. The incestuous hiring practices angered Farrell because they made a mockery of recommendations made in the aftermath of the highway deaths of the five teens who had escaped from the centre after overpowering an inexperienced female guard. To prevent another

tragedy, a coroner's jury had called for more experienced correctional officers to be hired. Other guards at the jail tolerated the favouritism, knowing that to speak out against the practice would only invite retribution.
Farrell decided to declare war on the jail's administration.

His first step was to apply for full-time work at the jail, though he
never intended to accept the job as it would have caused havoc with
his work for CSIS. His objective was to make a point and begin amass-
ing an incriminating paper trail. "I knew I wouldn't get the job,"
Farrell says. "But I had the experience and was more than qualified."
As he expected, just like Wihlidal, he was passed over for full-time
work. At first, he and his friend complained to the jail's senior administrators. But their complaints fell on deaf ears. Farrell and Wihlidal
were branded as troublesome malcontents and blackballed by management. Farrell hit back by raising a petition at the jail to call for a
probe into the "unethical and corrupt practices at York Detention
Centre." Only four other guards signed it.

Undaunted, he launched a letter-writing campaign. His correspondence to senior government officials, cabinet ministers and
Ontario Premier Bob Rae, opposing the jail's "unethical" hiring practices, would grow to be six inches thick. Farrell received scores of
polite but dismissive responses from bureaucrats. Ontario's minister of
Community and Social Services at the time, Tony Silipo, reassured
him that "management of the Centre is establishing objective criteria
for competitions." Farrell was angry. He wrote Silipo a stinging response,
telling the young minister that his "rhetoric and bullshit" wouldn't dissuade him from pursuing his complaint.

His experiences at the Rotherglen Youth Detention Centre had
taught him that the press could be a powerful but unpredictable ally
when confronting an obstinate bureaucracy. A little wary, he called
Alan Cairns, an experienced reporter at the *Toronto Sun*. Farrell knew
the combative tabloid was in an undeclared war of its own with Rae's
NDP government and that he had some ammunition for the newspaper. (Naturally, Farrell kept Cairns in the dark about his connection
to CSIS.) Unlike Rotherglen, where he fed information to the press
from the shadows, Farrell was prepared to go public with his allegations,

despite having sworn an oath of secrecy when he joined the jail. He also understood the decision could jeopardize his career with CSIS. It was a risk Farrell was prepared to take.

In June 1993, Cairns wrote a small story, buried inside the paper, about the "job scandal." The story triggered a swift and unpleasant response from jail administrators and unsympathetic guards. Farrell was called by a senior jail official and told that his part-time contract would not be renewed. Officials claimed the action wasn't linked to Farrell airing the jail's dirty laundry in public but rather to his "failure" to show up for scheduled shifts. A well-connected guard threatened to break Farrell's arm, and Wihlidal's car was tar-smeared with the words "Pig" and "Rat." Farrell hadn't cowered in the face of schoolyard thugs or fights on the basketball court or in the street. Now, he fought back, propelled by the echo of those past battles. He launched a wrongful-dismissal grievance against the jail and filed a complaint with the provincial ombudsman as well as the Ontario Human Rights Commission. And he issued a warning to a senior bureaucrat at the jail. "I will not let this issue rest until I have a straight answer," Farrell wrote. He kept his word: "I was determined that someone be held accountable for what was going on inside that jail."

Lunau was behind him all the way, urging Farrell to "get the fuckers." In fact, his boss insisted that Farrell go to the press with his complaints if he wanted to get quick results. And when Farrell's photo appeared in the *Toronto Sun*, Tommy Birkett, another intelligence officer assigned to SOS, congratulated him. "It's a tough fight, but someone's got to do it," he told Farrell.

Then Farrell lobbed another bomb at the jail. He and Wihlidal knew about a much darker episode hidden within the prison's walls. Several female guards told Farrell that they had been sexually molested by a male colleague. The assaults had taken place in the late 1980s. The women had kept quiet because they feared for their jobs. In early 1990, one of the victims reluctantly broke her silence and went to administrators at the jail for help. She was assured that the guard would be dealt with swiftly. He wasn't. A labour activist canvassed other women and soon compiled a long and disturbing catalogue of stories about a male guard exposing his genitalia and trying to force himself upon female guards. There were also allegations of rape. In 1990, the labour activist began writing to a string of bureaucrats, government ministers and Premier Rae, urging them to launch an independent probe into the sexual abuse "cover-up" and other misconduct at the jail. The complaints bounced from one ministry to another for three years before ending up in a bureaucratic black hole. The police were never called in to investigate. Meanwhile, the guard at the centre of the storm quietly left York in 1990, after he was confronted by one of his alleged victims.

By the time the sex scandal hit the pages of the *Toronto Sun* in 1993, the government had launched what it described as an "operational review" of the jail. At first, the probe didn't include the alleged sex attacks or questionable hiring practices, but rather, management practices and procedures, morale, safety concerns and staff complaints. When word of the review's limited scope leaked—courtesy of Farrell— the government quickly assured the public that the two issues would be examined. The report, however, would not be made public. Incensed, Farrell and Wihlidal raced to Silipo's Queen's Park offices clad in T-shirts bearing messages that blasted government secrecy. They were thrown out of the legislature for their trouble. They were soon pacing the sidewalk, brandishing placards that demanded the report be made public.

After the story broke, three female guards finally went to the police and filed complaints. On June 22, 1993, Lawrence Maxwell Dawkins, a stocky martial arts expert, was arrested and charged with three counts of sexual assault. Police believed that there may have been as many as fourteen other victims and were told by several women that they would not come forward because they still feared Dawkins. The former guard was eventually handed a suspended sentence and put on probation for three years for sexually assaulting a young female guard. Two other charges against Dawkins were dropped. Meanwhile, a senior jail official who repeatedly rebuffed calls for an inquiry into the sexual assault allegations and the hiring improprieties was reassigned. Prison officials belatedly acknowledged that there were, in fact, "personal" links between managers and a spate of guards the jail had hired. In one case, the jail admitted that the "wrong" guard had been hired. No one, however, was disciplined and Wihlidal was never hired on full-time.

Still, Farrell felt vindicated. He had appeared on local radio, on television and in newspapers, hammering home his point that a public institution was being run like a private club by a few powerful administrators. But he wasn't given his part-time job back and his pocketbook was hurting. He had to win his wrongful-dismissal grievance before he could claim total victory. It wasn't easy. First, the provincial ombudsman and Human Rights Commission told Farrell that they didn't have jurisdiction in the matter. Farrell badgered his union for months for a lawyer to help fight his grievance. The union, Farrell says, was reluctant to pursue the case, because it was preoccupied with thwarting plans to privatize the jail. A union lawyer told Farrell that he didn't have much of a case. Strapped for cash, Wihlidal accepted a small lump sum payment to settle his own grievance. Farrell was alone. A prison official negotiating on the ministry's behalf offered Farrell eleven thousand dollars to go away. He rejected the offer. "I told them that I was prepared to go to court," Farrell says. And that gambit finally worked. Farrell demanded and received $19,999.99 to settle the matter. He even asked that the payments be paid out in four cheques to avoid having taxes eat too deeply into his settlement, and prison officials agreed. Farrell received his last cheque on June 29, 1995. He was also handed a glowing letter of recommendation as part of the settlement. "Throughout John's employment at York Detention Centre, he has been a conscientious, committed professional with a genuine interest in working with people. I can confidently recommend him as a highly motivated individual who would be an asset to your team," wrote Shelley Upshaw, his former shift supervisor.

Farrell celebrated his victory with Lunau. But his boss had a word of caution: he didn't want Farrell to let the APIs or any intelligence officers know that he had won a settlement of almost twenty thousand dollars. Lunau was worried that the windfall might provoke resentment among his peers. Farrell agreed not to boast. To show his gratitude for their support, Farrell bought seven cases of beer for the SOS unit, including a case of Lunau's favourite Sleeman.

Soon, Lunau and Farrell would be raising a toast in celebration of another victory, this time against the service's arch-enemy: the Russians.

7

SOS CALLING

As Farrell waged a public campaign to expose nepotism and wrong-doing inside the York Detention Centre, his boss at CSIS was poised to welcome the jail-guard-turned-media-darling into the spy agency's inner sanctum: Special Operational Services. The move seemed at odds with Farrell's new-found public profile, but by early 1994, Lunau understood that his protege was getting restless. In Farrell's eyes, Operation Vulva was a lucrative gig, but despite the challenges of troubleshooting for his incompetent colleagues, he was bored with picking up "apple pies" and anxious to get more involved in SOS work.

Farrell had proven that he could manage the day-to-day mechanics of a highly classified mail intercept program. And his boss also entrusted him with many of his own pedestrian secrets. For instance, Lunau once jetted to Miami for a weekend getaway with a few of his fellow CSIS officers. Their benign mission: enjoy the sun and an NFL football game. Lunau told his family that he was away on a top-secret assignment and they believed him. To avoid an incriminating sunburn,

Lunau wore a baseball cap and long-sleeved shirt and slathered on the sunscreen. He enjoyed beer in the hot Miami sun in the company of friends, and knew his secret was safe with Farrell.

Lunau was also impressed by Farrell's ability to juggle his prison crusade, Operation Vulva and school. Farrell knew that a university degree was a crucial prerequisite to becoming a full-time intelligence officer. Lunau had promised him repeatedly that once he graduated, the doors to CSIS would officially spring open, and Farrell was close to finishing his criminology degree at SFU by correspondence.

Intelligence officers in Toronto understood that it was Lunau who really ran the SOS unit and that nothing was done without his consent or approval—he was not a man to be crossed. But Farrell had also caught the eye of Ray Murphy, long-time boss, on paper at least, of the SOS crew in Toronto. A former member of the RCMP Security Service, Murphy was a veteran of the spy wars who was content with his place as a kind of polite, titular head of the SOS unit. Lunau dubbed Murphy the "Governor General." His wave of silver hair and habit of wearing grey slacks, a blue blazer and striped ties did give Murphy a regal look. He knew that his job would soon pass to his faithful lieutenant, Don Lunau. The succession was inevitable and he didn't resist it. Lunau wasn't pushy or impatient with his boss. It wasn't his style.

An avid fisher and sportsman, Murphy often played hockey with senior RCMP officers, including the commissioner. Murphy's ties to the Mounties ran deep, and he never forgot them. Mementoes of his days with the "Horsemen" dotted his home in Ajax, Ontario. His old service revolver took centre stage in his living room. Awards and plaques that he won along the way were also proudly on display. Murphy's twenty-five-year union with his wife, Lorraine, was a rare thing at CSIS, where marriages often crumbled under the strain of the secret work.

But the new age of intelligence, with its reliance on computers, satellites, technologically generated research, and analysis were utterly alien to him (as they were for many of his colleagues). His skills had dulled. His underlings joked that Murphy's idea of undercover work was to put on a baseball cap. Indeed, it was Farrell's raw, sometimes unsophisticated, qualities that made him attractive to Murphy—his drive to get the job done no matter what.

In time, Murphy and Farrell would develop a close friendship, baptized over hours of conversation at the SOS boss's favourite watering holes around Toronto. Farrell enjoyed Murphy's company and knew that the aging spy was well-connected and could offer him guidance and perhaps even protection when he needed it. In return, Murphy would come to treat the industrious Young Turk as the son he never had.

With Murphy's consent, Lunau made Farrell an offer—full-time work with the SOS unit in Toronto, with the promise of becoming a staff member once he earned his university degree. His already remarkable career at CSIS was about to take a new turn.

For Canadian intelligence officers, Toronto is the Holy Grail; a subterranean world of safe houses, legends, codes, whispers, furtive glances, secret rendezvous, eavesdropping, stalking and memorable hair-raising moments.

As the Cold War flickered out, Toronto, not Ottawa, became the espionage capital of Canada. CSIS was still interested in Chinese, North Korean and Russian spies as technological and business secrets, rather than state secrets, emerged as the most sought-after prizes. But terrorists, not spies masquerading as diplomats, became the service's principle preoccupation. Toronto, with its rainbow of sometimes fractious ethnic communities—Irish, Somalian, Sudanese, Sri Lankan, Indian and all the nationalities of the Middle East, to name only a few— is a well of support for some of the world's most ruthless terror groups. Of course, Canada's largest and richest city has attracted millions of hard-working, law-abiding immigrants, but it is also home to outlaw immigrants and terrorists who have silently and often easily slipped into a country known for its tolerance and openness. They meld into the city's cultural mosaic while planning and raising money to execute mayhem abroad.

Another emerging threat is the growing influence and power of organized crime syndicates operating in the city. Asian gangs and Russian mobsters thrive in Toronto, where they are involved in racketeering, extortion, drug trafficking, and smuggling both people and weapons. Increasingly, CSIS is being called upon to assist police in monitoring the well-armed and well-financed tentacles of what is known in the intelligence trade as "transnational crime."

Toronto is teeming with spies, terrorists and criminals, and they are all targets of the service's Special Ops unit. Yet for all its allure, SOS work is, ultimately, just burglary with badges. The state-sanctioned break-ins arguably involve a touch more planning and a few more conspirators. But the objective is the same: get in and out without being detected and retrieve something of value. The government's burglars have one decided advantage over their private-sector brethren: when they break into a home, apartment or car of a suspected terrorist or spy, they don't usually carry a crowbar or hammer. CSIS's little-known band of technical wizards, called "techies," can cut custom-made keys to fit the lock of any car, home, apartment or office door in the country.

Once inside, CSIS's SOS cracksmen take careful steps to ensure that they leave behind no trace. Before anything is touched, everything in the house, office or apartment is videotaped by an officer who usually tiptoes in, camcorder in hand. Then come the techies, who install bugging devices quickly and quietly. When the mission is over, the team retreats to a nearby safe house to debrief before packing up and heading home. The information uncovered in the SOS unit's covert entries is passed on to officers manning the service's counter-intelligence and counter-terrorism branches.

Beyond the mystique of the work, there is another, more mundane reason why CSIS officers want a piece of the SOS action—money. SOS work often translates into overtime. Any officer with an ounce of ambition or thirst for a good paycheque pines after work in SOS. For a young intelligence officer making a starting salary of $38,670, working for SOS is akin to finding the proverbial pot at the end of the rainbow. For the chosen few, the spoils can be substantial, often as much as three thousand dollars extra a month.

Lunau began Farrell's initiation into the SOS unit by handing him relatively small assignments. Just days after he offered Farrell the chance to do such work, Lunau gave him a manila envelope. Inside, he found the names of individuals whom Lunau wanted him to check out. One of his first jobs was to delve into the histories of two Americans from New York City who had set up a telecommunications firm in Ottawa. Lunau wanted the background works on both men: corporate, property and personal lien searches, as well as credit and driver's licence checks. Ottawa, Lunau impressed upon Farrell, needed the work done fast and without a trace. Farrell mined his sources in the financial, credit and banking industries, which he had cultivated while working as a postal inspector. Two days later, he paged Lunau to tell his boss that the information was ready. Occasionally, Farrell would map out intriguing links gleaned from his inquiries for his boss, but more often than not, he just gave Lunau the raw data, no questions asked. Lunau would race out to Farrell's home on Kenworthy Avenue to pick up the material.

Lunau started to use Farrell to do such searches for two reasons. For one, other SOS members simply didn't know how. "They had absolutely no idea where to get the information. They wouldn't know their way around a public library, let alone how to do a property search," Farrell says. SOS officers often paged or called him, pleading for his help to track down the right office to conduct a corporate search in Toronto. "They would call me and ask, 'Hey, where's that building again? What floor do I go up on?'"

Secrecy was also paramount. Lunau didn't want a paper trail to exist that would link the searches to the SOS unit and so he turned to his mercenary. Farrell set up a front company, called Northlands Leasing, to charge Lunau and CSIS for the cost of conducting the searches, and incorporated another front company, called Canada Legal Services, to make the requests. This is how the scheme worked: Farrell deposited five hundred dollars or more into a bank account registered to his front company, Canada Legal Services. His front company entered into an agreement with, for example, the Ministry of Transportation, which dipped into the firm's bank account to extract its flat fee whenever Farrell or an intelligence officer made a driver's licence or motor vehicle registration check under the auspices of Canada Legal Services. As a result, there was no trace that it was CSIS making the request. Many legitimate businesses entered into similar arrangements with provincial agencies for convenience. CSIS did it not to save time or money but to shroud its work in another layer of secrecy. Lunau loved Farrell's idea and used the front companies regularly to conduct searches that he didn't want either the local police or the Mounties to get wind of. Turf wars between CSIS and the RCMP raged on as both agencies guarded their investigations and information jealously.

With Ray Murphy's blessing, Lunau began introducing Farrell to the other members of the SOS team: Michelle Tessier, Jack Billingsley and later, Cliff Hatcher, Tommy Birkett and Sandy Brown. Farrell was off the books—the only member of the unit who wasn't officially an intelligence officer—but no one seemed to mind. Unlike his frosty relationships with the other APIs, Farrell befriended his colleagues in the SOS unit. And they reciprocated by quickly accepting Farrell as one of their own. (They became so close that the SOS team, including Lunau, attended the funeral of Farrell's sister Josephine in Toronto.) They were a small, tightly knit group, each member with his or her own peculiar idiosyncrasies, personality and talents.

Tessier was a rare breed at CSIS: a francophone woman working in a male-dominated, anglophone region, in which anyone hailing from east of Cornwall, Ontario, was usually viewed as secretly harbouring separatist loyalties—but Tessier wasn't shy about her nationalist leanings. She chattered incessantly about politics and proudly wore a fleur-de-lys lapel pin. Her political sympathies, however, hadn't stopped her from teaching the children of former prime minister Brian Mulroney and his wife, Mila, how to ski. A natural athlete, Tessier enjoyed the company of her cat; long, relaxing, early morning runs along Toronto's beach-lined boardwalk; and museum-hopping vacations in Europe. Her skill and devotion to her work were evident to her colleagues. She was discreet, prompt and precise. Before joining the service, she had graduated from the Carleton University journalism program and had been asked to join the service's communications branch. She turned the offer down.

Tessier may have had a link to the Mulroneys, but Jack Billingsley was the man with the real connections. With his easy smile and quick wit, he was the bon vivant of the unit, and he had contacts everywhere—at the major banks, credit card companies and, particularly, among police forces. The slim, five-foot-nine, forty-something-year-old with thinning black hair had a healthy ego and always knew someone who could get useful information for the unit without much hassle.

Billingsley cultivated his vast network of sources, in part, by running a profitable travel agency he called For Members Only, which exclusively catered to CSIS employees and police officers. He drummed up business through word of mouth or by handing out his wildly popular calling card, which featured a stern-looking, big-chinned spook, drink in hand, wearing a fedora, dark sunglasses, sandals, multicoloured shorts, crimson sunburn and a heart-shaped "Mom" tattoo. A sheriff's badge adorned an undersized T-shirt that stopped just short of the agent's expansive midriff. The calling card's message: "Travel deals—Anywhere for Law Enforcement Personnel, Family and Friends Only."

Business was booming for the father of two, dubbed "Airport Man" by his grateful colleagues. Billingsley's cellphone rang endlessly with last-minute requests for cheap flights, hotel rooms, cruises and tours in Canada and overseas. The Caribbean and Cancún, where Billingsley salted away enough money to buy two beach-front condominiums, were popular destinations with his clientele.

At times, Billingsley seemed more travel agent than spy, but he was never reprimanded or disciplined for his lucrative extracurricular activities, despite widespread knowledge in the service that he brokered his deals largely on company time. He was, however, the subject of an internal audit. Tom Geiger, the number-three spy in Toronto, ordered the review after he learned how much time Billingsley was actually spending on his CSIS cellphone arranging trips. The bill was big. To make amends, Billingsley was ordered to write a cheque to the Receiver General of Canada. That was it—no suspension, no pay cut, no demotion to a dreaded desk job, no warning of possible dire consequences if he didn't close up shop and concentrate exclusively on his real job.

After he paid his bill, Billingsley and Farrell hatched a simple plan to keep the business humming without attracting any more irritating audits. The pair met at a parking lot in east-end Toronto and exchanged cellphones. Since Farrell wasn't a card-carrying intelligence officer, his expenses weren't as carefully scrutinized as those of the other members of the unit. From then on, Billingsley used Farrell's CSIS phone to make travel arrangements for all his sun-worshipping CSIS friends.

(Billingsley still enjoys a brisk business. Always eager to make a sale, he answers his phone swiftly, often halfway through the first ring. "Hi, it's Jack. What can I do for you?" he said cheerfully when I called.)

Farrell admired Billingsley's ingenuity and artful dodger–like street smarts. The pair shared the same philosophy when it came to their secret work: exploit any conceivable angle to make extra cash. Billingsley was attracted to Farrell's youth, calm demeanour and popularity with women. (Some years later, they enjoyed a wild week in Cancún together. Billingsley made all the arrangements, including prying whatever perks he could out of a charter airline that flew the pair to Mexico. Their room at a brand new beach-front hotel featured a twenty-foot balcony facing the ocean. Billingsley's condos were unavailable; they were occupied by senior CSIS officers and their wives.)

Like Farrell, Billingsley knew that SOS operatives were protected by a reassuring blanket of security that shielded them from any serious or lasting punishment. Billingsley was able to run his travel agency on company time because he was liked and protected by powerful CSIS officers like his boss, Don Lunau. He was an untouchable. Former Mounties, such as Billingsley, are members of a powerful clique at CSIS, where they guard their privileges and perks jealously. According to Dick Lewis, the former president of the CSIS employee association, Billingsley enjoyed another advantage that warded off punishment. He was a member of the "fair-haired boys club"—a select few intelligence officers who curried favour with the service's top brass. Less-favoured officers have been drummed out of the service because they refused to accept transfers, their memo-writing skills weren't quite up to snuff or they simply alienated the wrong people. The well-connected club, on the other hand, can do no wrong. This double standard, Lewis says, is a sorry part of the cultural fabric of Canada's intelligence service. New

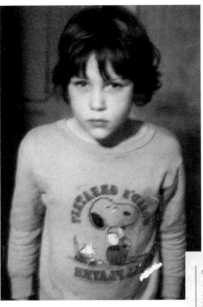

In Grade 6

John Farrell at five

Farrell driving to the basket on the
Neil McNeil team

A summary of his high-school basketball career

Farrell in the back row (number 22) with
the Simon Fraser team. Coach Jay Triano
is third from the right in the front row

The Farrell clan at Gwen's wedding in
1984. From left: Greg, Mary Lou, Art,
Claire, Carmelita, Annette, Patricia,
Louise, John's father, Gwen, her new
husband, Kevin, John's mother, John,
Cathy, Josephine, and Joe

Jesse Barnes, groomed to be a mob hitman, who ended up in possession of top-secret CSIS surveillance files that had been stolen out of a car belonging to a member of the service's watcher unit

Barnes outside the small home in Novar, Ontario, where he hid the files

Farrell's API identity badge

Kenny Baker, the API who trained Farrell in the etiquette of CSIS mail intercepts

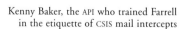

Pat Baker

The parking garage near CSIS's Toronto headquarters where Farrell
would meet with Don Lunau and Ray Murphy

Don Lunau

Angela Jones, the CSIS officer who
visited Jesse Barnes in prison.

CSIS's annual picnic at
Toronto's Centre Island

CSIS officers at play, at
one of their annual baseball
games in Toronto

Farrell with one of Richard
Garland's ex-girlfriends, from whom
he was ordered to retrieve one of
Garland's troublesome calling cards

Garland's fake card

GOVERNMENT OF CANADA

RICHARD D. GARLAND
FEDERAL AGENT

OFFICE OF: THE SOLICITOR
GENERAL
OF CANADA   TEL. 416•982•9390

FOR MEMBERS ONLY

905-824-5070
"TRAVEL FOR
LAW ENFORCEMENT PERSONNEL"

Farrell with Garland at Garland's wedding

Jack Billingsley's business cards for his travel agency

FOR MEMBERS ONLY
TRAVEL DEALS - ANYWHERE FOR
LAW ENFORCEMENT PERSONNEL, FAMILY
AND FRIENDS ONLY
• CRUISES
• TOURS
• DOMESTIC
• INTERNATIONAL
(905) 824-5070

Farrell with Findlay Wihlidal, his fellow whistle-blower on practices at the York Detention Centre

The Roehampton apartment building where the Russian sleeper agents, Ian and Laurie Lambert, lived. Farrell rented apartment 602 so CSIS could keep tabs on them

The bugging device disguised as a phone jack used by Farrell to spy on a postal worker suspected of leaking information to the media during the Grant Bristow affair

Ian Lambert's sports car, which CSIS briefly stole in order to bug, parked in front of the Parisienne condo, where Ian lived after he broke up with Laurie

The Lamberts, whose real names were Dmitriy Olshevsky and Yelena Olshevskaya

The Crown key

Farrell with Anita Keyes, Olshevsky's Canadian lover and now wife

CP/*Toronto Star* (Ken Faught)

The apartment rented by Farrell as a CSIS observation post, which was instead used by Heather McDonald, the daughter of a senior CSIS officer. Apartment 6C is on the left, top floor of the centre building

Farrell at home with friends. He's standing next to Renée Murphy, whom he coached so she could pass her RCMP entrance exam

Marchessault (right) with Cliff Hatcher, a member of the Toronto Special Ops unit

Jean-Luc Marchessault, at the far left in the front row, with his graduating class of CSIS officers

Farrell during his stint training to be a Durham Regional Police officer

Farrell handing back his CSIS-issue equipment to an officer in front of the intelligence service's headquarters on Front Street West in Toronto.

Deborah Baic

Uncredited photos courtesy of John Farrell or Andrew Mitrovica.

recruits quickly understand that there are one set of rules for the "fair-haired boys" and another less forgiving set of rules for everyone else.

Tommy Birkett, an intelligence officer assigned to the SOS unit, was also a member of that lucky fraternity. The married father of two was, in many ways, the antithesis of the new breed of intelligence officer that CSIS's founding fathers wanted to attract. Birkett was a natty dresser with blond hair and a fondness for Ralph Lauren suits. His family had money and owned a posh cottage in Muskoka and a condo in Florida. Birkett had little time or patience for the young, well-scrubbed university graduates who joined the service and received intelligence training under its umbrella. Birkett earned his stripes and sharpened his investigative skills by working long, lonely hours policing parts of Canada that most Canadians couldn't point out on a map. The clash of cultures between old and new still causes friction among CSIS officers. Mutual suspicion, mistrust and open disdain mark the tense relationship.

All the same, Birkett himself is a university graduate. Young intelligence officers who have worked with him in Toronto describe him as a soft-spoken officer who doesn't flaunt his family's wealth and can sweet-talk his way out of any bind. They also note Birkett's irritating sense of humour. In the summer, the SOS member often sat on a stool at East Side Mario's—a popular restaurant close to CSIS's offices—cradling a beer and pitching peanuts at colleagues who happened to walk by the open window.

Birkett quietly longed for a return to the days when cops were hard-nosed and sometimes meted out rough, swift justice—and he soon warmed to Farrell, who had a natural affinity for the work, and the street credentials and toughness to back up his bravado.

Cliff Hatcher was Jack Billingsley's brother-in-law—an imposing figure who at six-foot-four looked every inch a cop. His obvious physical prowess was married to an agile mind. Hatcher was polite and well-read, and his colleagues in the SOS unit considered him a finicky perfectionist who enjoyed spending hours renovating his home. If anyone represented the new breed of intelligence officer, Hatcher was it, even though he was also an ex-RCMP officer. Born in Newfoundland, he had been with the Mounties before becoming a spy, and had failed his first attempt to join the service. He enrolled at the University of Toronto and graduated with an English degree. He applied at CSIS again and was accepted. Hatcher was posted to Ottawa headquarters before moving to Toronto to work in the SOS unit. He loved to travel and shared ownership of the two condos in Cancún with Billingsley. (The pair had married sisters from Newfoundland whose maiden name was Farrell. They are not related to John.) Farrell admired Hatcher's quiet, self-effacing manner and his obvious loyalty to the service.

Like Hatcher, Sandy Brown attended the University of Toronto, where she studied Russian literature and was a member of the swim team. Young, athletic and bright, Brown seemed to be a natural fit for work in the SOS unit. But her private life was a concern. Brown had a child with an American Marine who was stationed at the U.S. embassy in Moscow, and she had developed a disconcerting habit of meeting men through Internet chat rooms. Brown told her Internet Romeos that she worked for Canada's secret service. Billingsley considered her Internet surfing for companionship a security breach and complained to Lunau. Lunau was furious with Brown, but she, too, escaped punishment because he had a soft spot for the pretty intelligence officer.

Farrell found himself drawn to the relaxing rhythm of SOS work. At least three days a week, Lunau, Murphy and gang got together at bars across the city—Lido's, the Beach House Bar & Grill, the Boardwalk Cafe, the Rose & Crown at Yonge and Eglinton or the Beverley Tavern on Queen Street—to spend long, leisurely afternoons enjoying more than a few drinks. Drinking, Farrell soon discovered, was an occupational hazard. Although Hatcher and Billingsley abstained, the other members of the team knew how to party on company time. It was not unusual, Farrell says, for bills to reach as high as eight hundred dollars at one sitting. Farrell, who was not immune to the lure of booze, joined in, especially as CSIS was picking up the tab.

The SOS members aren't the only truants. Other CSIS officers spend as little time as possible at their desks, preferring long, early-morning and mid-afternoon coffee breaks instead. A Starbucks coffee emporium at the corner of John and Queen streets in downtown Toronto is a popular retreat for CSIS's legion of caffeine junkies. The trendy coffee boutique is several blocks from CSIS's headquarters, but many of the officers don't seem to mind—they need the exercise, the coffee is great and it certainly beats working.

Since CSIS isn't a police force, drinking on the job, while frowned upon, is a popular habit. "This place stinks of a brewery," an intelligence officer once joked when a large pack of his colleagues returned from their leisurely liquid lunch. They were not amused.

But the drinking doesn't stop at lunch. Each year, CSIS arranges morale-boosting "official office functions" where attendance is encouraged and so, apparently, is drinking. Every July in Toronto, for example, CSIS managers throw a private picnic for intelligence officers on Centre Island, a short ferry hop from headquarters. Pictures taken at a recent picnic show cases of beer stacked high beside park benches. The picnic takes place on a workday. So, in effect, Canada's sober and responsible spies are paid out of the public purse to enjoy a little fresh air and bonding. It is all repeated in the fall, when CSIS managers organize a softball tournament at a baseball diamond near Toronto's beachfront. Once again, attendance is encouraged and the beer is plentiful. Most intelligence officers show up, but others choose to stay home. Everyone gets paid.

Farrell organized parties at the SkyDome hotel for an eclectic mix of people: CSIS officers, members of various police forces, correctional officers, drug dealers, paramedics, strippers, petty crooks and even the odd Canadian rock star. He got himself a "law enforcement" account from a local brewery, would order a few kegs of beer and rent a luxury box overlooking the field. The parties made him and CSIS a lot of friends, and became legendary even at the SkyDome hotel, where couples had been caught making love with the curtains open in plain sight of a stadium full of sports fans.

Lunau and Farrell often preferred to do their drinking in private. Shortly after Farrell became an API, the pair began having lunch together almost every day at noon. In the summer, they ate at the Boardwalk Cafe or Mr. Slate Sports Bar, a pool hall in the Beaches, where Lunau liked his burgers well-done. In the winter, they headed to Chinatown to enjoy a cheap all-you-can-eat buffet. Again, the drinking would begin at lunch and often didn't end until late in the evening. So much beer was consumed that Farrell came to believe that beer drinking, not hockey or baseball, was Lunau's favourite pastime.

It was at lunch that Farrell first noticed Lunau's constant hand-washing. He also coughed incessantly. It wasn't an illness, but another nervous tic. A keen observer of human nature, Farrell made his own connection between Lunau's quest for cleanliness and his work. The cough, however, remained a mystery to him. A fastidious man, Lunau dressed casually, with an ever-present fanny pack lassoed around his waist. He was fond of wearing a black windbreaker with a Porsche decal and dreamed of one day owning the European-made sports car, but had had to settle for a new Ford Bronco once his van packed it in.

The bond between Lunau and Farrell eventually grew so strong that it triggered envy among other members of the unit. They asked Farrell about Lunau's family, wife and habits—questions he always refused to answer.

Lunau once even did the unthinkable: he invited Farrell to his modest home in Pickering for dinner with his wife, Jennifer, his two teenaged stepchildren and his Siberian husky, Thunder. None of the other members of the unit had been invited to Lunau's home, and the invitation bothered them. Farrell knew that the dinner was a sign of the depth of Lunau's trust in him, and when Lunau gave Farrell a tour of his house before dinner, the trust was tested. Farrell discovered that furniture he had sold to CSIS for special ops work, including a futon couch, a bookshelf, a radio and a TV set, had found a new home: Lunau's basement. Farrell passed the test. He didn't tell a soul.

The pair eagerly swapped stories at dinner about Thunder and Farrell's burly German shepherd, Heidi. Lunau loved his dog as much as he enjoyed playing hockey at Moss Park Arena with other CSIS and RCMP officers every Tuesday afternoon. That evening, Lunau rambled on about his life. He told John that he had attended high school in

Toronto and then went to university; he had married twice; he met his second wife, Jennifer, a tall, slim, polite woman of Korean descent, at the office; they were wed at Toronto's city hall in the early 1990s in the presence of a handful of family and friends. And he confided that Jennifer's spicy cooking often gave him stomach cramps.

Lunau pampered his stepchildren. Like many fathers, he worried that his son was spending too much time in front of the computer, and wanted him to share his passion for team sports. His son took up martial arts instead.

After dinner, Lunau asked Farrell if he would throw a birthday party for his son. For Farrell, the request was really an order. Farrell called Tom Holmes, the manager of the Cineplex Odeon movie theatre at Morningside Avenue and Highway 401 in Scarborough, and arranged a special treat for Lunau's son and twenty of his boisterous friends: pop, popcorn and special seating in a theatre with an extra-big screen.[1] Farrell tried to think of the day as a long-term investment. Lunau, his good friend, might reciprocate one day.

Lunau wasn't the only SOS member to take advantage of Farrell's skills and contacts. When Billingsley's marriage began to fall apart (it ultimately ended in divorce), he asked Farrell to spy on his wife. Billingsley thought she was having an affair with a business executive, and he wanted proof. Farrell reluctantly agreed to tail the alleged lovers. The surveillance was done, Farrell says, on company time and with the approval of senior CSIS managers.[2] When Sandy Brown began an Internet relationship with a landscape architect from Boston, she asked Farrell to check him out with his police contacts south of the border. He did.

When Laurie, the eldest of Ray Murphy's three precocious daughters was getting married, Murphy asked Farrell for a particularly special favour.

---

[1] Holmes made the arrangements as a favour to John. He once dated one of Farrell's sisters.

[2] Later Billingsley intercepted the executive's cell-phone records to try to determine when, and how often, he was calling Billingsley's wife.

"Whatever you need, Ray," Farrell said.

A frugal man, Murphy asked Farrell if he could smuggle a load of cheap alcohol, preferably rum, from the United States into Canada for the wedding. Murphy told Farrell that he was paying for the reception and wanted to cut down on any unnecessary expenses.

"No problem," Farrell said. "Consider it done, Ray."

Farrell approached a Toronto prison guard he knew who had contacts with smugglers who ran alcohol and cigarettes into Canada through the Akwesasne reservation, which straddles the U.S.-Canada border near Cornwall, Ontario.

"I put a call in for two cases of rum," Farrell says.

Unfortunately, the smugglers were arrested before Farrell's shipment of rum arrived. Undaunted, he quickly moved to Plan B. Farrell drove down to Buffalo, New York, and met some law-enforcement contacts who helped him smuggle a case of six large bottles of rum back into Canada. The retail price for each bottle was eighty dollars. The cost to Farrell: fifteen dollars. Farrell charged CSIS for his mileage to and from Buffalo, before dropping the rum off at Billingsley's home in Mississauga. Billingsley drove the contraband to CSIS's offices, where he met Murphy in the underground parking lot. "They did a trunk-to-trunk," Farrell says.

Murphy invited Farrell to the wedding, but he didn't go. He was worried that he would end up tending bar or be asked to deal with unruly guests.

Farrell's unofficial membership in the exclusive, no-holds-barred world of Special Ops was christened over drinks, favours and promises. Farrell believed that eventually Lunau would arrange Farrell's official induction into the SOS unit. For now, he was content to enjoy the ride.

8

OPERATION STANLEY CUP

On a pleasant afternoon in July 1994, Farrell had finished his morning mail runs and was enjoying a lunch of cereal and toast, when the private line in his bedroom rang. He picked up the receiver, hoping it wasn't Lunau. He was tired and wanted to spend an afternoon away from postal stations, white supremacists, APIs and CSIS's downtown headquarters. But it was Lunau, and he sounded unusually serious.

"John, I want you to shave, put on a clean shirt and tie and get down here as soon as possible."

This must be important, Farrell thought, if Lunau wants me to shave.

So he hopped into the shower, dragged a razor across his face, donned a shirt and tie and headed to the underground parking lot for his hastily arranged appointment with Lunau. He also quickly brushed Heidi's hairs out of his car since Lunau had mentioned that Murphy would be joining them. Farrell didn't want the stolid SOS chief's blue blazer and grey slacks to get covered in dog hair. As Farrell zoomed down the ramp into the underground lot, he called Lunau on his private line.

"ETA, two minutes," Farrell told Lunau.

"Great. We'll be right down."

Farrell parked and waited. Minutes later, Lunau pushed through a glass door into the lot. Murphy followed him half a minute later. The senior intelligence officers slid into Farrell's compact car. Lunau sat in back and Murphy up front. Both men looked stern, though Farrell sensed an excitement simmering just beneath their veneer of seriousness. Lunau began the briefing.

"John, Ray's going to ask you to do some stuff," Lunau replied.

"No problem, Donnie, whatever you need," Farrell said.

Murphy took over. "We need you to do an operation. It involves renting an apartment next door to two high-profile targets. This is a very sensitive operation, and we are getting our instructions from Ottawa."

The instructions came from Keith McDonald. (Farrell would meet McDonald later that year at a funeral home just outside Barrie after Lunau's father died. They would also share small talk over a couple of pints of beer at a tavern in town after the funeral.) Murphy and Lunau would not, and could not, have enlisted Farrell in such a sensitive operation without McDonald's consent. Murphy was emphatic. The service needed Farrell. And they needed him to get that particular apartment. "It's imperative that we get this apartment, John. We will do anything it takes to get it. Money is absolutely no object," Murphy said. "You go up there, and you work the superintendent and get that goddamn place."

Farrell could see that his bosses were thrilled, but he had no reason to share in their excitement. The request was simply another order that had to be obeyed. And his calm was ruffled only slightly when Murphy told him the identities of the two targets, Ian and Laurie Lambert. The husband and wife were spies, working for the Russian Foreign Intelligence Service, the SVR (formerly the KGB). The Lamberts' real names were Yelena Olshevskaya and Dmitriy Olshevsky.

For CSIS, Russian intelligence officers still represented the zenith of the spy game. Veteran spies like Murphy and Lunau spent careers searching, indeed yearning, for an assignment like this one. The Russians were considered the most skilled and accomplished adversaries in the Byzantine world of espionage. The duel with the Russians would test the service's patience, determination and will. CSIS dubbed the caper Operation Stanley Cup. And like winning the cherished hockey trophy, the operation would mark the pinnacle of many careers. Lunau and Murphy knew they would be judged, perhaps even remembered, by its outcome. To ensure their success and cement their legacy, they turned to a young man who wasn't even a full-fledged intelligence officer.

Ian and Laurie Lambert's presence in Canada seemed to be the remnant of a time when the world was still divided by two irreconcilable ideologies: capitalism and communism. By the late 1980s, the Soviet Union had emerged from the suffocating grip of totalitarian rule. Glasnost had taken root and become part of the world's lexicon. Its architect, Mikhail Gorbachev, the savvy, telegenic Soviet leader, had become a media darling around the globe. He was someone, the West declared, it could do business with. Between East and West, the old hostilities, the distrust, the fear of nuclear annihilation eased. The Cold War thawed at a dizzying pace, and the world sighed with relief. In an instant, however, that relief turned to dread. On August 19, 1991, eight Communist hardliners attempted to oust Gorbachev in a *coup d'état*. In a brave show of defiance, reformer Boris Yeltsin stood on a tank and urged his country to resist. Yeltsin prevailed. The Communist Party was dissolved. The Russian Federation was born. The Cold War was finally over. Or so it seemed.

In many ways, the reassuring words and images were a mirage. Silent warriors in the shadow war of espionage remained hard at work. And Canada, a supposed docile backwater in the game of international intrigue, remained part of the covert battlefield. This nation has always been a magnet for spies, particularly Russian spies. Canada's democratic society and its proximity to the United States, the principal target of several other nations, have made it an attractive destination.

Throughout the Cold War, Soviet intelligence agencies had enormous success in penetrating Western governments, spy services and defence contractors to collect political, technological and military secrets. The demise of the Cold War saw Russian spymasters shift their resources to non-military industries, attempting to pilfer technological and scientific secrets as a means of rejuvenating the decrepit Russian economy. The expansion of East-West scientific exchanges and joint business ventures offered Russia even more opportunities to steal scientific and technological information generated by Western governments and industry at considerable cost.

Though its former satellite states are increasingly gravitating to the West's orbit—either through the proposed expansion of the North Atlantic Treaty Organization (NATO) or the European Union—Russia's intelligence services remain determined not only to prevent Moscow from becoming a marginal player in Europe but also to ensure that its country's leadership continues to exert influence over the continent's future. As a result, Russia's espionage officers remain a formidable adversary and a potential threat to the security of the West.

The Lamberts were two in an unknown legion of foreign spies in Canada. The attractive young couple lived in Toronto's uptown, where they fit right in. They had a taste for fine clothes, good food and expensive cars. In the early 1990s, the Lamberts rented a one-bedroom apartment at 77 Roehampton Avenue, Suite 601. The gleaming ten-storey building, with its marble foyer and semi-circular driveway, is a stone's throw from Yonge Street, just north of Eglinton. The neighbourhood is filled with brand-name designer stores, chic restaurants and nightclubs. The couple often went window shopping, hand in hand. They occasionally shared brief but affectionate kisses during their regular evening walks. They were, it appeared, very much in love.

Ian, who had the physique and rough-hewn face of a middleweight boxer, was a photo enlarger for Black Photo Corporation in Markham, Ontario. In his spare time, he studied politics, international relations and psychology at the University of Toronto. Laurie was demure, almost coquettish. With her fine, dark hair, high cheekbones and slim frame, she was often mistaken for a model. But her beguiling looks belied her less than glamorous work as a clerk at the Gerling Global Life Insurance Company. The couple did their banking at a branch of the Canadian Imperial Bank of Commerce (CIBC) at 2576

Yonge Street, where they also kept a safety deposit box (CSIS would try unsuccessfully to burrow into it). To their very small circle of friends, the Lamberts were a charming, if ordinary, Canadian couple.

The Lamberts were, in fact, highly trained members of an elite Russian espionage unit that slipped operatives into Western countries using assumed identities and built "legends" to mask their espionage. Directorate S of the SVR dispatched officers, who worked alone or posed as couples, to gather political, economic, scientific, technological and military intelligence from target countries. The Lamberts received regular instructions from headquarters—known as the Centre and located in Moscow—through coded messages sent via short-wave radio. The couple also had contact with another spy, known as a Line N officer, working under diplomatic cover at Russia's embassy in Ottawa.

In spy parlance, the Lamberts were "illegal residences." Constructing airtight legends was crucial to the success of their covert mission. They not only had to appear to belong in Canada but also to know enough about this country's people, geography and history so as not to raise suspicion among friends, neighbours and co-workers. They needed a history, too; a place in Canada to call their own, where they were born and raised. The two spies stole the first building blocks of their legends from two dead infants. The theft, although unseemly, was routine spy craft and a tactic employed by espionage agencies around the globe.

The real Ian Mackenzie Lambert's death certificate reveals that he was born in Toronto on November 24, 1965, to Mackenzie Archibald Lambert and Miriam Elizabeth Helen Orson, who both hailed from Scotland. The baby died on February 17, 1966, and was cremated at the Toronto Necropolis and Crematorium four days after his death. His ashes were buried in a "common ground" plot and marked only with a tiny stone chiselled with the number 72A. The nondescript marker was concealed by several inches of unkempt grass and earth in a tree-shaded section of the sprawling cemetery in Toronto. The real Laurie Catherine Mary Brodie was born on September 8, 1963, in the small parish of St. Willibrords in Verdun, Quebec. Her parents were Melvin Brodie and Thelma McDougall. She died on August 7, 1965, in Toronto and was buried in a Windsor cemetery.

Using forged travel documents, the Lamberts entered Canada in the late 1980s. Ian spent time at an apartment in Vancouver and one at 600 de la Gauchetière in Montreal before meeting up with Laurie in Toronto. Credit, banking and provincial records show that the Lamberts began building their legends in earnest in 1990. The first and perhaps most important step was to get married. A marriage licence is a symbolic commitment, not only between husband and wife but to a society. And with it comes an important measure of legitimacy and respectability.

In a small civil ceremony at Toronto's Old City Hall on December 10, 1991, Ian Lambert and Laurie Brodie tied the knot. The spies asked two co-workers to witness their short exchange of vows. On the one-page marriage certificate, the Russian agents provided details of their legends to the unsuspecting Justice of the Peace who performed the ceremony. On the document, both Laurie and Ian declared that they had never been married. Ian listed his age as twenty-five, while Laurie gave hers as twenty-eight. Ian gave his religion as Anglican, while Laurie claimed to be a Catholic. The newlyweds' distinctive signatures suggested long and careful practice. Ian's penmanship was bold and firm, while Laurie had a more graceful, feminine hand.

The marriage certificate also offered up hints that the two spies may not have been as well-trained or at ease with their legends as expected. Ian, for example, incorrectly listed his mother's maiden name as Green. He also incorrectly listed his job as a "printer." For her part, Laurie jotted down "unknown" in response to a query about the birthplace of her parents. Despite the curious errors and omissions, an official with the Office of the Registrar General certified that the information provided on the certificate was "correct and sufficient" and registered the marriage of the two Russian spies on Christmas Eve, 1991. In return for their perjury, the Lamberts received a wonderful and much needed Christmas present: marriage licence C933673.

With their marriage licence in hand, they began adding to the pieces of ID and other plastic that fill most Canadians' wallets and are proof, on paper at least, that we exist. The Lamberts collected social insurance numbers, driver's licences and passports in the dead children's names. Laurie was issued a driver's licence on December 20, 1990. Ian obtained his a month later, on January 31, 1991. In 1993, in a move that surely attracted some uncomfortable attention, he paid over twenty thousand dollars cash for a two-door, red Mazda MX-3 Precidia. He bought the high-powered sports car from Gyro Mazda, a small dealership close to the couple's apartment. He and Laurie also began applying for and receiving a batch of credit cards. Ian took out a card with Canada's oldest department store, the Hudson's Bay Company. He also carried credit cards with IKEA, Visa and MasterCard. Ian's cards had meagre spending limits. Laurie was the shopper. The limits on her credit cards topped four thousand dollars. By 1996, Laurie had a purse full of credit cards, including American Express, Visa, Eaton's, the Bay and IKEA.

Once the couple, with their methodically built histories, were comfortably settled into their new apartment, Ian started school, enrolling at the University of Toronto's Woodsworth College in the winter of 1992. Lambert may not have known the college's ideological pedigree, but it was entirely appropriate that a Russian socialist should register there. The college was named after J. S. Woodsworth, the Canadian clergyman, labour leader and socialist who helped found the Co-operative Commonwealth Federation (CCF), the country's first mainstream leftist party. In his first year, Ian took only one course, but it was a class that would undoubtedly improve his understanding of his "adoptive" country: Introduction to Canadian Politics. At first, Lambert was a good and conscientious student and his marks reflected his enthusiasm. He scored a respectable 77 per cent, earning himself a B+ in a class where the average grade was C+. The following year, Lambert signed up for four courses: Introduction to Politics; Political Theory; Politics and U.S. Government; and Introduction to International Politics. Again, the courses seemed well-suited for a spy trying to ground himself in the history and politics of the nations he was dispatched to. His grades, however, were mediocre. He scored two Cs, a B+ in political theory, but a dismal D+ in economics.

In general, Lambert chose large classes where he could remain anonymous and avoid striking up potentially tricky friendships with inquisitive students. In 1994, he took only three courses, but it was an eclectic selection. He studied psychology, took an introductory course in international relations and a class called Global Political Geography. The academic promise Lambert had shown in 1992 evaporated by 1994. His grades plummeted. He scored an anemic 57 per cent in his psychology course.

Ian's problems at school paled in comparison to another potentially catastrophic difficulty the couple wrestled with. Both of the Lamberts had difficulty keeping their legends straight. The telling errors and gaps on the marriage certificate were a clear sign. Ian compounded those blunders with a breathtaking error. When he applied for one of his credit cards he gave his full name as Ian Mohammed Lambert, not Ian Mackenzie Lambert. Why the experienced intelligence officer made such an extraordinary mistake remains a mystery. Ian even got into a serious traffic accident in Toronto in November 1995, which attracted the attention of police. He was charged, but escaped with a seventy-five-dollar fine and a few demerits. Co-workers wondered why he wore his wedding band on his right hand—which was a Russian tradition. When a co-worker pointed out that the ring should be on his left hand, the spy briefly dropped his guard.

"What are you talking about? I have it on the proper hand," he protested.

Ian's hard-to-pin-down accent seemed strangely at odds with his Scottish Anglican background. And some colleagues noticed it changed dramatically when he joined them for a drink or two after work. One female co-worker once gently confronted Lambert about the sudden change. He dismissed her queries with a joke. "Ah, that always happens when I get drunk," he said.

She didn't buy the explanation, but didn't pursue the matter.

Laurie told co-workers that she was born in Canada but had travelled to Sweden with her mother after her parents separated, returning later to this country. Oddly, a close friend said, she had difficulty recalling her time in Sweden. And the self-proclaimed opera buff rarely went to the opera in Toronto. Co-workers also wondered how the couple were able to maintain their rather expensive lifestyle. The apartment in the tony neighbourhood, the upmarket leather jackets and the expensive car seemed out of step with their moderate income. The Lamberts' apparent difficulty with their legends would soon bear consequences.

Two CSIS officers, posing as husband and wife, made the first attempt to become the Lamberts' next-door neighbours. They failed. So Murphy and Lunau turned to Farrell to rent apartment 602 at 77 Roehampton Avenue. Fidgeting uncomfortably in Farrell's tiny car in the underground parking lot at CSIS headquarters, they hammered out a cover story. Farrell would pose as an IBM systems analyst who had recently moved back to the city and was looking for an apartment to suit his single and active lifestyle. If he was going to have to hang out at the apartment for long hours, Farrell demanded that it be furnished with an unlisted phone number and cable television. Lunau and Murphy agreed.

Operation Stanley Cup was Farrell's first big taste of SOS work, and he, as always, was determined to do a good job. When their brief meeting ended, Lunau handed Farrell one thousand dollars and wished him good luck. Luck, he told his boss, was never the key to a successful operation—planning and attention to detail were.

He may not have needed any luck, but Farrell did need help finding Roehampton Avenue, since he rarely ventured to that part of the city. He pulled out his thick Perly's map book and charted a route. As he made his way up Yonge Street, he went over his cover story. He also sped through a mental check list of do's and don'ts. Farrell worried about being followed. He gunned through a number of busy intersections just as traffic lights moved from amber to red. He also made a few dizzying U-turns. Satisfied, he slowly turned onto Roehampton Avenue. As he leaned over his steering wheel, Farrell's eyes scanned the south side of the street, searching for number 77.

The building's superintendent was busy doing his daily chores when Farrell arrived at the well-manicured entrance and buzzed the super's apartment in vain. Luckily, a female tenant arrived, and Farrell smiled benignly as he followed her into the building. He found Marty, the superintendent, hunched over a mop in the basement. Farrell introduced himself and apologized for the intrusion.

"Do you have any apartments for rent?"

"Yes, there are two," Marty replied. "One is on the second floor and one is on the sixth floor. I think they're both available. Would you like to take a look?"

"That's very kind of you," Farrell said, as Marty laid down his mop and escorted him up the elevator. As they went, Farrell told Marty that he had just returned from British Columbia and was anxious to move into the neighbourhood. The pair made a quick tour of both apartments. Suite 602 was tiny, barely over 700 square feet, and the rent was $940 a month, including utilities and an underground parking spot. Farrell told the super he liked it.

"I may have made a mistake," Marty told Farrell. "It might already be taken." He went to check and Farrell's heart sank. As he reached into his wallet prepared to offer a five-hundred-dollar bribe for the place, Marty, his instant friend, emerged with good news.

"John, it's all yours."

Farrell handed Marty five hundred dollars as a down payment and another five hundred as a tip. "This is for being so kind," he said.

The super politely refused. "John, it's really not necessary. I hope you enjoy living here," Marty said, handing him a copy of the lease.

Farrell drove home, removed his tie and called Lunau, who was anxiously waiting by his phone at CSIS headquarters. "Everything is set," he said.

"Great, John. I knew you could do it."

Two minutes later, Murphy called to congratulate Farrell and fire questions at him.

"Are you sure we are on the sixth floor?" Murphy asked.

"Yes, of course," Farrell said.

"What's the super like?"

"He won't be a problem. Everything's fine."

"Just great work, really great work," Murphy repeated.

It had taken Farrell less than an hour to accomplish what Lunau and Murphy seemed to have waited a lifetime for: to get close to two Russian spies. Despite his success, Farrell's workday was not over.

Operation Vulva churned along. Lunau dropped by later in the day with the mail intercepts that Farrell had to return.

After meeting his stable of APIs, Farrell scooted over to a Canada Trust branch at 2453 Yonge Street to open an account, depositing the nearly three thousand dollars that Lunau had given him to cover the first and last month's rent, as well as other expenses. Farrell couldn't resist flirting with the pretty bank clerk as she made out the $1,880–money order he would later hand Marty. His banking done, he headed home to fill out the lease application, listing another of the front companies that Lunau had asked him to set up—Housing Unlimited—and a close friend as a reference. The fictitious firm allegedly specialized in finding apartments for corporate executives, so the service could rent apartments without leaving a paper trail to CSIS. Housing Unlimited and Farrell shared the same pager number. When someone called the bogus company requesting a reference check for Farrell or another intelligence officer, he simply disguised his voice and reassured the caller that the applicant was a responsible, mature and conscientious client. The scam had the added advantage of alerting Farrell to who was making the inquiries and how detailed they were.

By this time, Farrell was juggling several front companies that he had set up for Lunau and the service. The firms shared the same mailing address: a post office box number on Danforth Avenue. CSIS paid the fees associated with setting up and maintaining the front companies. With Lunau's consent, Farrell also created a sham credit check company to occasionally alter key information on his credit statements. Posing as an official from the front company, Farrell would call Equifax, a firm that houses credit information on thousands of Canadian citizens and businesses, to update client addresses and phone numbers. The client was, of course, John Farrell. Farrell routinely altered the information to conform with the legends he was using on missions for CSIS.

The young operative was simultaneously managing Operation Vulva, conducting credit and other checks for Lunau and renting observation posts for Operation Stanley Cup. Farrell's long day began at half past four in the morning when he raced to Niagara Falls and Hamilton to intercept the mail of three high-profile CSIS targets. As his workload grew, so did the financial rewards. He was often pulling in over $1,200 tax-free a week for "professional services" rendered.

The morning after he'd secured the apartment on Roehampton, he met with Marty to settle the lease. Marty was finishing his breakfast when Farrell buzzed his apartment. The super's wife invited him in as if he were an old friend. Marty told Farrell that the apartment building's property managers, Elsberg Investments Limited, had to do a standard credit check before the apartment was officially his.

"No problem, Marty," Farrell said.

"Look, I'm going to give you the keys anyway, because you're the kind of person we want living here."

"That's very kind," Farrell responded, smiling broadly.

With the precious key in hand, Farrell called a thrilled Lunau and made arrangements to hand it over, along with a copy of the lease.

Farrell moved into the apartment on August 1, 1994, with the help of a friend. Lunau had given him about four hundred dollars to rent a van to move some of his belongings into the apartment. His cash register instantly began ringing when Lunau told him the service was prepared to pay for any belongings he brought from home to furnish the apartment. Farrell scooped up everything in sight: cutlery, a coat rack, shoe stands, dishes, a futon couch, books, clothes, hangers, shoes and cleaning supplies. All told, Farrell made over five hundred dollars and split the money with his buddy.

Murphy and Lunau had also dropped off bookshelves, a bed frame, a desk, lamps and chairs at Farrell's house to add to the move. Most of the paraphernalia came from a secret CSIS warehouse, located near a large RCMP detachment in Newmarket, where the service stores furniture, cars and other items used in covert operations.

Farrell couldn't believe it. "Think about it," he says. "Two of this country's top spies arrive in their CSIS cars to deliver furniture to the home of a guy who, on paper, isn't an intelligence officer but is going to be living next door to Mr. and Mrs. Stanley Cup. It was so Mickey Mouse."

Farrell's disbelief turned to anger when he discovered that the furniture

Lunau and Murphy had delivered was stickered with government bar codes in order to keep track of its whereabouts. The bar codes had "CSIS" stamped on them and identified the furniture as the property of the solicitor general. What if, Farrell asked Lunau and Murphy, the Russians decided to slip into his apartment while he was away and spotted the scores of stickers emblazoned with the words "CSIS" and "Solicitor General"? The pair sheepishly shrugged their shoulders and thanked him for noticing the lapse. Farrell carefully peeled off the offending stickers, put them in an envelope and handed them to Lunau.

Like nervous parents, Lunau and Murphy repeatedly reminded Farrell of his primary responsibilities: to carefully watch and note the Lamberts' comings and goings and to help CSIS break into the Russians' apartment to install sophisticated bugging devices. Farrell should carry himself, Lunau said, as if he belonged in the upscale neighbourhood and exclusive building. Murphy urged Farrell not to betray any nervousness if he bumped into the Lamberts. "Be yourself," Murphy said.

Farrell wondered what his reaction would be when he first encountered the Russian spies. He worried about whether he was being watched in return. He wondered if the Lamberts already knew that he was working for CSIS. He wondered whether he was in danger. He wondered if it was worth risking his life for twenty dollars an hour. The stakes were high for Lunau, Murphy and the service, but ultimately he was the one living just steps away from two potentially dangerous Russian spies. For the first time in a long time, Farrell was nervous.

As he drove into the underground parking lot at Roehampton Avenue after returning from his pre-dawn intercepts in Niagara Falls and Hamilton, Farrell took a quick peek at spot 48. If Ian's red Mazda, sporting licence plate number 696 WKM occupied the space, he knew the Lamberts were home. Farrell often arrived back at his apartment door carrying a bag full of groceries as the spies enjoyed their morning showers or fed their cat, Murphy. By carefully listening with his ear pressed to the wall, Farrell knew that the Lamberts got up at seven on workday mornings, that Laurie was usually the first one in the bathroom, and that she enjoyed taking long showers. Ian often lingered in bed. The couple always spoke English at home, and their conversations were sometimes heated.

When the couple emerged from their apartment at eight to begin their days, Farrell raced to his peephole and watched silently as they walked toward the elevator. That his first glimpse of the Russian spies came courtesy of a peephole seemed appropriate. As he peered out, Farrell sized up his adversaries. The service had painted the Russians to be almost superhuman, but the Lamberts appeared harmless. To him, Laurie looked plain, pale and bored. Ian was short, pudgy and grim-faced. Watching the spies as they stood waiting for the elevator, waiting to begin another day of lies, Farrell found his thoughts turning to his father, Joseph. During the Second World War, his dad had served in the merchant marine in North Africa, Europe and England, and the wound he'd received on behalf of his country had poisoned his life and that of his family. A wave of raw anger hit Farrell, directed at the two Russian operatives. It was the only time he felt at one with the overriding mission of the service. Farrell dutifully jotted down the time of their departure in a small notebook and then entered the data into a computer that CSIS had given him.

Farrell waited awhile after the Lamberts departed before heading out to meet with the APIs to pick up their mail intercepts. His next destination was a brief meeting with Lunau to pass on the letters and any details about the Lamberts he'd gleaned. Then, it was back to the apartment for a nap before speeding to the airport to pick up special packages. Later, Lunau dropped by Farrell's home to deliver more letters. Day after day, Farrell followed this routine. There was, however, one important addition to it: Farrell began intercepting the Lamberts' mail at Postal Station K at 2384 Yonge Street just days after he moved into the apartment. The couple received only a few pieces of mail a week, mostly bills and never any correspondence from overseas.

No one, not even Lunau or Murphy, was allowed to enter Farrell's apartment without his permission. Though he'd handed a key over to his bosses, Farrell made it clear that for his own safety, he needed to be in charge of comings and goings. Ray Murphy, however, broke that cardinal rule. Apparently with little to do, the SOS chief loitered in the apartment wearing his Toronto Maple Leafs baseball cap and helped himself to a few of Farrell's beers. In the meantime, CSIS posted as many as six watchers to keep an eye on the Lamberts twenty-four hours a day, seven days a week. Farrell often overheard the PSU crew "chiefs" contact the watchers using secure radio frequencies to note their locations or pass on anything unusual. On one occasion, for example, a watcher noticed a police officer hovering around 77 Roehampton Avenue. SOS was notified to shoo the officer away before he attracted too much attention.

Among the watchers assigned to the caper was the error-prone Richard Garland. Another watcher who worked on Operation Stanley Cup was a young, attractive black woman whose previous experience included stints at a Second Cup coffee shop and as a waitress at the Royal York hotel. Farrell had recently bumped into her at Montana, a popular singles bar in downtown Toronto. The woman, not knowing who Farrell was, told him that she worked for CSIS. "Oh, really. What's that?" Farrell asked.

"I was just granted my top-secret clearance," she giggled.

This was one of the people charged with watching the Lamberts, at the time the most important intelligence operation in Toronto. Farrell told Lunau about the incident, and he brushed it off. Farrell and the talkative watcher would soon meet again.

Late one afternoon in September 1994, Lunau and Murphy arranged to meet Farrell in a nondescript van parked in a municipal parking lot near the Lamberts' apartment. The SOS veterans often used the convenient spot to discuss the operation with Farrell. Lunau and Murphy were busy briefing the watcher when the van's side door slid open and Farrell got in. The watcher's jaw dropped when she saw Farrell. He greeted her with a knowing smile.

There was no time to settle an old score, since Lunau wanted the pair to follow a young woman who was visiting the Lamberts' apartment to water plants while the Russians were away. As they shadowed the woman from the Lamberts' apartment to a nearby street before cutting off the chase, Farrell and the watcher held hands. Along the way, she pressed Farrell for information.

"Garland got you this job, didn't he?" she whispered.

"No one got me this job. If I were you, I would learn to keep my trap shut."

Already the subject of one probe by the service's internal security branch, Garland was about to become the target of another. His latest offence: he'd had hundreds of calling cards printed describing himself as a federal agent. The official-looking cards bore Garland's name and were adorned with two small Canadian flags. The cards described the lowly watcher as a federal agent working out of the office of "The Solicitor General of Canada." Garland had the cards made up, Farrell says, because he was miffed that U.S. investigators routinely described themselves as federal agents, while watchers had no such impressive-sounding title. Garland was about to take a trip to Tucson, Arizona, where he was scheduled to give testimony in a case against Denis Leyne, a Canadian banker accused of shipping munitions and arms to the Irish Republican Army (IRA). Before leaving for the States, Garland showed Farrell a mock-up of his new calling card. Farrell tried, unsuccessfully, to convince him to abandon the notion. Garland travelled to Tucson, testified on behalf of the service and returned with a letter of recommendation from the U.S. prosecutor, praising the "federal agent" for his professionalism.

The warm afterglow of Garland's successful trip down south soon evaporated when CSIS's internal security branch got wind that the watcher was spreading his bogus calling cards around the city, as well as showing his CSIS ID to get into bars and nightclubs, and frequently blabbering on in a drunken stupor about his secret work. Marty Dengis, an investigator with the internal security branch, got Lunau's approval to question Farrell about Garland's curious habits. Farrell kept his mouth shut. Dengis told Farrell that the service had retrieved all but two of the five hundred cards that Garland had made. What the service and Dengis didn't know was that the printer had given Garland an extra fifty cards, which he had also handed out throughout Tucson and Toronto. Some of his favourite recipients were young ladies whom he met while trolling the city's bars, including a food and beverage manager at a downtown Holiday Inn. When Lunau learned of Garland's latest security breach, he called in Farrell.

Farrell knew the woman from the Holiday Inn and arranged to meet her at My Apartment, a popular downtown pickup bar. In telephone conversations with Farrell before their date, the young woman, named Julie, described Garland in unflattering terms and said that he had told her one evening that he was an undercover agent. "He told me, 'I work for CSIS. Lots of times they fly me out of the country at a moment's notice and I don't know when I will be back in the country. It's pretty dangerous. Don't tell anyone.' Can you believe it, John?" Julie asked. She said Garland had showed her his CSIS ID, a service handbook and a large gun case and claimed he was also a government pilot who flew senior officials to Washington and Ottawa. "Little did I know that he was a pathological liar," Julie told Farrell.

At the club with Julie, Farrell bided his time. As the night wore on, the din got louder and the young woman got tipsy. Farrell made his move when she paid a visit to the ladies' room and left her purse behind. He rifled through the handbag and plucked out Garland's calling card. The next day, he handed it to his relieved boss. Garland was suspended for six weeks but kept his job. (The whereabouts of the other forty-nine cards remained a mystery.) Cats and CSIS operatives share a trait: they both apparently have nine lives.

Soon after Farrell moved into his apartment on Roehampton Avenue, CSIS began preparing to break into the Lamberts' apartment to install electronic listening devices. The first task was to smuggle the equipment into the building. Farrell ferried three engineers with CSIS's technical services branch—Alex Yu, Dean Weber and Mike Israel—from a parking lot at nearby Northern Secondary School to the building. He made three trips in his compact car, crammed with electronic gear and an engineer. Israel was in his mid-fifties, the oldest of the bunch. The ex-military engineer was a safe-and-key expert. Weber was the jokester. With his curly hair, glasses and permanent smile, he looked more like a friendly accountant than a government-paid technical wizard. Yu was a rarity at CSIS, a visible minority. In the service's lingo, the British Columbia Institute of Technology graduate was a CBC (Chinese-born Canadian).

The techies brought along fifteen large aluminum cases filled with sophisticated electronic instruments and tools. Farrell wanted to use a dolly to deliver the equipment in one trip via the service elevator. But "the three amigos," as Farrell called them, had other ideas. In order to avoid an accident that might damage the contents of the cases, they wanted to use the main elevator and ship the cases to the sixth floor, two at a time. Farrell worried they would be spotted. He lost out. The engineers and Farrell carried the cases up in the main elevator and paraded by the Lamberts' door and into his apartment. The move took half an hour to complete. All the while, Farrell stewed.

Once inside, he draped a bed sheet over the large living room window because CSIS hadn't bothered to pay for curtains. Lunau arrived as the engineers unpacked their gear. The techies conducted a variety of tests, including measuring the thickness of the walls. Israel also carefully examined the front door locks.

Suddenly there was a loud knock on the door. Lunau motioned to everyone to stop what they were doing and gently tiptoed to the peephole.

"It's the landlord," Lunau whispered to Farrell. "Get rid of him."

Farrell opened the door a crack and told Marty that he was on the phone. "I'll drop by later, okay?"

"No problem," Marty replied.

The techies went back to work, installing equipment in the kitchen. Lunau also had Israel put another chain lock on the door to prevent the curious superintendent from slipping into the apartment unannounced. The gear that CSIS's engineers installed in Farrell's apartment was borrowed from the service's sister intelligence agency, the Communications Security Establishment (CSE). The CSE is the little-known arm of the Department of National Defence that eavesdrops on Canadians and the world. From its six ultra-secret listening posts across the country and its headquarters in Ottawa, the agency acts as a sort of massive vacuum cleaner in the electronic haze, sucking up the Internet traffic, cellphone calls and fax transmissions of diplomats, crooks and terrorists. (And now ordinary Canadians. In the aftermath of the September 11 terrorist attacks against the United States, Ottawa lifted the ban on the CSE's ability to intercept the communications of Canadians. It is a troubling development, since the multi-million-dollar agency with nearly one thousand employees does not require judicial warrants to conduct electronic surveillance, because it is part of the military. In 1995, Ottawa grudgingly created a tiny team to keep tabs over the agency after Jane Shorten, a former CSE analyst, blew the whistle on abuse of the espionage service's extraordinary powers. The CSE and CSIS are wedded to one another, indispensable partners in espionage.)

Farrell was glad when the techies installed their listening devices. It meant he didn't have to rouse himself from bed or the couch every time the Lamberts moved or had a conversation. But Farrell's peace was soon disturbed again by the building's inquisitive superintendent. Marty noticed that Farrell was often away from the apartment, and Marty never saw his athletic and handsome tenant in the company of a woman. Farrell told him that his girlfriend was an Air Canada flight attendant based in Vancouver, which appeased him for a time. Then Marty had a change of heart and hit Farrell up for the five-hundred-dollar tip he'd turned down. Farrell put him off for awhile, but then Lunau emphatically said no. To soothe Marty's disappointment, Farrell took him to Cheaters, a local strip club, and ordered a string of drinks and table dances.

By the fall of 1994, Operation Stanley Cup was consuming most of Farrell's time. And yet he still hadn't come face to face with the Russians. Around half past five one evening in October, Farrell carefully parked his new car, a used Porsche, in the underground parking lot. He grabbed his groceries out of the back seat and made his way to the elevator. The doors opened. The elevator was empty. Farrell pressed the sixth-floor button, closed his eyes and leaned his weary head against the wall, and nearly slipped into sleep. The elevator stopped on the main floor. Ian and Laurie Lambert got in.

Farrell woke up. Heart racing, he said hello. The Lamberts looked preoccupied and nodded their heads, smiling half-heartedly. "Snobs," Farrell thought. His palms moistened as the elevator slowly made its way up to the sixth floor. He remembered Murphy's admonition to keep calm. "Be yourself, be yourself," Farrell silently repeated. Then he realized that the Russians had no idea that he was a CSIS operative. He was just a kid from Parma Court. They were two Russian espionage officers, and they didn't have a clue.

The Lamberts got off the elevator first. Farrell followed steps behind to avoid making the spies feel uncomfortable. The Lamberts stopped at their door, and Laurie dug into her purse, searching for her key. Farrell arrived at his door and couldn't resist the urge to catch another glimpse of his quarry. Laurie looked up and caught Farrell's eye. She grinned, seeming to acknowledge that the young man in the elevator was actually her neighbour.

The Lamberts disappeared into their apartment, Farrell into his. He locked his door and made notes of the encounter for Lunau. He sat on the couch, turned on the television and cracked open a beer. Farrell would never get that close to the Lamberts again.

Preparations continued for the covert entry into the Lamberts' apartment. Farrell regularly met with Lunau and Murphy at nearby pubs—the Rose & Crown, Duke of Kent and Chick n' Deli—to discuss the operation. They ordered Farrell to canvass the underground parking lot and record licence plate numbers and models of cars until he had compiled a complete list of the other tenants in the building. The objective was to unearth any confederates who might be offering the Lamberts help. To that end, Lunau also instructed Farrell to conduct mail cover checks on all the tenants at 77 Roehampton. The service, Farrell says, did not obtain the necessary judicial warrants to intercept the mail of hundreds of tenants who had absolutely no connection to the Lamberts, but that fact didn't stop Lunau. He ordered Farrell to photo-copy the names and addresses of every tenant in the apartment building from mail that passed through Postal Station K on Yonge Street.

His late-night trips into the bowels of the apartment building unnerved Farrell. Underground parking lots can be foreboding places. The large cement columns offered a host of convenient hiding places. He worried about who was behind the wheel when the sudden screech of tires pierced the eerie silence. He decided a weapon might make him feel more secure. Lunau sometimes carried a small handgun in his fanny pack, though CSIS officers are not police officers and are forbidden to carry weapons. Lunau was a sure shot. He often invited Farrell to join him at shooting ranges, trips Farrell always declined. But he did get a semi-automatic weapon from a sporting goods store.[1]

Lunau called Farrell that October to share some good news. Ottawa had given him the green light for the covert entry. Lunau spent four days drawing up plans for the operation. His blueprint set out in meticulous detail every aspect of the break-in, from the number of officers involved, their precise tasks, where they would be positioned and how they would communicate with each other, to contingency plans in the event the operation had to be aborted. Fine-tuned by Michelle Tessier, the plan was sent to Keith McDonald in Ottawa for approval.

From phone and mail intercepts, the service had learned that the Lamberts had made plans to join friends out of town. The intercepts also revealed that the Russian spies had asked a couple who lived just blocks away to drop by the apartment to water the plants and feed Murphy, their cat. Lunau could hardly contain his excitement. The watchers set up shop around the apartment building. On Lunau's instructions, Farrell had rented apartment 111 on the ground floor of 100 Roehampton Avenue, directly across the street, under the name of John Turner. The apartment was used by the watchers, techies and SOS members as a safe house. Farrell even persuaded the landlord to trim a tree that was obstructing the service's view of the Lamberts' home. (Farrell would later rent an apartment on the sixth floor and another on the seventh floor in the same building because they offered unobstructed views of the Lamberts' apartment and Roehampton Avenue. Linda Smith, a CSIS officer assigned to Operation Stanley Cup, moved into one of the apartments. Smith, who now works as an investigator

---

[1] Farrell obtained a permit for a .22-calibre Squire Bingham weapon, serial #A499511

with the British Columbia Securities Commission, later sublet the apartment to her sister. She once complained to Lunau, Farrell says, that the techies used binoculars to watch her undress in the apartment.)

Background checks on the other tenants at 77 Roehampton were completed. No other fifth columnists were found. But Farrell discovered that Richard Garland had rented a bachelor apartment at 100 Roehampton Avenue and that the neighbourhood was teeming with CSIS officers not linked to the undercover operation. It was so bad, Farrell says, that Lunau was always bumping into intelligence officers on streets near the Lamberts' home.

On a Thursday evening in late October 1994, Lunau assembled the SOS unit in Farrell's apartment for a briefing. Tessier, Farrell, Israel, Weber and Yu were present. Two intelligence officers, who previously worked in the Toronto region, were dispatched from Ottawa to attend as well. Everyone stood as Lunau, wearing his trademark black windbreaker emblazoned with the Porsche insignia and reading from handwritten notes, went over the plan.

Tessier and Yu were chosen to slip into the Lamberts' apartment at precisely 11:45 p.m. using a key that Israel had made. (Farrell had tested the key to make sure it worked.) Tessier was fitted with a small microphone tucked under her wrist and an earpiece that allowed her to communicate with Lunau. Yu would videotape the Lamberts' apartment. Farrell's job was to carry an air mattress to the elevator. Lunau wanted the mattress to act as a shield, helping block other tenants' view of the break-in. "I thought it was a ridiculous idea. Who moves furniture that late at night?"

Farrell was also supposed to be the "muscle." Lunau told him to knock out anyone who tried to wiggle by the mattress.

"With what?" Farrell asked. "Your fist," Lunau said bluntly.

Another officer would watch the emergency exit for any movement in the apartment stairwell, while a second intelligence officer would stand guard in the hallway opposite Farrell. Lunau would remain in Farrell's apartment, kitty-corner to the Lamberts', watching events unfold through the peephole. There was only one contingency plan if the mission was compromised: Farrell would take the fall.

"I was the one with the criminal record and history of B and Es. So if the caper went sour, I was the fall guy," Farrell says. (He agreed because he was confident that Lunau would intervene and prevent the police from laying any charges.)

The briefing lasted five minutes.

"We go at 11:45 sharp," Lunau said. "Any questions?"

Silence fell on the team as they synchronized their watches. It was 10:30 p.m. Lunau made one final and surprising announcement.

"John was never here. He doesn't exist. Does everyone understand?" His team nodded in agreement.

Farrell made one final check and knocked on the Lamberts' door. No one answered. Lunau gave the signal to move at 11:44 p.m.

Two officers quickly took up their positions in the hallway and at the emergency exit. Tessier and Yu were the last to emerge. Tessier fumbled nervously with the key before quietly stepping into the Lamberts' apartment. She let out a muffled shriek. Lunau caught his breath.

"What's wrong?" he whispered into his microphone.

Murphy, the cat, had frightened her, Tessier replied. Yu closed the door behind them. Tessier flicked on her flashlight and began making notes while Yu videotaped the entire apartment. Lunau ducked his head out the door and motioned for Farrell to return to the apartment, ordering him to man the peephole. It was late and Farrell was tired. He fought to stay awake, but boredom and fatigue eventually won the battle and he dozed off. His head hit the door with a loud thump. Lunau, startled by the noise, ordered everyone to freeze.

"What was that?" he barked.

Farrell was still half asleep.

Lunau contacted the watchers positioned around the apartment by walkie-talkie tuned to a secure frequency, demanding to know if they had heard or seen anything untoward.

"Nothing going on down here," a watcher replied. "But we are freezing our asses off."

"What was that?" Tessier anxiously asked Lunau.

"I don't know," he said. "I'm trying to find out."

The commotion woke Farrell, who kept his mouth shut.

Round one was over in fifteen minutes. Tessier and Yu retreated from the apartment. Apart from Tessier's shriek and the mysterious thud, the operation was going well. The unit gathered in Farrell's apartment for a debriefing. Farrell gulped Coca-Cola to fend off sleep and further mishaps.

At half-past midnight, round two began. Again, Farrell slipped out first, followed by the two officers. This time, Yu, Weber and Tessier quickly entered the apartment carrying several aluminum cases of electronic listening devices and video equipment. Murphy, the lonely cat, was startled again by the intruders and the twang of the doorstop. Lunau kept his eye firmly pressed against the peephole. He beckoned Farrell back into the apartment to take a turn watching the hallway. The techies worked furiously next door installing the electronic bugs and video surveillance equipment.

"It was like we were all sitting in a bomb shelter waiting for a bomb to explode," Farrell says.

Lunau was in constant contact with the watchers, getting updates on anyone entering or leaving the apartment building. He also called Ottawa. Farrell listened as the techies flipped on the television and radio to calibrate their equipment.

At 1:20 a.m., Yu, Tessier and Weber emerged from the apartment.

By 3:00 a.m., the exhausted team finished packing their equipment and was ready to bug out. Farrell pushed the button for the elevator and signalled to Lunau when it arrived. Tessier and the techies hurriedly got in. Lunau, Farrell and the other intelligence officers followed later. The unit met in the underground parking lot, where a van pulled up to carry the equipment, the techies and the officers home.

Impatient and tired, Farrell simply wanted to go back to his east-end home and walk his dog. He desperately needed a few hours' sleep before meeting the APIs at his home later that day. Lunau wanted to buy him breakfast at the Sunset Grill, a regular haunt of the SOS boss in the Beach neighbourhood. Farrell shook his head.

"John, did you at least find it exciting?" Lunau asked.

"Sure," was all Farrell could summon up.

Later that day, Lunau arrived at Farrell's home to drop off some mail and handed him one thousand dollars in cash as a reward.

"You did a good job last night," Lunau said. Farrell took the money and went back to sleep.

9

ROMEO AND THE CROWN KEY

J ust weeks after Don Lunau had successfully executed the break-in
of the Lamberts' apartment, he and Ray Murphy faced an unexpected crisis. The sophisticated listening devices that the SOS team had
planted soon confirmed what Farrell had heard by pressing his ear
against the wall: the Lamberts were at each other's throats. The angry
spats were real, loud and becoming all too frequent. The Russian spies
were edging close to the inconceivable: a split-up.

Love, or at least lust, had come between them. It turned out that
Ian was smitten with Anita Keyes, a tall, attractive accountant who
worked with him at Black Photo. The pair had met in early 1994.
From there, the affair had followed a familiar arc: furtive glances led
to flirtatious small talk, then lunch, dinner and ultimately bed. Ian
was leading a *second* secret life.

Laurie, his wife, lover and fellow spy, began to press him about his
unusually long absences from home. Ian lied, claiming he was busy at
the library. His betrayal wounded Laurie to her core. Their marriage
may have been arranged by Russian spymasters, and their identities

may have been stolen, but Laurie's love for Ian was genuine. One after-noon, in the fall of 1994, Farrell listened intently while Laurie con-fronted her husband with evidence of the affair. The quarrel exploded violently, and the screams jolted their eavesdropper. As the fight sub-sided, Farrell heard Laurie's muffled weeping. The marriage was over.[1]

The breakup posed problems for CSIS. It would be harder for the ser-vice to track the spies while they lived separate lives. It would mean renting more apartments to keep tabs on the pair, making more mail intercepts, dispatching more watchers to tail them and spending more money to keep Operation Stanley Cup running smoothly.

Laurie, the telephone intercepts revealed, planned to remain at 77 Roehampton until she found a new and cheaper place to live. Ian and Laurie divided up their treasured possessions. She would keep Murphy the cat and the short-wave radio used to contact their bosses in Moscow, while he'd get the expensive sports car.

In late 1994, Ian packed his belongings and moved to a shabby high-rise next to a rundown government housing project at 921 Midland Avenue in Toronto's east end. The apartment building was called The Parisienne, though its white, decrepit facade called up few associations with the City of Light. Ian shared Suite 615, a small, two-bedroom apartment, with a friend from Black Photo. (The roommate had been Ian's witness at his wedding to Laurie.) His new place was a twenty-minute drive and a far cry from the upscale shops, restaurants and yup-pies at Yonge and Eglinton.

On November 24, 1994, Laurie signed a six-month lease to rent a bachelor suite at the Manhattan Towers at 75 Broadway Avenue. The rent was a modest $481.64 a month. Laurie moved into Suite 417 on New Year's Day, 1995. Her move to Broadway Avenue, just a block north of Roehampton, was a stroke of luck for CSIS. Vacant apartments

---

[1] At the time, CSIS wasn't sure if the breakup was a pre-arranged ploy to make it more difficult to trace the pair. The service concluded later that the split was the product of very real human fragilities and desires.

were hard to find in the popular neighbourhood, and the service could still rely on its safe house at 100 Roehampton to watch over her until a suite in the Manhattan Towers came up for rent.

In the meantime, Lunau and Murphy hatched a scheme to get much closer to at least one of the estranged Russian spies: the SOS veterans wanted young John Farrell to take advantage of the breakup and seduce Laurie Lambert. Romeo spies, as they are known in the world of espionage, were a favourite tool of the SVR and other intelligence services and used seduction and romance, rather than the crude techniques of sexual compromise and blackmail, to illicit information from lonely government officials, diplomats and businessmen. The service had learned that Laurie was making plans for a brief trip to Los Angeles—why not send John down there at the same time, book him into her hotel and hope that "love," however fleeting, flourished.

His bosses broached the delicate subject to Farrell during a regular rendezvous in the underground parking lot at Front Street.

"John, I have a very big favour that I need you to do for me," Ray Murphy said. "I put in for you to go to Los Angeles to keep an eye on Laurie. And if you get the chance, I want you to sleep with her."

Farrell thought that Murphy was joking, something he often liked to do. "What do you want me to do?"

"I want you to get close to her and fuck her," Murphy said. "John, do it for your country."

Farrell laughed. He thought Murphy's plan didn't make much sense. What were the odds of Laurie Lambert's former next-door neighbour conveniently showing up at the same hotel while she was vacationing in California? And if he did, wouldn't she be immediately suspicious?

Lunau and Murphy assured him that the service would happily cover all his expenses. CSIS knew the swank Los Angeles hotel where Laurie had booked a room. Farrell's bosses argued that the mission was relatively painless: strike up a relationship with the jilted Russian spy, take her to bed and troll for useful pillow talk. Despite his reservations, Farrell agreed to go. Money, not country or the idea of sleeping with a Russian spy, tipped the scales.

Murphy was ecstatic. But his excitement was tempered by two

critical considerations. Strictly speaking, CSIS is a domestic, not a foreign, intelligence-gathering agency. That Farrell would try to seduce a Russian intelligence officer in the United States without the FBI's consent or co-operation could upset relations between the two services and lead to a messy diplomatic spat. Farrell's bosses, however, were prepared to take that risk. Murphy needed the approval of McDonald and other senior CSIS officials before the Romeo caper could proceed. He told Farrell that he expected a call from Ottawa later that evening with a decision. Farrell headed home, packed his bag and waited by the phone.

It rang at about half past seven that evening.

"They wouldn't go for it," Murphy said, sounding disappointed.

Farrell breathed a sigh of relief and unpacked his bag.

It took months of patience and persistence, but on March 6, 1996, Farrell struck gold. Using his *nom de guerre*, John Turner, he signed a five-month lease for a one-bedroom apartment on the seventh floor of the Manhattan Towers. He gave the building's superintendent, Rose Haslam, $331.07 as a deposit and was so anxious to move in that he politely declined the super's offer to paint the apartment. Farrell moved into Suite 715 on March 16, after making out two money orders to cover the first and last month's rent, and severed his lease at 77 Roehampton.

Lunau ordered Farrell to keep a low profile at the new building. He didn't want to raise suspicion in Laurie's mind about why her former neighbour had suddenly taken up residence in the building.

Many officers at CSIS's Toronto office realized that when it came to fitting out and furnishing these observation posts the service was an open till for enterprising persons. One young intelligence officer based in Toronto was no exception. She sold Farrell a used futon, lamps and end tables for his new apartment. Sale price: three hundred dollars, covered by a cash advance from Lunau. CSIS also paid

Farrell's mom two hundred dollars for her used dishes and to clean the place. Lunau even got into the act by selling a pair of lamps to Farrell for the apartment.

Once the service had learned of Laurie's new digs, Lunau ordered Farrell to conduct mail cover checks on every resident in the apartment building. Again, to Farrell's knowledge, CSIS did not secure the necessary judicial warrants. Farrell went, as instructed, to Postal Station K and photocopied the back and front of letters addressed to each resident in the building. He passed the information to Lunau in a plain manila envelope marked "Private, DL." Lunau ran the names through a variety of CSIS databases to see whether the unsuspecting residents were friendly or not. The residents, it turned out, were all friendly.

The service had lost a lot of valuable time as Farrell spent fruitless months searching for a vacant apartment close to Laurie. A few days after he moved in, Lunau arranged for Yu and Weber to plant electronic bugs in the apartment. Farrell and Lunau helped carry the equipment into the building using a side entrance in the underground parking lot. The move went well. Yu and Weber installed the sensitive equipment, which could penetrate the layers of concrete that separated the apartments, in an armoire in Farrell's bedroom.

Farrell was now splitting his time among several apartments that he had rented for CSIS as observation posts and safe houses, and he was still overseeing Operation Vulva. By any measure, Farrell was among CSIS's busiest and most productive operatives.

His deepening involvement with CSIS began to trouble senior officials at Canada Post, who knew about it through his invoices for work on Operation Vulva. Matters came to a head when Farrell ran into his old nemesis, Ron Flemming. Farrell was visiting Canada Post's administrative offices at 1200 Markham Road when Flemming confronted him, demanding to know why Farrell was interested in a "relay key." (Relay keys are used by letter carriers to open mail boxes that dot city streets and store undelivered mail.)

Farrell told Flemming to take a hike. But Flemming wasn't done. He warned Farrell that he would do everything in his power to have the Canada Post "contractor" fired.

Farrell told Lunau about the angry exchange. "I'm the one who decides who gets hired and who gets fired," Lunau said, and he called Keith McDonald. "Keith will walk over and talk to the boys at Canada Post and tell them to keep their hands off of you," Lunau assured Farrell. They did.

But McDonald's intervention didn't end Canada Post's worries about Farrell's temper and his tendency to go public. Don Bick, Mike Thompson's successor as divisional manager of Canada Post's Security and Investigation Services for York Region, called Farrell to harangue him about his alleged unauthorized use of a postal inspector's badge and car, and the fact that he'd been hired as an API. (Lunau ordered Farrell to record the conversation.) Farrell angrily denied the charges.

"What concerns me is that you were hired in the first place," Bick said. "Yeah, I have some concerns, real concerns about the type of business you are in."

"What type of business am I in?" Farrell replied.

"You know, the CSIS [business]," Bick said. "[I'm] concerned about down the road and embarrassment about you losing your cool. That concerns me."

Bick's comments are remarkable because they confirm that Farrell and the other APIs were controlled by CSIS, not Canada Post. His concern that Farrell might embarrass Canada Post "down the road" was, to say the least, prescient.

Ian Lambert spent little time at his dingy apartment at The Parisienne. He preferred the company of Anita Keyes and her two young children, Jesse and Kayla. Ian routinely visited Keyes at her home in Port Hope, Ontario. Later, he helped his lover move into a small Valley Woods Road townhouse, just off the busy Don Valley Parkway in north Toronto. Keyes's two children warmed to Ian, and Keyes welcomed his presence in their lives. A messy separation from her husband had cast a sad pall over the family. Jesse, a shy but bright boy, gravitated to the gregarious

Russian. Kayla, who protected her mother fiercely, was happy that Ian was attentive and kind.

Meanwhile, Lunau ordered Farrell to rent yet another apartment, this time in Ian's new building. Farrell made a pilgrimage to The Parisienne and turned on the charm with the building's superintendent. It was fruitless. The building only offered condos for sale. Farrell delivered the bad news to Lunau, Murphy and Birkett over drinks at the Mr. Slate Sports Bar. Lunau assured Farrell that the service would pony up the money to buy a unit. It didn't. So Lunau moved on to Plan B. Farrell was instructed to conduct a property search on the building so the service could draw up a list of the condo owners. Lunau had another SOS member contact each owner to ask if their unit was for rent. Unfortunately, the approach failed: none of the condos was available.

Exasperated and out of options, Lunau had his trusted API rent an apartment on the seventh floor in an aging high-rise on Gilder Drive, directly opposite Ian's new home. At least the apartment gave CSIS a clear view of Ian's car, which sat in an above-ground parking lot.

Farrell loathed spending time at the cockroach-infested apartment. The fifteen-storey building looked like a slum. New immigrants on fixed or low incomes filled the building, and the thick odour of curry permeated the hallways. Wet laundry hung from scores of balconies, while bedsheets doubled as window curtains. Pigeon droppings caked the balconies. Farrell paid $631.62 a month for a filthy one-bedroom apartment. With his mother's help, he spent a day cleaning mouse droppings off the stove and painting his new flat a gaudy shade of lilac, billing CSIS fifty dollars a gallon for the paint and two hundred dollars for his mother's cleaning services.

The CSE was anxious to train a bevy of electronic listening devices on Ian's new home. Farrell's job was to meet the CSE crew in front of the building and escort them to his apartment. Six CSE engineers and technicians from Ottawa arrived from Toronto's Pearson airport in a rented van. The crew was wearing slacks, expensive loafers and open-collared shirts. Farrell sat on the curb with his head bowed as the large cube van pulled into the driveway. He was wearing a green army jacket, a baseball cap flipped backwards and new, white sneakers, attempting to blend in with the surroundings. The CSE technicians, on the other hand, resembled a band of befuddled plainclothes cops. Farrell approached them. "You guys wanna buy some drugs? What are you looking for? You name it, I got it," he whispered.

The frightened technicians scampered back into their van. One techie shouted at Farrell to get lost, while the others waited anxiously for their tardy CSIS escort to arrive.

"I'm kidding. I'm here to meet you. My name is John."

Farrell and the CSE technicians marched into his apartment, carrying several large aluminum cases. Leading a parade of electronic snoops and their equipment was becoming something of a habit for Farrell. This time, however, an unusual piece of machinery caught his eye. The technicians brought along a device that looked like a small refrigerator and weighed enough that they had to use a dolly to move it to his apartment. He assumed the monolith was some sort of listening device.

It took the technicians a little over four hours to install all their electronic gizmos. They also hooked up a state-of-the-art security system in Farrell's bedroom that would instantly tip the service off the moment anyone tried to tamper with the equipment. (The radio traffic emitted by CSE's bulky equipment did catch the attention of a letter carrier who delivered Ian's mail at The Parisienne. The postal worker, who carried a portable police scanner, was also a ham-radio buff, whose home was filled with top-of-the-line radio equipment. One day, while Farrell was intercepting Ian's mail at a nearby postal station, the letter carrier approached him to point out that the radio traffic in the area had recently multiplied ten-fold. Not only that, the letter carrier said, he was picking up what appeared to be government or military communications from vehicles around The Parisienne. Farrell feigned ignorance, insisting he was merely conducting a fraud investigation.)

On their way out of Farrell's place, the CSE technicians took turns wiping their feet and checking the soles of their shoes for cockroach eggs.

Farrell spent several uncomfortable nights at the Gilder Drive apartment, watching over the CSE's equipment and spying on Ian from his living room window. CSIS was particularly interested in Ian's sports car because the service planned to steal the red, six-cylinder 1993 Mazda MX-3 Precidia and temporarily replace it with an exact duplicate while its owner slept. While the substitute filled the parking space, CSIS technicians would plant electronic bugs and tracking devices under Ian's car.

From his perch on the seventh floor, Farrell was asked by Lunau to pinpoint the times when Ian left his car unattended. Lunau also needed to know if a small, flashing red light in the car was a high-priced alarm system designed to fend off thieves and nosy spies. (It turned out the light was part of the car's expensive stereo system and not an alarm.) Lunau and an SOS team waited until well after the light in Ian's bedroom went off before pouncing. Tommy Birkett obtained a key for Ian's car from a source at a Mazda dealership in Toronto. Using that key, a CSIS officer opened the driver's door of the car, slipped in and drove out of the parking lot. A second Mazda, its engine purring, quickly slid into the vacant parking spot.

CSIS technicians spent several hours installing the listening devices and a Global Positioning System (GPS), which allowed the service not only to eavesdrop on Ian but to track his movements across the city. Before sunrise, the sports car, laden with the invisible bugs, was quietly returned to its spot in the parking lot. The mission had gone off without a hitch. Ian Lambert never caught wind of the fact that CSIS had turned his car into a giant beacon.

In August 1995, fresh from the success of his car caper, Lunau began planning to break into Ian's condo at The Parisienne. Because Farrell and the service had failed to rent a place in the building, executing a covert entry would be problematic. Lunau's solution: order Farrell to steal a Crown key. Designed for use by letter carriers, the special key can open the main door to almost every apartment building and many mailboxes across the country. The small, easily concealed device can be a useful tool in the hands of spies and thieves.

Industrious crooks are increasingly interested in mailboxes because they can contain easy loot. Money, jewellery, credit cards and other valuables routinely make their way across countries, continents and oceans in the mail. U.S. police believe that some ruthless street gangs have forsaken robbing banks, preferring instead to steal Crown keys. Los Angeles gangs, for example, have terrorized letter carriers, holding them at gunpoint and knifepoint, demanding the Crown keys attached to their mailbags. The gangs have used the keys to steal tens of thousands of pieces of mail. In 1995, two Winnipeg thieves tried to fashion their own Crown keys to steal credit cards from mailboxes but were caught by police.

Stealing a Crown key is a serious criminal offence and carries a possible ten-year jail sentence. But that disturbing fact didn't daunt Lunau, who was a practitioner of the service's unofficial Ways and Means Act: if there was a way to get things done, it didn't matter what means you employed.

Lunau broached the subject of stealing the key during lunch with Farrell, telling him that he had read a newspaper article about how biker gangs were getting into the illicit Crown key business.

He asked Farrell what the keys could be used for.

Farrell told Lunau that apart from opening mailboxes, the keys could be extremely useful when SOS teams were tracking targets. "I told him that, let's say, a target walked into an apartment building—you didn't have to wait to be buzzed up, you could just use the key to open the front door and make it look like you belonged in the building."

Lunau's next question was how could Special Ops get one.

Farrell told his boss that letter carriers attached the keys to long chains hooked on to their mailbags. The keys were also stored in locked or unlocked cabinets at postal stations across the city, but it was unlikely that the supervisors would let him sign one out.

If they wanted to get their hands on a key, they were going to have to steal it.

"No problem," Lunau said. "Just get me one."

The day after that lunch, Farrell drove out to Postal Depot 1 at 340 Matheson Boulevard East in Mississauga. En route, he went over in his mind's eye how he would steal the Crown key. He also prepared a simple contingency plan in the event that a supervisor or postal worker discovered what he was up to: run.

In fact, he decided to steal two Crown keys—one for Lunau to use and one for himself to use for special ops work—from a small cabinet in the supervisor's office. Failing that, he was prepared to use a pair of wire cutters to pilfer the keys from the mailbags of preoccupied letter carriers.

There were two large mail depots on Matheson Boulevard and both were teeming with postal workers; the supervisors' offices were usually beehives of activity. From a thief's perspective, the busier, the better. Farrell expected to slip in amid the confusion and bag the Crown keys without anyone noticing. The cabinet that housed as many as forty Crown and relay keys at Depot 1 was often left invitingly open.

And it went as Farrell had predicted. He scooped up two Crown keys from the open cabinet, dropped them into the pocket of his track pants and simply walked out. It took less than a minute.

While working as a postal inspector, Farrell had discovered that the serial numbers on Crown keys were not recorded at many postal stations, making the job of finding errant keys difficult. As well, only cursory background checks were done on low-paid ad-mail workers, who all carried Crown keys. In fact, Farrell was once asked by a senior Canada Post official in Scarborough to conduct urgent CPIC checks on five hundred ad-mail workers who had already been on the job for six months. Letter carriers, Farrell also learned, were subject to equally skimpy background checks.[2]

As a precaution, Farrell went home and, using a cordless drill and a concrete bit, filed off the serial number on one of the keys. He then drove to a postal station in Toronto's east end to meet with the APIs before making his way to the Rose & Crown pub for lunch with Lunau. His boss was already there when he walked in. Farrell sat down and slipped him an envelope marked "D. L. Private." Inside, his boss found a Crown key without a serial number.

Farrell told Lunau that he had stolen one for himself and Lunau nodded. The theft was their secret in a business filled with secrets.

---

[2] Many ad-mail workers claimed to have lost Crown keys while delivering junk mail. These keys often went unreported by Canada Post, Farrell says.

(Farrell used his Crown key for work, particularly when he went look-ing for apartments for CSIS. He used the key to get into apartment buildings to snoop around without the superintendent's knowledge.) After lunch, the pair left the pub separately before meeting up again at a nearby municipal parking lot, where they exchanged batches of mail. Lunau was anxious, Farrell says, to try out the key. So they met later in the day at an apartment building near Ian's condo, where Farrell patiently showed his boss how to use the key. At first, Lunau turned the key the wrong way, but he got the hang of it on his second try. Farrell told him that, in some apartment buildings, the key acted like a mas-ter key, opening all the mailboxes at once. This caught Lunau's atten-tion and fancy. Some days later, the pair went to an apartment complex near Laurie's new flat and practised using the key to open mailboxes.

The RCMP Security Service had collapsed under the weight of damning revelations that its members stole political party membership lists and dynamite. Stealing a small Crown key may not be as sexy as stealing dynamite, but it was, nonetheless, an unconscionable act. It was ordered and countenanced, Farrell says, by a senior official of a spy service that has repeatedly pledged to uphold the law and prevent the abuses of the past.

But the Crown key wasn't the only piece of Canada Post property that Farrell says Lunau ordered him to steal.

Denis Leyne was a successful Canadian banker who divided his time between a gleaming office tower in downtown Toronto and his million-dollar mansion in the city's west end. The strapping fifty-year-old embodied the spirit of Irish wit and humour, enjoying his drink and the company of family and friends. His friends say Leyne had a fierce pride in Ireland and a passion for the country's history, its Gaelic lan-guage and his Cork ancestry. He also had no love for the English. CSIS believed that the senior vice-president of the Canadian Imperial Bank of Commerce (in charge of the bank's operation for Ontario, excluding Toronto) was leading a double life as a terrorist linked to the ruthless Irish Republican Army (IRA).

Suspicion about Leyne's connections to the IRA dated back to

1973, when he was first questioned by police about his links to another Toronto man convicted of trying to buy a Stinger missile from an undercover FBI agent. In 1991, the CIBC abruptly fired Leyne, insisting that the banker, who had spent thirty-five years patiently climbing to the upper rungs of the industry, simply didn't fit into its future plans. Leyne suspected his dismissal was triggered by an international police probe into weapons and munitions purchases for the IRA. Then in 1992, Leyne was arrested as he stepped off a flight from Toronto at LaGuardia Airport in New York City. He and five other men were charged with a variety of offences connected to the purchase of a heat-seeking, surface-to-air Stinger missile and 2,900 detonators from a firm in Tucson, Arizona. Leyne and the other defendants denied the charges, and in 1994, a jury acquitted them.

Leyne returned to his Toronto home embittered and angry, and he denounced his prosecution as an orchestrated campaign to subdue an Irish Canadian who peacefully supported the IRA's "just cause." He singled out CSIS and the Mounties for spearheading the drive to discredit the Irish community. "The RCMP and CSIS have been very active in the Irish community, attending social events, public houses . . . wherever they feel they can gather information," he told the *Winnipeg Free Press*. "It's an orchestrated attempt to cow the community [telling them] to be complacent, to be inactive, to keep your mouth shut."

Leyne's acquittal and his stinging accusations did little to dissuade the service from spying on him. And one of the CSIS officers who kept track of Leyne was Don Lunau, who enlisted Farrell's help in 1994 to intercept Leyne's mail. This time, for unknown reasons, Lunau didn't want Farrell to visit a postal station to do it, and he asked him whether there was another way to intercept mail. Farrell told Lunau that Leyne's mail could be seized from a relay box before it was picked up by a letter carrier. There was usually a twenty-minute window of opportunity between the time the sorted mail was dropped into the relay box and when the letter carrier arrived to pick it up and deliver it. To get into the box, the carrier used a relay key. The message to Farrell was unmistakable: Lunau now wanted him to steal a relay key. But this time Farrell had a close call.

He picked a small postal station at 2985 Lakeshore Boulevard West in west-end Toronto as the best spot to lift the key.[3] Showing his postal inspector's badge, Farrell identified himself as an investigator with Canada Post and struck up a friendly conversation with the station's supervisor, who was standing too close to the cabinet storing the keys for Farrell to risk the theft. He told the supervisor that he was in the area making the rounds, checking the security of relay keys and would drop by the following morning.

Before Farrell returned the following day, the supervisor unexpectedly received a call from the York Control Centre, which monitors the movement of mail and postal workers across the city. He mentioned that he had just been visited by a fellow named Farrell, who was asking about relay keys and carrying a badge that identified him as a postal inspector. A Canada Post official told the supervisor that Farrell had left the Crown corporation years ago.

"What the fuck is going on here?" he asked Farrell when he walked in the door. "You don't work for Canada Post anymore."

Cursing his bad luck, Farrell insisted that he still worked for Canada Post and asked the supervisor to call the Security and Investigation Services office at 491-4472 to verify it. It was a rash move, but Farrell felt he had little alternative but to rely on the good graces of his former mates to get him out of a jam. When the call went through, Terry Parnell, a secretary with the Security and Investigation Services, vouched for Farrell. Farrell kept visiting the station until he was able to steal a relay key.

Farrell spent two days watching the relay box housing Leyne's letters, carefully noting the times when the mail was dropped off and the letter carrier arrived. Farrell established that he could safely open the box any time between nine and nine-thirty in the morning. Wearing a Canada Post T-shirt, baseball cap and jacket, Farrell used the spindly key to open the relay box that sat in the middle of a small knoll near

---

[3] It is now a Goodwill store.

Leyne's home in Etobicoke. (The box is no longer there.) He took the whole mailbag, dumped it into his car and drove to a nearby school parking lot where he quickly flipped through the mail and plucked out Leyne's letters. He spent the next two weeks intercepting Leyne's mail from the relay box. The whole operation reeked of criminality, from posing as a postal inspector and wearing Canada Post clothing, to stealing the relay key and opening the box. And it was all done with the consent, knowledge and approval, Farrell says, of Don Lunau.

Farrell placed Leyne's mail, along with the other API intercepts, in a manila envelope and handed it to Lunau in the underground parking lot at Front Street. Later Lunau ordered Farrell to intercept parcels and registered mail addressed to Leyne at a local postal station. When the operation was over, Farrell slipped into the postal station and returned the relay key. He needn't have taken the risk, since no one had reported the key missing. In February 1995, Leyne died of a massive heart attack at his home.

Lunau reassembled the same SOS crew that had broken into the apartment on Roehampton Avenue to try to surreptitiously slip into Ian's dank new home. This time, however, Tommy Birkett and Ray Murphy tagged along. The gang of spies—including Farrell, Tessier, Lunau, Yu and Weber—met in a large parking lot directly opposite Ian's condo at 11:30 a.m. on a warm August afternoon in 1995. The intelligence officers and technicians arrived in separate cars before herding into a large, grey Ford van for a briefing. Birkett was sent on a coffee and doughnut run.

Lunau told his crew that there would be two entries. The first wave would videotape the entire apartment and select the best location to plant the electronic bugs. The second wave would install the bugs. A team of watchers, Lunau said, were posted around the building. The techies had cut a set of keys for Ian's apartment. Tessier and Farrell, posing as a couple interested in buying a condo, would enter Ian's building using a Crown key. (Lunau handed Tessier the key during the briefing.) Not one of the team asked how the service had gotten its hands on Canada Post's key—that remained Lunau and Farrell's little secret. Once the couple had established that Ian and his roommate weren't home, the other officers would swiftly move in. Tessier was again fitted with a small microphone and earpiece to communicate with Lunau. Everything was set. Lunau gave Farrell and Tessier the signal to go.

Walking hand-in-hand, they crossed Midland Avenue, heading toward the apartment building's main entrance. A small car caught Farrell's attention. He turned and watched with horror and amazement, as his mother and brother Greg drove by, honking wildly. Mary waved enthusiastically at her surprised son. Farrell kept walking.

"Who was that?" Tessier asked.

"Oh, just my mom and brother," Farrell said.

Unnerved by the incident, Tessier fumbled for the Crown key when they got to the front door. Farrell whipped out a small key chain.

"Allow me," he said, as he opened the door with his own key.

Tessier was startled but knew better than to ask silly questions.

Lunau and two other intelligence officers waited patiently as Tessier and Farrell quickly walked through a deserted reception area, skipped down a flight of stairs and made their way to the rear entrance, where they opened the door. Lunau and the others slipped into the building. Tessier and Farrell then hurried up to the sixth floor. They knocked on Ian's door to make sure no one was home, then took up their positions in the emergency stairwell between the fifth and sixth floors. Tessier brought the microphone concealed in the cuff of her shirt to her mouth and whispered to Lunau that the building was "all clear."

But as Lunau and the other SOS members were about to walk into a waiting elevator, the crew heard another elevator jolt into action. It stopped on the sixth floor, where a gaggle of people hopped in. Lunau waited for the elevator to stop on the main floor. The SOS chief was about to announce the "all clear" again, when Farrell thought he heard some rustling on a lower floor. He tiptoed down the stairwell, opened the emergency exit a crack and spied a janitor replacing hallway lights. Farrell watched silently as the janitor headed for the fourth floor on foot. Tessier alerted Lunau, who raced up to the fourth floor and saw the janitor changing light bulbs. Lunau silently cursed the janitor and called off the break-in.

The SOS members huddled together for a quick debriefing in a nearby parking lot. Lunau decided to take another stab after lunch. This time, he told his crew that he planned to use a pair of unstained, bifolding doors, which he had bought at a hardware store earlier that morning to shield the covert entry. Farrell shook his head. At Roehampton, he'd had to wield an air mattress, and now Lunau was asking him to carry a door. He thought the idea was inane.

As the SOS crew prepared to make their way to a nearby Kenny Rogers restaurant for lunch, Lunau decided to tuck his brand new doors in an anteroom near the janitor's basement office. Farrell, the experienced thief, knew his boss was making a big mistake.

"Donnie, the doors are a heat score," Farrell said.

"What do you mean?" Lunau replied.

"They're going to get stolen. You leave anything lying around here and you're going to get ripped off."

"John, you're fucking paranoid," Lunau said. "Let's go eat."

The eight SOS members commandeered a large table at the restaurant. Lunch lasted ninety minutes. Lunau fretted over his chicken and french fries, musing openly about calling off the mission. But Ottawa was anxious for results. After consulting with McDonald by phone, Lunau decided to go ahead with the break-in. Farrell whispered to Tessier and Birkett that the doors would be gone by the time they returned.

Tessier used the Crown key to get into the apartment building. Farrell raced to the back entrance and let in the rest of the crew, while Tessier took up her position in the stairwell. Farrell and Birkett quickly headed for the janitor's office.

"Shit, the doors are gone," Birkett said, trying to conceal a grin.

Lunau let out a small yelp.

"I hate to tell you, 'I told you so,' Donnie, but I told you so," Farrell said.

Lunau immediately called Murphy, who was anxiously sitting in the parking lot.

"The fucking doors are missing. We're coming out," he moaned.

Lunau and Murphy spent ten minutes mulling over their dwindling options before calling Ottawa to inform them that the break-in was being aborted for "unexplained" reasons. Farrell had never seen his boss so abrupt with his crew.

Lunau told Farrell that he was going to try to break into Ian's apartment again, but next time he wouldn't invite him along for the ride. Instead, Farrell could go on standby to assist in other break-ins. He occasionally spent whole days at doughnut shops or delicatessens across the city with Birkett and Dean Weber, CSIS's locksmith. The three of them munched on doughnuts and twiddled their thumbs, waiting for Lunau to call.

John Farrell knew Tom Geiger as the chief of Technical and Support Services, providing assistance to the SOS unit. (Geiger later became the director general of Toronto Region, effectively assuming the mantle of the region's top spy.) Geiger knew about Farrell's role with SOS and his involvement with mail intercepts, and he gave him a frantic phone call one day—so frantic that he didn't follow protocol and call Lunau first. The watchers, Geiger explained, had spotted Laurie Lambert dropping a letter into a mailbox inside the Eaton Centre in downtown Toronto and another into a box on University Avenue, near the insurance company where she worked. He wanted the mailbags seized and Laurie's letters intercepted immediately.

Geiger's call surprised Farrell. Curious, he asked how Geiger had gotten his cellphone number. The answer? Farrell's name was listed in the agency's personnel directory beside "mail warrants." Geiger's call is yet another important piece of evidence that the API program, ostensibly operated by Canada Post, was really a surrogate operation controlled by CSIS. John Farrell may have been receiving cheques from the Crown corporation, but CSIS was his real paymaster.

Farrell told Geiger that he would call him back in a few minutes, and he raced to a pay phone to inform Lunau about Geiger's unorthodox request. "It's your call, Donnie, what do you want me to do?"

Miffed, Lunau told him not to help Geiger.

Geiger's harried call to Farrell came as Operation Stanley Cup was reaching its climax. Despite their estrangement, Laurie and Ian Lambert had travelled together back to the SVR Centre in Moscow in early 1996. The trip suggested that either the pair of sleeper agents were about to decamp entirely or that they were finally being activated. Murphy's money was on them leaving the country; and it looked like a safe bet, since the pair had hurriedly closed their bank accounts when they returned from Moscow.

The Lamberts' mission was a shambles. The carefully prepared facade of the happily married couple had crumbled. After Ian left her, Laurie had become fond of Dr. Peter Miller, a Toronto physician who thought the woman he was dating was Swedish. The pair had met while attending a dinner honouring Scottish single malt whisky.

Ian was spending most of his time with Keyes at her townhouse, where the pair shared each other's quiet company and the occasional marijuana cigarette.

While Ian and Laurie found refuge in their new lovers, CSIS, prodded by the fact that Ian had told friends at work that he was planning to move to Switzerland, was preparing to swoop in and help make their arrests before they had a chance to leave the country again. The service rented a townhouse just steps from Keyes's home to keep an eye on Ian and his girlfriend. The townhouse sat directly above the entrance to the underground garage where Ian often parked his sports car. The ubiquitous watchers were also on Laurie's trail as she made her way to and from work from her apartment at the Manhattan Towers.

Lunau called Farrell at home two days before Ian and Laurie were to be arrested. He was blunt: "John, I don't want you going anywhere near Ian's or Laurie's places in the next few days. They're both going to be arrested. There may be a lot of media around, and I don't want anyone near them or their apartments."

Lunau told Farrell that other members of the SOS unit would also be tipped off to the impending takedown.

May 22, 1996, began comfortably for Ian Lambert. He awoke in Anita Keyes's waterbed and stayed there as his lover showered and dressed. Keyes was surprised when Lambert decided to call in sick, since he had never taken a day off work before. She headed to the office and found another surprise waiting for her. A man and a woman were sitting in a car in the company parking lot, and they seemed to be watching her.

After Keyes left, Ian rolled out of bed and threw on a pair of jeans and a T-shirt. He was preparing breakfast when the phone rang. Leonard, the building superintendent, was on the phone, asking if Ian would be kind enough to pop down to the visitors' parking lot and move his car because workmen were about to begin repaving the lot.[4] Ian grabbed his car keys and headed out the door, smiling and nodding hello to the neighbours. When he got to his car, he opened the door and slipped into the driver's seat: oddly, his key wouldn't fit into the ignition. He peered around the steering wheel to take a closer look. A lock had been installed on the ignition to prevent him from starting the car. Before he could move, a group of well-armed Mounties and immigration officers sprinted from a nearby van and surrounded him. He was pulled from his car as the police shouted that he was under arrest. CSIS is not a police force and therefore cannot carry arms or make arrests. The Mounties also have the tactical training to handle tricky and potentially violent arrests. The short, strapping Russian colonel fought back and was bruised badly in his struggle. Finally, he was thrown into a police van and it sped away. CSIS officers were also present to make sure that Ian Lambert's days as a spy in Canada were over.

Laurie Lambert had no idea her estranged husband was being bundled up by the Mounties as she prepared to begin another day of work at the Gerling Global Life Insurance Company. A dedicated and popular employee, Laurie had won a promotion and become a member of a special projects team working on improving productivity at the firm. The Mounties and immigration officials swooped in on her as she walked along Broadway Avenue to the subway station. Unlike Ian, she didn't resist but calmly accepted her fate. Her secret life as a Russian sleeper agent had also come to an abrupt end.

Like an army of ants, CSIS officers seized Laurie's computer and personal files from work and descended on her bachelor apartment.

---

[4] Leonard later apologized to Keyes for his involvement in the ruse.

Rose Haslam, the superintendent, says that as many as six officers hauled most of Laurie's belongings out of her suite in boxes soon after her arrest. "They cleaned almost everything out, except some furniture," Haslam said. Later, Laurie's boyfriend, Dr. Miller, dropped by to retrieve whatever CSIS had left behind.

On May 27, 1996, Neil MacDonald, a CBC television reporter with solid connections inside the service, broke the news of the Lamberts' arrest. His story of spies, intrigue and betrayal transfixed and entertained the country for the next two weeks. Other reporters scrambled to dig up more details about the mysterious Russian spies. The splash the story generated boosted morale at CSIS.

Meanwhile, the federal government moved swiftly to deport the Lamberts. But Ottawa faced a big problem: it had little evidence that the couple had engaged in actual espionage during their years in Canada. And while Keyes, the apparent victim of the callous game called espionage, chose to remain silent, Miller launched a spirited public campaign within days of the arrests to have Laurie remain in Canada. He claimed that shortly after her arrest, CSIS had promised her safe haven in the country, only to renege on the deal after skittish politicians nixed the offer. Laurie Lambert hired Clayton Ruby, a prominent Toronto attorney, to vigorously oppose any effort to boot her and Ian out of the country. Ruby argued that the Lamberts' arrests and detention were unconstitutional, since the pair could be deported before the defence attorneys had had an opportunity to properly challenge the government's evidence against them. The Lamberts, it appeared, were bracing for a long and expensive fight to remain in Canada.

Then, on June 6, the Russians waved the white flag. With their lawyer by their sides, the pair briefly appeared in federal court in Toronto and admitted that they were spies and would no longer contest Ottawa's efforts to ship them back to Russia. Through their lawyer, they told the packed courtroom that they wanted to return home rather than face years in custody while their legal battle slowly wound its way through the courts. Laurie, wearing a white tank top and long flowered skirt, waved goodbye to Miller, who whispered, "I'll see you again." Laurie shrugged and raised her hands toward him, her fingers outstretched, before she was hustled away to a holding cell. Ian silently left the courtroom, his hands cuffed behind him. Keyes stayed away from the proceedings and the media frenzy. Outside the courtroom, Miller said that the Lamberts had made the right decision. "This is their safest choice, their best opportunity to restart their lives, which they wish to do," he told a throng of reporters.

On June 7, an immigration adjudicator ruled that the Lamberts were neither Canadian citizens nor permanent residents but people for whom "there are reasonable and probable grounds to believe are or were members of an organization that . . . is or was engaged in acts of espionage and subversion against democratic government." The Lamberts, this time dressed in sombre blue prison clothes, chatted quietly, laughing occasionally, as they sat waiting for the adjudicator to seal their fate. Their public ordeal appeared to ease the hard feelings that had led to their separation. At one point during the hearing, Laurie leaned toward Ian and brushed his cheeks with the fingers of her cuffed hands.[5] A convoy of RCMP vehicles took the spies back to jail. Four days later, a plane carrying Yelena Olshevskaya and Dmitriy Olshevsky touched down in Moscow as thunder, lightning and rain lashed the airport. The pair were whisked away in a van with blackened windows.[6]

Farrell heard the news of the Lamberts' return to Moscow on his car radio as he headed out to train for a marathon. He turned up the volume and listened to a news report that sketched the rough outlines of the spy saga. For a moment, he felt good. He thought of his father, Joseph, who had died in 1992. He would have been proud of the role his son had played in nabbing the two Russian spies. Then Farrell clicked off the radio.

Lunau gathered Farrell and the SOS team, even the CSE technicians from Ottawa, for a celebratory lunch at the Chick n' Deli restaurant on

---

[5] Harold Levy and Dale Brazao, "Russian spies ordered deported. Couple—and their secrets—leaving 'as soon as possible,'" *Toronto Star*, 8 July 1996, p. A13.
[6] Olivia Ward, "Deported spies return to Russia," *Toronto Star*, 12 July 1996, p. A1.

Mount Pleasant Road in mid-town Toronto. The party of twelve toasted their success with round after round of beer, and at one point, Lunau sidled up to Farrell and congratulated him again for his fine work.

"John, you did an extraordinary job. I owe you a lot," Lunau said.

The pair shook hands. Murphy told Farrell that he was the unit's ace and that the service could not have pulled off the operation without him. "You did an outstanding job for us, John. We're really proud of you," Murphy said, as he patted him on the back.

One of the enduring mysteries of the Lamberts' sojourn in Canada is how CSIS twigged to their presence in Toronto. Intelligence operations involving illegals are shrouded in extraordinary secrecy. The Lamberts' true identities and mission were known only to a handful of officers in the SVR. Illegal residences are immensely time-consuming operations that normally involve years of detailed training and meticulous planning. As such, the cost of such missions is huge, as is the cost of failure—exposure usually generates unpleasant diplomatic fallout. Time and money are invested in illegals to ensure their success, not failure. So how did the Lamberts fail? Were they betrayed by an unknown traitor in the SVR or did they simply slip up and invite suspicion that ultimately led to their exposure as spies?

Documents filed by CSIS with the court when Ottawa sought to deport the couple offer a hint of the answer. "The service became aware that a legend had been prepared for a future Directorate S operation based on biodata of Ian Mackenzie Lambert and Laurie Catherine Mary Brodie, two deceased Canadians," CSIS wrote in its twenty-four-page brief to the Federal Court of Canada. The tantalizing sentence suggests that the Lamberts were betrayed.

But the answer to the riddle of how the Lamberts were unmasked is more complex than CSIS's ambiguous sentence implies. Intelligence sources familiar with Operation Stanley Cup confirm that the Lamberts were unearthed by a combination of events. A Russian defector, the sources said, supplied information that an operation involving illegals was afoot in Canada. The defector, however, did not know the identities of the SVR officers planted in this country.

Finding them would be akin to unearthing the proverbial needle in a haystack.

Laurie and Ian had applied for their Canadian passports on June 3 and June 6, 1994, respectively. Their passport photos captured them carefully coiffed and wearing stiff, half-hearted smiles. David Nimmo, a long-time professor and the director of Woodsworth College, acted as guarantor for Ian. Laurie asked Dr. Fraser Tudiver, a physician at Sunnybrook Health Science Centre, to be her guarantor, and he obliged. Laurie's application was error-free. But Ian had trouble with his. He had to correct the spelling of Lambert on the very first line of the application, an unusual mistake for someone to make. Further down on the form, he scratched out "Toronto" as his place of birth and replaced it with "East York" in capital letters. He also listed his occupation as "student." But Ian's perplexing errors alone were not enough to lead CSIS to the sleeper agents. According to Anita Keyes, the service's big break came when a municipal clerk in Quebec—who was updating birth and death information onto a computer—typed in the real Laurie Catherine Mary Brodie's date of death. The clerk was surprised when a social insurance number for Laurie Lambert (née Brodie) popped up on the computer terminal. The SIN was 275 008 482. A long-dead baby with a social insurance number: that unusual but important piece of information eventually ended up in CSIS's grateful hands.

Rather than scooping up the Lamberts instantly, the service waited and watched, certain that the two had confederates working with them in Canada. Along with the Lamberts, CSIS arrested an eighty-year-old woman in Verdun, Quebec, whom the service suspected had been spying on behalf of the Russians since the Spanish Civil War. Given her age and the awkwardness of charging a senior citizen with espionage, Ottawa decided not to prosecute her. The service suspected that the leader of the spy ring was a Toronto dentist who lived and practised near the Lamberts.

Only the arrest of the Lamberts was reported in the press, conveniently leaked at a time when the service's budget had been cut sharply by Ottawa. The story served another important purpose: it reminded Canadians that although the Cold War had been extinguished, this country was still vulnerable to covert operations. But it turns out Operation Stanley Cup was very nearly botched. Just days before the Lamberts were arrested, two CSIS officers arrived at the dentist's front door as he entertained friends at a lively dinner party. The officers accused him of being the ringleader of a network of Russian spies in Canada and demanded to know the details of his relationship with the Lamberts. Apparently the service suspected that the dentist had implanted secrets in Ian's teeth. While acknowledging that he knew the Lamberts, the startled dentist immediately handed over Ian's dental records and persuaded the CSIS officers that they had made a terrible mistake. Miraculously, the poorly timed ambush did not scuttle the two-year counter-intelligence undercover operation.

Operation Stanley Cup was an expensive triumph. A lot of the agency's resources had been devoted to nabbing two very human Russian spies. Tessier, Birkett, Hatcher, Murphy and Lunau were all promoted. Yu, Weber and the other techies earned thousands of dollars in overtime. Murphy was sent to Ottawa to take over as the national director of training of new SOS recruits, and Lunau became chief of Special Ops in Toronto, the job he had been groomed for since he joined the service— the only job, Farrell says, his boss ever really wanted.

There was no promotion, however, for Farrell. Lunau promised him permanent work with the SOS unit, but Farrell was beginning to realize it was a hollow pledge.

10

DIMA AND THE DEFECTOR

Sitting at her round, wooden dining-room table, Anita Keyes takes a calming puff of a cigarette and cradles a glass of Scotch as she quietly casts her mind back to the frenzied days when she was at the centre of a spy story that transfixed a nation. In the years since her relationship with a Russian spy became fodder for headlines, much has changed in her life. There has, however, been one constant: the public portrait of Anita Keyes as a crestfallen woman wounded, her heart pierced by deceit and betrayal.

That sympathetic picture is true—up to a point. To be sure, Keyes was deeply shocked by the arrest of Ian Lambert—but not by the fact that her lover was a spy. She was surprised that he got caught. Keyes had duped both CSIS and the media. She had known for months before his arrest that Ian was a spy. She stayed silent because, she says, she was in love.

The extraordinary affair had a very ordinary beginning. Keyes and Ian Lambert met while working at Black Photo in Markham, Ontario. At the time, Keyes was emerging from a failed marriage. The custody battle over her two children had drained her financially and emotionally, and she sought refuge at work and in the company of friends and co-workers. At Black's, she led a team of employees involved in electronic imaging. One member of the team was Ian Lambert.

She noticed that Ian was a courteous, attractive young man. Brief snippets of small talk in hallways and the office lunchroom eventually led to a proposal: Keyes asked Lambert if he would be interested in a drink after work. Lambert was taken with Keyes's wit and maturity. For her part, his patient ear was a soothing antidote to the painful residue of a failed marriage. Their quick courtship flourished over an agreeable mixture of intimate get-togethers and long walks. On their second date, Lambert blurted out, "I am going to marry you." Surprised, Keyes just smiled.

Lambert told her that his marriage was disintegrating and that her presence in his life was ordained by fate. The relationship was certainly convenient for the spy. He knew that Keyes was a lonely woman, vulnerable to the overtures of a young man adept at playing a variety of characters. Lambert was, Keyes agrees, an accomplished chameleon. The veil of deceit that shrouded him was so persuasive that she never doubted that her new lover was Canadian. Once, after a few glasses of Scotch, she did detect a subtle shift in his accent and jokingly quizzed him about it. "He said he had lived in Germany when he was younger and he had a German nanny and that all left him with a trace of an accent," she says, and she had believed him.

Soon, they began taking weekend trips to Syracuse and Rochester in upstate New York, visiting craft shops and museums and staying at posh resorts.[1] Keyes even accompanied Lambert to his classes at the University of Toronto. "I sat in with him on his history and psychology classes. I loved it," she remembers. She thought Lambert excelled at university. He didn't. She was also by his side when he asked Professor

---

[1] CSIS, Keyes insists, never notified the FBI of Lambert's presence in the United States.

Nimmo to sign his passport application. They often dined at Gio's, an Italian restaurant on Yonge Street, which, with its graffitied walls, loud music and friendly ambience, became one of their favourite haunts. The affair may have buoyed her spirits, but it also caused her unexpected problems at work. Black Photo, she says, gave her—not Lambert—a surprising ultimatum: end the relationship or leave the firm.

"I just snapped and told them that I had enough of the place and left," Keyes says.

When Laurie found out about her, Keyes says, she attacked Ian, punching him and biting his ear. He raced to Anita after the fight to display the scores of cuts, bruises and bites to his face, back and ear.

After his violent showdown with Laurie, Ian decided not only to abandon her but also his career as a spy. He went AWOL in Mexico City a few months after the blow-up. (Lambert told Keyes he was meeting his mother.) Nervous spymasters in Moscow couldn't reach their missing officer. The Russian intelligence operation fell apart not as a result of the millions of dollars CSIS poured into Operation Stanley Cup, but because a man fell in love with a woman, though that delicious truth never made its way into press reports, which lavished praise on CSIS for its so-called intelligence coup.

When Lambert returned from Mexico he moved into Keyes's townhouse. Soon after they began living together, Keyes noticed an unusual clicking sound on her telephone and had Bell Canada check it out. The inspection revealed a possible tap on the phone. "I mentioned it to [Ian] at the time," she says. Strangely, he didn't seem perturbed by the discovery. Days later, Keyes received a note from her landlord advising her that technicians from Ontario Hydro needed access to the townhouse to conduct an inspection.

"I realized later, of course, that it was a trick by CSIS to plant a bug in the house," Keyes says.

Ian's relationship with Keyes not only rocked Laurie but angered his worried bosses. In early 1996, the two spies were summoned back to the SVR Centre after almost seven years in Canada. (Why CSIS risked letting the pair slip permanently from their grasp remains a mystery.)

Ian told his bosses that he was in love with Keyes and wanted out of the espionage game. Ian's superiors gave him two equally unpalatable choices: either he dump Keyes or recruit her to work with him as a spy. Keyes laughs at the notion of being recruited into the world of espionage.

"It's ridiculous," she says. "It's absolutely ridiculous."

Ian told his superiors that both options were unthinkable. Moscow ordered him to break off the affair. He refused, and he and Laurie were told to bug out of Canada immediately. Indeed, when the pair returned from their meeting at the Centre, Laurie began closing bank accounts and paying off outstanding bills.

But where were the spies headed? Keyes believes that the couple were likely bound for Israel with their Canadian passports to gather commercial secrets. The SVR's decision to pull their agents, Keyes says, forced CSIS's hand. "That's why they [CSIS] jumped."

But before the spies departed, Ian decided to tell Keyes the truth.

He chose to make his confession at the exclusive Camberley Club high atop the Scotia Plaza at 40 King Street West in downtown Toronto. The club, which catered to monied businessmen and Hollywood actors searching for privacy, occupied the twenty-eighth and twenty-ninth floors of the bank tower. (It closed in 1999.) The club's suites were large and tastefully decorated, but perhaps most importantly, the Camberley assured guests that they would not be disturbed.

Keyes thought that Lambert had simply planned another romantic weekend getaway, until Ian confessed through a torrent of tears that he was a Russian spy. On bended knee, he told the woman he loved that his marriage to Laurie was a sham and that he and his wife had been sent to Canada as sleeper agents. He divulged his real name, his rank in the Russian military (the youngest person, he claimed, ever to make colonel in the Russian forces) and some details of his intelligence training. Dmitriy Olshevsky told Keyes that he had fallen in love with her and really did want to marry her. He pleaded for her forgiveness. Keyes was stunned.

"Most people, I think, search their whole lifetime for true love, and I really believed that I found it when I met him. So for him to suddenly tell me that he wasn't who I thought he was, well, it would have been much less painful if he had just taken a knife and stabbed me," Keyes says.

She struck her lover and sobbed uncontrollably for several minutes with fury and an almost sickening sense of betrayal. But then the anger ebbed away. Although wounded by his mountain of lies, Keyes told Olshevsky—or, as she affectionately calls him, Dima—that their love was more powerful than his deceit.

Asked now why she stayed with Dima and, indeed, protected him, Keyes says, "I loved him." There is little doubt, however, that Dima's secret life, rich with intrigue and risk, thrilled her.

Dima told Keyes that he was a reluctant spy. Senior Russian intelligence officers, he insisted, had plucked him out of a university classroom in St. Petersburg, where he was studying journalism. He had caught their eye during a successful two-year stint in the military. He had little choice but to say yes when the powerful officials came calling. "Dima said, 'If you get asked and you refuse, you may as well kiss your career goodbye,'" Keyes says.

Yelena Olshevskaya was one of the bright students in Dima's study group at the university. The pair dated briefly before intelligence chiefs persuaded them to marry and serve their country overseas. "He wasn't in love with her," Keyes insists. "But Yelena fell in love with Dima."

The couple spent several months in Vancouver and Quebec perfecting their French and English, before settling in Toronto. "He was familiarizing himself with the country," Keyes says. Dima even told Keyes about his clandestine visits to Mexico in 1993 and Zurich in 1994 where he met with senior Directorate S officers to discuss the intelligence operation and obtain forged travel documents. But Dima didn't tell Keyes everything. "We decided very early on that I would not ask too many questions," she says.

Still, Keyes never envisioned that her lover would be arrested and end up in jail. It was only when CSIS came calling that she truly understood the profound reverberations that Dima's arrest would trigger in her life and his.

Keyes was hunched over a photocopier at her office at an accounting firm when two CSIS counter-intelligence officers, Frank Ayres and Elena Pascual, quietly slipped by security and approached her to ask if they could speak to her for a moment.

"What's this about?"

"Anita, we work with the Canadian Security Intelligence Service," Ayres said, as he and Pascual handed their calling cards to the stunned accountant. Before the officers arrived, Keyes knew little about Canada's spy service or the broad powers it wields.

"Is this a joke?" Keyes giggled.

A cleaning lady was standing behind Keyes, enthralled by the unfolding drama.

"Look, is there somewhere we could talk?" Ayres said. Keyes ushered the intelligence officers into her office.

Ayres asked Keyes about her work at Black Photo, then began peppering her with questions about Dima. Keyes demanded to know what this was all about. Pascual could see that Keyes was becoming upset, and she pulled a small carton of juice from her purse.

"Are you okay?" she asked, proffering the juice box.

The service knew that Keyes was diabetic, and Pascual had brought the juice along in case she went into shock. At that moment, Keyes realized she had been under surveillance. She also understood why her garbage, with her disposable syringes and empty medication boxes, routinely went missing from her front stoop. She had even mentioned the disappearances to Dima.

Ayres told Keyes that her boyfriend was a Russian spy and produced a slew of documents, including the real Ian Lambert's death certificate. Keyes said nothing as Ayres paraded the evidence of Dima's subterfuge before her eyes. The CSIS officer angered Keyes only once, when he suggested that Dima was still seeing Yelena. As Ayres continued his questioning of Keyes, a co-worker popped his head into her office to say that a Mr. Fudge was on the phone, demanding to speak to her urgently.

"I don't know anyone called Mr. Fudge, and I can't talk to anyone now," Keyes said. "Anita, he said he won't leave a message," the co-worker insisted.

The caller was Dima. He was desperately trying to reach Keyes from the Toronto jail where he was being held after his arrest. Not realizing, she didn't take the call.

Hours later, a bevy of CSIS officers and Mounties invaded Keyes's townhouse, searching for evidence. Keyes looked on in silence as government agents seized most of her bedroom furniture, CDs, computers, a printer, an espresso maker, lamps, phones, her treasured key and matchbook collections, two wall clocks, a VCR, desks and a stereo. They also found back issues of a CSIS newsletter that Dima subscribed to and hauled them away. Officers ripped open walls and insulation throughout the house, removed the box-spring cover in her daughter's bedroom and drained the waterbed, thinking that Dima may have hidden incriminating documents beneath it. They tore into ceilings and searched the freezer and refrigerator, where they found a small stash of marijuana and hashish. (Keyes says she and Dima smoked the drugs during their lovemaking to bolster their orgasms.) The officers also found eight thousand dollars in U.S. currency hidden under a desk. They put Dima's beloved red sports car onto a truck, took it away and stripped it bare. "It was not a pleasant experience," Keyes says.

CSIS gave Keyes receipts for Ian's car and all her belongings. The service and the Mounties returned most of it, including the drugs and money.

To ease the shock of Dima's arrest and to curry favour with her, CSIS put Keyes and her children up at the Prince Hotel for several nights. For the most part, Keyes enjoyed her stay at the hotel, inviting friends over and ordering room service. Why shouldn't she pamper herself, she thought, when CSIS had abruptly invaded her happy life and the service was picking up the tab.

At the hotel, Bill Walker, then head of human sources—a branch of CSIS that cultivates and pays sources who provide information to the service in Toronto—along with Ayres, Pascual and Alan Jones, an officer with CSIS's internal security branch, took turns questioning her: Ayres and Pascual on the first day, Walker and Jones the next. Keyes says that CSIS knew intimate details about her life before she met Dima, and pressed her about her knowledge of Dima's activities. Ayres told Keyes that the service had been watching her and Dima for over two years. She didn't believe him. (It was true.) "They said he was still active, still in contact with Yelena," Keyes says. "They said that he had been lying to me all along."

While Keyes was being questioned in a comfortable hotel room, Dima and Yelena ended up in less inviting quarters: the Metro West Detention Centre. Keyes visited Dima several times before he implored her to stop coming. He was sure the cell was bugged.

Keyes says her interrogation by CSIS turned into a negotiation, with the service trying to cut a deal with Dima to mine his knowledge of Russian espionage activity and tradecraft in exchange for him staying in Canada. Keyes and her lawyer willingly played the role of conduit, passing on information to Dima while he and Yelena sat anxiously in jail.

Keyes and Dr. Miller, Yelena's boyfriend, made a pact during their lengthy discussions with CSIS: the service would have to agree to provide a refuge for both Dima and Yelena or there would be no deal. "We decided early on that the four of us would support each other," Keyes says. "It was all for one and one for all." Keyes credits Miller, an Oxford University–educated physician, for supporting her in the tumultuous days after Dima's arrest.

It became clear during the negotiations, Keyes says, that the service had set its sights on Dima because of his senior rank in the SVR. Walker, she says, could hardly conceal his excitement at the prospect of snaring a top Russian spy. His job was to recruit human sources, and Dima would be an invaluable catch. The veteran CSIS officer told Keyes that his role in the caper was the crowning achievement of his long career. "He was like a kid in a candy store," she says. Walker told her, "I've been looking for this for twenty-five years. This is my dream to be involved in something like this, to catch a spy."

To have any chance of securing that coveted prize, CSIS knew that Keyes was indeed the key. "I knew they would use me to get him to play for Team Canada," she says. Walker even offered her money in exchange for her co-operation. "He was actually quite comical. He started out by putting money on the table." The senior CSIS officer told Keyes that the money was hers, no strings attached. Keyes glared at Walker with disdain as she snatched the three thousand dollars cash off the table. The service made her sign a receipt.

Walker assured her that the service understood that she was the unwitting victim of a consummate scam perpetrated by an experienced espionage officer. (When the story hit the news, two CSIS officers even took Keyes to see her ex-husband to reassure him that she hadn't co-operated with the spy but had been duped. Again, Keyes remained silent.)

CSIS wasn't the only intelligence service that was interested in Dima. The FBI also made a proposition to him. Keyes says that CSIS slipped her an envelope, on the back of which were the names of two FBI agents who were anxious to meet Dima. The agents subsequently met with her lawyer and offered Dima a new life, identity and job in exchange for his valuable information. In the end, Keyes and Dima turned down the FBI's offer for one powerful reason: she did not want to uproot her children.

Eventually, CSIS did carve out a deal with Dima, Keyes says. The service wanted to sequester him in a safe house for six months and question him about his training, as well as the SVR's techniques and operations in Canada and overseas. He would also be trotted out before American and British intelligence services for more rounds of questioning. In exchange for his information and co-operation, the service agreed to provide Dima with a new identity and safe haven in Canada with Keyes and her children. Yelena would be offered the same deal. The carefully prepared arrangement, however, fell apart when nervous politicians in Ottawa would not approve it. The decision devastated Keyes, Miller and the security service. Keyes demanded an explanation from Walker for the abrupt about-face. The shell-shocked CSIS officer told Keyes that politics had prevailed over principle and that Ottawa didn't want to upset the Russians by securing the defection of two of their spies.

CSIS had reeled in their big catch, but Ottawa let him wiggle off the hook. Canada's spymasters shook their heads with bewilderment and anger. Despite wanting to cut a deal, Dima was about to be handed back to the grateful and vengeful Russians. Just days after the negotiations collapsed, word of the arrest of the two Russian spies was leaked to the press. CSIS, it seems, had to salvage something from the aborted attempt to lure Dima over to play, as Keyes put it, for "Team Canada."

With no other option but a legal battle, Dima and Yelena reluctantly capitulated in court. Dima's uncomfortable stay in prison also contributed, Keyes says, to his decision to abandon the legal battle to remain in Canada. His co-workers at Black Photo had tried to boost his spirits by sending him a music video filled with messages of support sung to the wildly popular theme song from *Mission: Impossible*. It had little effect. Dima, Keyes says, became despondent in his tiny cell at the Metro West Detention Centre.

The penalty for their failure in Canada was swift and harsh. Not only were the Russian spies disgraced, they had also stuck their embassy in Ottawa with a forty-thousand-dollar legal bill before they gave up and took the Aeroflot flight home. After several weeks of gruelling interrogation in Moscow, Dima and Yelena were forced to pay hefty fines, which effectively drained their bank accounts. Their travel documents were stripped from them, and they were banned from leaving the country for five years. The Russian press was filled with unflattering stories about the intelligence debacle. "There were some very nasty articles written about their failure, their betrayal and the huge cost to the public," says Keyes. "Dima was not viewed as a hero."

But after the media frenzy in Canada died down, Keyes quietly made arrangements to visit her lover in Russia. In August 1996, just ten weeks after his sudden arrest, she boarded a plane in Toronto for St. Petersburg via Frankfurt, Germany. In a curious twist, Russian authorities permitted her to resume her relationship with the humiliated spy. It was the first of many visits that she has made to Russia. Both Dima and Yelena had resigned from the SVR by the time she arrived.

That first reunion at St. Petersburg airport still brings tears to Keyes's eyes. "When he met me as I was coming through customs, he took me in his arms and he kissed me for so long and so passionately that everyone in the airport applauded," she says. Two others were there to greet her: Miller, who'd arrived in Russia a week earlier, and Dima's wife. Keyes was convinced that Yelena was still very much in love with Dima, but she need not have worried. Yelena embraced her.

A senior Russian intelligence official contacted Keyes shortly after her arrival and politely asked if there was anything that she needed or that he could do to make her stay in the country more comfortable. Despite the apparent hospitality, the couple were followed by Russian intelligence officers. (And when Keyes got back home, she learned that the SVR wanted to repossess Dima's red sports car. She had to scrape the money together to pay the pesky Russian officials for it.[2])

Keyes's August trip to Russia was unsettling. She was welcomed into Dima's world and family with open arms, but what a world it was. Russia, reeling from the cataclysmic transition from communism to capitalism, was awash with corruption and crime. For Keyes, confronting first-hand the lawlessness that marked the new Russia was an unnerving experience. Dima was struggling to build a new life, she says, out of the ashes of his career in espionage. He had set his mind on opening a photography studio. To get the business off the ground, however, he was forced to pay bribes to a coterie of bureaucrats.

If she and Dima were to have a life together, she thought, it would have to be in Canada, not Russia.

Still, in early 1999, Keyes made another trip to Russia—to marry Dima. The marriage took place on January 16 at the Wedding Palace, a restaurant and dance hall in Dima's hometown of Pskov, in northwest Russia, a city of breathtaking beauty, towering churches, monasteries and an epic fortress painstakingly rebuilt after the devastation of World War Two. Keyes even sent wedding invitations to Michelle Gagné, a young counter-intelligence officer, and another CSIS officer whom she had befriended years earlier, though they didn't show up.

Among the beaming couple's honoured guests in Pskov were Keyes's Toronto attorney, Mark Trenholme, Miller and Yelena. Two years earlier, Miller had travelled to Russia to wed his love. Now, they were both happily bearing witness to the marriage of Keyes and Dima.

---

[2] Keyes sold the sports car to a friend in early 2002 for five thousand dollars.

In the often ruthless and unsparing world of espionage, the double courtships and marriages were a first. For Keyes, they were also a fitting end to relationships born in deceit, nurtured in turmoil but sustained by love. "The world may have forgotten about us, but we never abandoned our love for each other. Peter married Yelena and I married Dima. Why shouldn't we?" Keyes says, as a smile crosses her face.

A picture of the two married couples was taken at the wedding ceremony in Pskov. In it, Miller sports a faint grin while Yelena, looking demure and serious, clasps her husband's hand. Dima and Keyes, arms entwined, stand shoulder to shoulder with the Millers. It is an astonishing image. Three years earlier, the Russians' hands were locked in cuffs as they were hauled to and from jail after their arrest. Now, those hands sport wedding bands exchanged in Russia, the very nation that dispatched the spies to engage in acts of "espionage and subversion against a democratic government."[3]

The scene was idyllic. A fresh layer of snow had fallen in Pskov the night before the ceremony, giving the wedding hall a picture-postcard look. The long wedding ceremony was performed in Russian. Dima's brother-in-law, Misha, stood beside Keyes and whispered the translation into her ear. The bride, her hair tinted blond and cropped short, wore a simple, stylish cream-coloured suit instead of a formal wedding gown. The groom opted for a green three-button jacket, dark tie and slacks. Yelena wore black. Dima's sister, Anya, was Keyes's maid of honour, while Dima had a friend, Oleg, stand up as his best man. The ceremony was awash with symbolism and tradition. Dima and Keyes walked under a handwoven towel, signifying their union and passage together into a new chapter of their lives. They dipped small chunks of freshly baked bread, a Russian symbol of abundance, into salt, a reminder of the bitter lessons of life, before taking eager mouthfuls. They shared champagne toasts and then smashed their glasses. Applause

---

[3] Cathy Simmie was the immigration adjudicator who presided over the Lamberts' fifteen-minute deportation hearing. "I'm satisfied that you have no right in law to remain in Canada," she told the two Russian spies.

and cheers broke out as they slipped simple, custom-made wedding bands on each other's hands and shared a long kiss. After the ceremony, the wedding party made a brief pilgrimage to a monument honouring Russia's war dead, a custom observed by all newly married couples since the war. The solemn gesture held special significance for Dima, a former colonel in the Russian military and reluctant spy.

At the lavish wedding reception, the sombre mood quickly evaporated. The forty invited guests, including Dima's parents and younger sister, sat at long tables festooned with plain china, crystal glasses and red, white and blue napkins in honour of the Russian flag. Dima's family handed the new bride a bouquet of roses as a gesture of love and friendship. No one from Keyes's family attended the wedding. Her brother, Kevin, an attorney in Calgary, wanted to make the trip, but his cautious law firm barred him from travelling to Russia for security reasons. Her parents, who enjoy a quiet retirement on a farm in Morrisburg, near Cornwall, Ontario, remained distant. "They have not been involved in my life since I was eighteen," Keyes says with regret.

Tipsy guests, including Miller, took turns serenading the couple with robust versions of Russian folk songs. Keyes gave Dima a nickname —"lobster"—because the crustaceans mate for life. Dima had a local baker prepare a special cake that symbolized the two nations that were being joined in matrimony. The base of the cake featured a Russian flag and a maple sugar leaf. Two hearts adorned the top of the cake.

After the wedding, Miller and Keyes began the long and frustrating process of trying to secure Canadian citizenship for their spouses. Russian officials, Keyes says, have finally lifted the travel ban that was imposed on Dima and Yelena in 1996. Freeing the pair from internal exile, Keyes says, is a critical step in the unpredictable road back to Canada.

In early March 2002, Yelena travelled to London, England, to spend a week with her husband and his family. It was her first trip outside Russia since her arrest. Immediately upon her arrival, officers with the British domestic spy service, MI5, tried to contact her to arrange a meeting. Miller politely, but firmly, rebuffed the attempt.

Spurred by Yelena's trip, Miller and Keyes have approached Canadian officials in Russia and Canada to persuade them that Dima and Yelena no longer pose a risk to the country's security and should be granted citizenship. In fact, in early 2000, Yelena had been questioned for forty-five minutes by a Canadian immigration official in Russia about the possibility of emigrating. Canadian officials questioned the legitimacy of her marriage to Miller, Keyes says. (Dima was scheduled to meet with officials at the Canadian embassy in Moscow in February 2002 to discuss his prospects of returning to Canada. The meeting was postponed.)

Is it possible that Dima and Yelena are still players in an elaborate ruse engineered by Russian spy chiefs or that their marriages to Keyes and Miller are a diabolical ploy to get the former spies back into the country to resume their covert work or travel overseas using Canadian citizenship as cover? It seems highly unlikely. First, Dima and Yelena's cover is blown— permanently. CSIS knows the former spies are trying to get back into Canada, this time officially. If they do succeed in emigrating, they are likely to be watched with the same zeal that greeted them during their unofficial stay. Second, only a conspiracy buff could possibly believe that the marriages are a charade. Though their decisions may, to an outsider, appear perplexing and naive, Miller and Keyes are not witless.

Keyes bristles at any suggestion that her husband may still be a spy. "It is a lie," she says angrily. "He quit his job when he met me. His whole life changed when he met me." There is little evidence to dispute that passionate claim.

Finally, if Dima and Yelena returned to Canada—and that seems highly unlikely given the firestorm that would likely trigger—they would be allowed in only with the blessing of CSIS. Ultimately, the service will decide the couples' fates. If the service warns the Canadian government that the former spies continue to pose a risk to Canada's national security, they will not be allowed to enter the country. It is as simple as that. If CSIS wants another opportunity to debrief the pair with the media's gaze no longer trained on them, then the door to Canada might be opened wide.

Keyes says CSIS is still very anxious to pick her husband's brain about Russia's intelligence service. The service was so keen to get their hands on Dima, she adds, that they repeatedly advised her on how they could arrange his escape from Russia. "I have been advised by a number of people, including CSIS, on how they could get him out of there," Keyes says, refusing to elaborate. The service tried to persuade her to co-operate by sending cards and gifts to her home every Christmas—even a bottle of Scotch to send to Dima.

Keyes became close to her CSIS handlers, particularly Gagné, a junior officer based in Toronto. But that friendship ended when Keyes began her attempts to have Dima join her in Canada through official channels. The service turned nasty, Keyes says, threatening to block any attempt to have her husband obtain Canadian citizenship.

Her fight, however, got an unexpected boost on December 15, 2001, when Dima's sister, Anya (who speaks five languages and is now working as an interpreter in Toronto), and her husband, Misha, arrived in Toronto carrying work visas. The new immigrants were sponsored by Keyes and briefly stayed at her townhouse. The couple have since moved to Burlington, Ontario, and Anya is expecting her first child.

Still, Keyes says, the uncertainty over Dima's future is beginning to test the fibre of their relationship. Living with the "Russian Dima" is taxing her patience. Now it's Keyes who lives a double life: one in Pskov with Dima and his American cocker spaniel at their small dacha, and the other in Toronto with her children and job. Her transatlantic trips and the separation from her husband have taken an undeniable toll. Keyes is strapped for cash and weighed down by a mountain of debt and many lingering questions. But she has no regrets.

"So many surreal things have happened that sometimes, I think, is it all real or have I been dreaming?" she whispers. "I have a blessing because I have two children. And I have a love that is so amazing that it is worth waiting five or ten years for him, if that is what it comes down to."

Anita Keyes is, if anything, a determined woman.

Defectors are to intelligence services what whistle-blowers are to reporters: a coveted breed. In return for their only cache—information—they face life-altering retribution. They often lose their savings, their families, their identities, even their lives. They are shunned and have their reputations vilified. They can sink into depression and contemplate suicide. Their motives and loyalties are questioned. And when their usefulness is extinguished, they are often abandoned.

That was the unenviable prospect that Dmitriy Olshevsky and Yelena Olshevskaya faced throughout their ultimately fruitless negotiations to remain in Canada. The Russian spies surely understood that their only worth to their suitors was the intellectual property they could offer for sale or barter—the secrets stored in their minds. The pair knew they would be shunted between intelligence services like chattel, forever beholden to their handlers for reassurance and manipulative acts of kindness. The remainder of their lives, although made more comfortable by their new-found allies, would likely be filled with doubt, regret and more than a hint of fear.

That was largely the fate of the Soviet Union's most celebrated defector to Canada, Igor Sergeievich Gouzenko, a twenty-six-year-old cipher clerk who is credited with triggering the Cold War after he walked out of his country's embassy in Ottawa on September 5, 1945, with more than a hundred documents stuffed under his shirt. The documents Gouzenko spirited from the legation revealed a vast Soviet spy ring operating in Canada. Gouzenko took his trove of documents to the offices of the Ministry of Justice and the *Ottawa Journal*, both places told him to return the following day.

With Soviet security officers searching for him and the incriminating documents he had stolen, Gouzenko dutifully paid the incredulous ministry and newspaper offices another visit the next day, pleading for sanctuary. Again, he was rebuffed. Frantic KGB officers stormed into his apartment, while Gouzenko and his frightened wife found refuge with a neighbour. Finally, just before midnight on September 7, Gouzenko and his family were rescued by local police and offered protection.

Gouzenko chose to defect when he learned that he and his family were about to be forced to return to the Motherland. His only currency with Canadian authorities was the documents he had squirrelled away. Beyond exposing a nest of spies who yearned for Canada's atomic secrets, Gouzenko's documents plunged relations between Moscow and Ottawa into a tense freeze and paralyzed Soviet espionage operations in this country until the early 1960s. In exchange for his testimony and secret papers, Gouzenko and his family were given new identities and protection. In rare public appearances, Gouzenko wore an odd-looking mask fashioned from a sack, with cut-out holes for his eyes and mouth. For the remainder of his long life, he had to shield himself from Soviet spies bent on killing him. By the early 1970s, when his notoriety had waned and his revelations had lost their lustre, Gouzenko pestered journalists with phantom evidence of new conspiracies in a desperate attempt to recapture the moment when he was an important man. He died in June 1982 near Toronto, old, blind and largely forgotten by Canadians.

Gouzenko's death in obscurity cannot diminish the important place his defection still holds in the history of Canada's role in the espionage wars. The arrest and deportation of Olshevsky and Olshevskaya is certainly another celebrated chapter in the world of espionage. But had the service bagged the two spies, the couple may have rivalled Gouzenko for the information they could have delivered on Russian intelligence operations and techniques.

Gouzenko wasn't the only Russian to defect to Canada. A few years after CSIS's birth, fortune shined on the spy service. In a story never before revealed, Anatoli Gayduk, a disgruntled Soviet diplomat, waltzed in to see the Mounties in Ottawa in the early 1990s. He said he was prepared to make an extraordinary deal: in exchange for political asylum, he was willing to provide intimate details of KGB operations and to identify scores of high-ranking Soviet intelligence officers working in Canada. This time, the would-be defector wasn't told to come back the following day. In the vernacular of espionage, the Soviet diplomat was a "walk-in," a spy who willingly and literally walks into the welcoming but skeptical arms of a rival intelligence service and offers his knowledge, albeit at a hefty price.

Gayduk, who worked as a trade officer, was really a KGB major operating out of the Soviet mission in Ottawa. He was young and married with children; he was also the KGB's Line X officer, meaning he was responsible for gathering scientific and technological secrets in Canada. Protocol dictated that the Mounties hand the walk-in over to CSIS. It was up to the service to determine whether Gayduk was a bona fide defector or "bait" dangled in front of spymasters to hoodwink them into believing they had a treasure within their grasp: a double agent.

Gayduk was legitimate and he turned out to be the service's biggest espionage catch since Gouzenko. This time, the defector's motive wasn't disillusionment with the repressive Soviet dictatorship, but greed. And in order to prevent the political and diplomatic earthquake that Gouzenko's public revelations triggered, CSIS chose to keep word of Gayduk's defection a well-guarded secret.[7]

Gayduk gave up the entire KGB "residency" in Ottawa to CSIS—that is to say, he identified all of the Soviet intelligence agency's key spies working out of the embassy under diplomatic cover. "He was a smartass and cocky, but he fingered a bunch of guys," a veteran counter-intelligence officer remembers. He revealed the identity of the KGB "resident" or station chief in Montreal, Victor Baturov. He also gave up details of KGB field operations in Canada and the KGB resident in Ottawa, a dour fellow by the name of Valeri Botcharnikov. Information from the defector and other sources uncovered some disquieting contacts between Bocharnikov and a senior CSIS officer.

Officers from various branches within the service were pulled in to conduct the lengthy debrief of Gayduk. An intelligence officer familiar with the case says the new civilian service seemed taken aback by its unexpected blessing and the motherlode of information that Gayduk eagerly offered up. "CSIS was stuck with him, and frankly it didn't know what to do with him," the officer says. For instance,

---

[7] Peculiarly, Gayduk's name does not appear in any of the booklets produced by the Department of Foreign Affairs listing the names of consular, trade officials and other diplomats working out of the Soviet or Russian embassies or consulates in Ottawa and Montreal.

during his debriefing, Gayduk identified Valentine V. Izbitskikh, the KGB's Line N officer, who was responsible for providing support to illegals or sleeper agents silently operating in Canada. The defector not only provided CSIS with a wealth of information about KGB activities in Canada, sources say, but also corroborated information provided to Western intelligence services by another important defector, Oleg Gordievsky. Gordievsky was the KGB resident or station chief in London.

Like Gordievsky, who secretly co-operated with British intelligence from 1974 to 1985, Gayduk was offered up to sister spy agencies in the United States, Britain and Australia to have his brain picked. In return for his co-operation and tour of Western capitals, the KGB officer was paid a million dollars U.S. by the service, sources say. But, surprisingly, little was done about the Soviet spies in Canada whom the defector identified. "Nothing happened when the defector identified these [Soviet intelligence officers]," a CSIS officer says.

Veteran CSIS officers believe that the government's inaction may have been a by-product of the doubts that percolated within the service's senior ranks about the defector. "They always doubted him [the defector]," a counter-intelligence officer says ruefully. Gayduk, who was disliked by his CSIS handlers because he was lazy and arrogant, was given a new identity and protection and is still believed to be living in Canada.

Intelligence sources say that CSIS's record on enticing other Russian officers to defect is checkered at best. While the service devoted millions of dollars and limitless resources to follow, watch and ultimately arrest Ian and Laurie Lambert, other high-profile prospects were literally offering to walk right into CSIS's arms after the collapse of the Soviet Union during the early 1990s. But the country's spymasters rejected the promising overtures time and time again, privately concluding that once-aggressive Russian intelligence agencies, while still posing a threat to Canada's national security, were disoriented and unsure of their role in the new Russia. Canadian authorities and CSIS were turning to Moscow to help fight a new and emerging threat: the ruthless Russian Mob. Ottawa, sources say, was in no mood to alienate its new allies in the war against organized crime. "They [CSIS] didn't want to make any waves. So what the Russians wanted, the Russians got," a veteran CSIS officer says.

In the new spirit of co-operation, the two services made high-profile visits to each other's capitals to exchange intelligence and discuss other ways to join forces. Publicly, of course, CSIS basked in rare praise and glory for nabbing the two Russian spies.

One of the promising candidates whom the service apparently took a pass on, intelligence sources say, was Sergei Tretyakov. Working under diplomatic cover at the Soviet embassy in Ottawa in the 1990s, Tretyakov became the KGB's top spy in Canada after his predecessor, Leonid Ponamerenko, was apparently compromised by Gordievsky.

Tretyakov was well-suited for a life in espionage. His father was a career diplomat with numerous postings abroad; Tretyakov was, in fact, born in the United States. Growing up, he mastered English and French, speaking both languages fluently and without a trace of an accent. He obstensibly followed in his father's footsteps, joining Russia's diplomatic corps, all the while working for the KGB.

As the Soviet Union began to crumble, senior KGB officers, including Tretyakov, were offering their services, expertise and knowledge to CSIS in exchange for political asylum in Canada. As the KGB resident in Canada, Tretyakov was privy to most of the espionage agency's intelligence operations in the country. He was, to the chagrin of several intelligence officers, never recruited by the service. "We gave him [Tretyakov] to the service [CSIS] on a platter but they wouldn't take him. He was willing to meet. He was willing to talk. He figured that his career was finished, but we were told to let him go because the service thought he was baiting us and that we didn't have the money," says one veteran officer.

In October 2000, Tretyakov decided to take his chances with the Americans. At the time, the tall, hefty, balding forty-four-year-old was serving as first secretary in Russia's mission at the United Nations. He kept a low profile at the busy diplomatic mission; few of the bona fide diplomats had any dealings with the spy, who shared an apartment in the Bronx with his wife and teenaged daughter. Unlike their

Canadian brethren, America's intelligence services wasted little time before recruiting Tretyakov after he and his family failed to return to Moscow. His defection quickly turned into an intelligence coup. Shortly after Tretyakov was accepted into the CIA's resettlement program for valuable defectors, the FBI obtained the contents of a KGB case file that led them to finger Robert Hanssen, one of the bureau's top spy hunters, as a mole. The twenty-five-year FBI veteran was arrested on February 17, 2001, and charged with spying for the Russians since the early 1980s.

Although Louis Freeh, the FBI director at the time, denied any connection between Tretyakov's defection and Hanssen's arrest, intelligence experts on both sides of the Atlantic credited the career Russian spy with exposing the FBI agent's costly treachery. (Two months after Tretyakov defected, Evgeny Toropov, a Russian diplomat in Ottawa, also defected and made his way to the United States, leading to speculation that he, too, may have been involved in identifying Hanssen as a mole.)

In his two decades as a Russian agent, Hanssen betrayed the identities of more than fifty people who had spied for the United States. Many of them were jailed and at least two were executed. Hanssen was paid about $1.4 million in cash and diamonds for his information. He used the bulk of the money to pay for his upscale home and private school tuition for his six children. (The married Catholic also spent a total of about eighty thousand dollars to wine and dine a stripper.)

Apart from the human toll exacted by Hanssen's treason, expensive counter-intelligence operations were also compromised. Hanssen alerted his Russian handlers, for example, to the existence of a $500-million surveillance tunnel beneath the Soviet diplomatic compound in Washington D.C. But perhaps most damaging of all, the FBI agent sold Russia details of a super-secret plan for how the U.S. president, Congress and the federal government would operate in the event of a nuclear attack.

In a monstrous blunder, the FBI failed to investigate Hanssen even after his brother-in-law and fellow FBI agent, Mark Wauck, went to senior FBI officials in 1990 with his suspicions that his sister's husband was a Russian spy. Wauck told his bosses that Hanssen kept thousands of dollars hidden in the basement of his home and was spending too much money for someone on an FBI salary. The warning fell on deaf ears and Hanssen continued betraying secrets to the Russians for another decade.

Tretyakov's defection didn't surprise the Canadian intelligence officers who befriended him during his tour in Canada. It did, however, anger them. "We could have had him years earlier," one officer says. "He may have known about Hanssen's relationship with the KGB when he first approached us. And we could have perhaps saved lives and operations."

In the mid 1990s, another senior Russian intelligence officer, working clandestinely in Canada, made it clear that he was also willing to change sides. Colonel Alexandre A. Fedossev was the GRU resident, Russia's military intelligence station chief, in Canada. (Relations between the GRU and the former KGB were notoriously bad. The enmity, jealousy and bitterness between the two Russian intelligence services mirrored CSIS's strained relations with the RCMP.) After his young daughter suffered serious injuries in a car accident while on a brief visit to Russia, Colonel Fedossev quietly approached a veteran counter-intelligence officer. He had brought his disabled child back to Canada with him and said that he would do anything to help her, including betray his country. The excited officer reported the offer to his superiors in Ottawa, who ordered a psychological assessment of the GRU resident to determine whether he was a plant or making a legitimate offer. "They kept him waiting for an answer," a CSIS officer says.

A year later, the service decided against recruiting Fedossev; he was just too expensive, they said, and the Americans were skeptical of him. "They never talked to him, but they figured that he was an awful big dangle and that the service would be left with egg on its face," a counter-intelligence officer says.

Then, as Fedossev and his family headed to Mirabel Airport to leave Canada permanently, the service had a sudden, inexplicable change of heart: it asked its officer to "pitch him," that is, to offer the colonel a belated invitation to work for CSIS. Fedoseyev was surrounded by GRU officers and his successor when the CSIS officer arrived at the airport. The officer approached him in the airport parking lot, even though he knew it was too late. Fedossev extended his hand and told the officer, "It's all right."

Counter-intelligence officers who later watched the service pour resources into Operation Stanley Cup were perplexed by their superiors' decision to move so hesitantly to recruit Fedossev. "Recruiting the GRU resident would have meant recruiting God," says one officer who is still angry at the service's reluctance to pitch the colonel earlier. "The information he would have provided would have dwarfed whatever the Lamberts could have given us."

Sergei V. Machine, another GRU officer, who worked as vice-counsel of the Russian mission in Montreal and provided support to illegals operating in Quebec, also wanted to defect to Canada in the early 1990s. "He wanted to stay in the worst way," an exasperated officer says. "We could have recruited him a thousand times, but CSIS wouldn't touch him."

CSIS officers were increasingly frustrated by Ottawa's timidity in moving against Russian intelligence officers operating in Canada. Occasionally, the Russians were so disdainful of their Canadian hosts that they brazenly refused to boot out agents when Ottawa politely asked. An example: Gannadiy Matveyev was a KGB officer working at the Aeroflot office in Montreal in the 1990s. Matveyev was identified by successive CSIS counter-intelligence officers as a middle-ranking KGB officer, but despite repeated requests that he be ejected, the Soviets simply snubbed their noses at Canadian authorities, and the spy remained in Canada.

In the eyes of many CSIS officers who had waged the long, silent war against the Soviet Union, the service was abandoning its once celebrated mission—catching Russian spies—not with a bang but a whimper. Igor Gouzenko would not have been amused.

11

"HOUSTON, WE HAVE A PROBLEM"

C SIS enjoyed some rare praise in the aftermath of Operation Stanley Cup. Top officials at the intelligence service said little publicly about the role the agency had played in nabbing the two lovestruck Russian spies. They didn't have to. The service knew that it could rely on a string of faithful former officers and friendly academics to spread the news, and in the days following the arrest and deportation of Ian and Laurie Lambert, they did not disappoint. David Harris, briefly CSIS's chief of strategic planning before becoming a media favourite, proclaimed the operation an unqualified triumph. "Catching them [the Lamberts] is one heck of a major achievement," Harris told the *Toronto Star*.

Harris probably didn't know about the list of important defectors that the service had failed to exploit. He wouldn't have known that in its celebrated effort to snare the two Russians, CSIS had illegally intercepted the mail of scores of Canadians who lived in apartment buildings occupied by Ian and Laurie Lambert; that the service conducted extensive background checks on an untold number of unsuspecting

Canadians in a fruitless bid to determine whether the spies had confederates working with them; that a senior CSIS officer had ordered John Farrell to steal Crown keys that were used during an aborted break-in into Ian's apartment; that another CSIS officer had encouraged him to seduce Laurie in a scheme to elicit information from the lonely Russian spy—or that the service very nearly botched the whole counter-intelligence operation by questioning a startled dentist days before the Lamberts' arrest.

Farrell knew these sorry truths about Operation Stanley Cup and more. And it bothered him that everyone associated with the coup was benefiting, no matter the blunders they made. He still remembers with disbelief meeting Sandy Brown, an SOS member, who was with her young son, in July 1996, rollerblading near an outdoor swimming pool along the winding boardwalk adjacent to Toronto's lakefront. Brown actually told Farrell that she had helped herself to a souvenir as Operation Stanley Cup wound down—Laurie Lambert's new Rollerblades. Farrell understood the impulse to keep a souvenir of a memorable caper, but this was not only rash, but stupid. "Donnie let you take those out of the evidence room?" Farrell asked. "He doesn't know," she replied. (Brown returned the Rollerblades after an inventory check of the Lamberts' possessions seized by CSIS after their arrests revealed that they were missing. The Rollerblades were returned to the Russian embassy in Ottawa.)

Lunau seemed to sense Farrell's mood and tried to make sure his faithful lieutenant had little time to grumble. Another crisis was brewing in Operation Vulva, involving Kenny Baker, the veteran postal inspector and API who had trained Farrell. The first hints came in late 1995, as Baker's already fragile health began to worsen. Once, Farrell had to find him when he wandered into a washroom at a busy shopping mall after getting lost on his way to a postal station. Farrell's concern grew when the cheery Second World War veteran began to address him as "Sergeant." Often, Farrell had to shout to get his colleague's attention.

Baker's driving habits deteriorated, if that was possible. One morning, as Farrell made his way to a postal station along the express lanes of Highway 401, he noticed scores of angry motorists in the collector lanes honking wildly and swerving dangerously to avoid a car that seemed to have come to a near standstill. Farrell looked across the lanes of traffic and spied Baker slowly meandering from one lane to another, apparently oblivious. In a bid to save Baker's life, Farrell raced through a point on the busy highway where the express and collector lanes merged, honking and shouting at the beleaguered veteran to pull over to the emergency lane. When Farrell finally reached the befuddled Baker and saw the confusion in the old man's face, he felt sorry for him.

After twenty-five years of service with Canada Post and CSIS, Baker was unceremoniously dumped from the mail-intercept program. Patrick Bishop, a former military policeman who had become the manager of corporate security for Canada Post in Toronto, delivered the bad news. He called Baker at home to tell him that he was fired. Baker's widow, Pat, remembers the phone call. "That upset him terribly," she says. "It would have been better if they called him into an office and sat him down and talked to him instead of waiting until he got home and phoning to say: 'That's it. You're through.'"

Baker called to tell Farrell how hurt he was by Bishop's call. He vowed to exact his revenge for the shoddy and cavalier way in which he had been treated, and the veteran API had the ammunition to cause Canada Post and CSIS a great deal of trouble, neatly stored in his small, black notebooks, which were emblazoned with large gold shields and the words, "Canada Post Postal Inspector." A daily account of Baker's highly classified work as an API, the notebooks were stored inside a leather satchel in his car. He had logged critical details of every mail intercept that he had conducted as part of Operation Vulva since joining CSIS in 1989. Baker had recorded the hours he had worked on the ultra-secret program; the names and addresses of targets; the warrant numbers; the times and dates he had met with Farrell, Lunau and other CSIS officers to drop off and pick up mail; even the names of CSIS officers who had attended pool parties in his backyard. And, of course, he had noted the location of every single postal station where he had intercepted letters. Notebook after notebook was filled with the kind of sensitive information that could prompt unsettling questions about the intimate relationship between Canada Post and CSIS, and the service's activities and presence at postal stations across the country.

Baker was so angry he confronted Bishop at his office in Mississauga the day after his firing. Waving a handful of notebooks, Baker threatened to blow the whistle on Operation Vulva. "Listen, I've got these documents," he shouted.

Baker also warned Bishop that he was prepared to expose the dubious financial arrangement between CSIS and Canada Post that saw APIs earn thousands of dollars each year without paying a single cent in tax. Baker swore that he would hand-deliver his incriminating notebooks to top union officials at the super postal facility at 280 Progress Avenue. "He was going to blow the whistle on everybody," his widow confirms.

Farrell had understood from his first day of training that Baker was a security risk—he had watched with bewilderment as Baker routinely compromised the secrecy of the mail intercept program. He had warned Lunau that he was courting danger by hiring cronies and washed-up postal inspectors. CSIS might be able to deny its relationship with a sick, forgetful API, but not the evidence he possessed. Pat Baker knew her husband's notebooks were explosive: "Canada Post doesn't want [the public] to know that they are involved with [CSIS]," she says. "CSIS has a very bad name in this country."

Farrell learned that Baker, after his joust with Bishop, met with at least two union officials at 280 Progress to discuss his long-standing role in Operation Vulva. Baker was coy with them and didn't reveal much about the program or the existence of his notebooks. The union officials were receptive, but puzzled. To them, Baker appeared confused, and they couldn't grasp the significance of his broad hints. CSIS caught a lucky break. Farrell called Lunau to discuss Baker's mangled overture to the postal workers.

"Houston, we have a problem," Farrell told his boss. "Kenny's upset. He's threatening to go public."

To soothe Baker's wounded pride, Lunau decided to offer him a pat on the back, a congratulatory toast and perhaps even a plaque. Bishop had handled Baker crudely. It was up to Lunau to repair the damage.

As a first step, Lunau handed Baker a temporary reprieve, allowing him to work for another two weeks. He wasn't to intercept any mail, but he was paid his usual twenty-dollars-an-hour fee. In the meantime, Lunau was busy assessing the damage Baker's notebooks were likely to cause the service if they fell into the hands of the media or union officials; it was clear that CSIS needed to retrieve Baker's troublesome notebooks and destroy them.

Once again, Lunau turned to Farrell, calling him at home to discuss his next assignment.

Just to be clear, Farrell asked Lunau how he was supposed to get the notebooks.

"Any way possible," Lunau replied.

Farrell pondered the possibilities for a moment, before suggesting that he could break into Baker's car and steal the notebooks while the veteran API enjoyed a refreshing beer with him at a bar.

"Perfect," Lunau told Farrell. "Whatever you do, John, get the fucking notebooks."

Farrell arranged to meet Baker at O'Tooles Roadhouse and Restaurant near the corner of Kennedy and Ellesmere in Scarborough. (It is no longer in business.) The APIs occasionally met Lunau at the smoke-filled sports bar to share a few drinks and gossip. The pub was also a short drive from Baker's home. Farrell was confident that Baker would feel comfortable there and let his guard down, making the job of stealing his notebooks easier. Baker liked Farrell and believed his young boss was his friend. And Farrell had been kind to Baker, making allowances for his snail-slow pace on the job and often overlooking the fact that the frail API regularly padded his expense account. The pair met almost every day for three years to exchange mail, and they were close. But, ultimately, Farrell owed his allegiance to the CSIS officer who was paying him: Don Lunau.

Baker arrived at the pub unshaven and wearing a blue bomber jacket. He sidled up to the bar and greeted his friend. Farrell consoled him over how shabbily he'd been treated by Bishop and CSIS. Baker removed his jacket and ordered two pints of his favourite British ale. When he was partway into the first one, Farrell slipped his hand into the jacket and fished out the keys to the grey Mercury Grand Marquis which Baker had parked in front of the pub. While Baker sipped on his beer, Farrell excused himself to go to the washroom. He skipped out of the bar instead, opened Baker's car door, snatched the fifteen notebooks and any other documents he could find and tucked the loot into a small, leather bag, which he then dropped into his compact car parked conveniently beside the large vehicle.

It took him less than a minute.[1]

He walked back into the pub and sat down beside Baker, offering him a quick toast before taking a big gulp of his beer. Baker thanked Farrell for his generosity and for taking the time to meet him.

"No problem, Kenny," Farrell said. "I hate to see a good man like you get fucked over." Then Farrell pretended that his pager went off and excused himself again. Outside the pub, he called Lunau, who was waiting anxiously by his phone at CSIS headquarters.

"Donnie, I've got everything. What do you want me to do with it?" Farrell asked his boss.

"Destroy it."

"You don't want any of it?"

"No," Lunau said.

"You want me to read the stuff?"

"No. Just destroy them all."

When Farrell sat down beside Baker again, he apologized for the interruption and offered to buy him lunch. Baker took a pass, saying his stomach was acting up. The pair chatted a while longer before Farrell told Baker he had to get back to work.

"You're a good kid, John," Baker told Farrell.

"Don't get weepy on me," Farrell said. "I'll catch up with you later."

Farrell headed home and ripped each notebook in two before

---

[1] In case Baker caught him inside the car, Farrell had brought along a small gift (a pen) and a farewell card signed by Lunau and himself. The plan was to apologize to Baker for lifting his keys and explain, a little sheepishly, that he and Lunau wanted to surprise the former API by leaving behind a token of their friendship.

slipping them, one by one, into a shredder that CSIS had bought for him and which he kept in his bedroom. In less than two minutes, Baker's long history with the service had been destroyed. He could now be safely dismissed as an absent-minded, bitter old man with an axe to grind.

Baker only realized that his notebooks were missing several days after his lunch date with Farrell. The fate of the notebooks was a mystery to him, but according to his widow, he never suspected his good friend John.

A week after the theft, Lunau asked Farrell to arrange a going-away lunch for Baker and his wife at the St. Andrew's Fish & Chips shop in Scarborough. The homey, family-run restaurant, in a tiny suburban shopping centre near the Baker home, was one of Kenny's favourite spots. Lunau wanted Farrell to make the arrangements because he feared Mrs. Baker's wrath. She had called Farrell several times to curse the service for the "ugly" way her hard-working husband had been treated. Lunau brought Farrell along to the lunch for protection.

He picked up Farrell on his way to the restaurant and seemed ill at ease as they pulled into the shopping mall. He showed no sign of nervousness, however, when he greeted Baker and his wife with a warm handshake and smile. He turned on the charm, telling Baker that the service would always be grateful and indebted to him for the contribution he had made to the program.

"You've done a great job for us, Kenny."

"Thanks very much, Don. I appreciate that," Baker replied, he and his wife getting teary. Farrell was moved by Baker's reaction and sickened by Lunau's performance. Lunau even promised to get Baker a plaque to commemorate his work for the service. No one dared to raise the topic that had really brought them all together: Baker's notebooks. Mrs. Baker insists that before the lunch, her husband had decided not to blow the whistle on the service, fearing the storm and backlash that the revelations undoubtedly would have triggered. "I was afraid of him doing it," she says. "I don't think he could have gone through the strain of it, to be quite honest. And they wouldn't have given him an easy time."

Having placated Baker, Lunau was anxious to leave. But lunch dragged on for over ninety minutes. When it was over, Lunau bid the Bakers goodbye and slipped into a sporting goods store next door to buy a hockey stick and tape.

A few months after he was fired, Baker was admitted to hospital. He was very ill and the doctors were mystified. Despite a battery of tests, they couldn't make a diagnosis. Baker's condition worsened. A persistent cough sometimes left him gasping for breath. Eventually, both of Baker's legs had to be amputated. (Lunau joked, Farrell says, that there was now no risk of Baker taking CSIS to court because "he didn't have a leg to stand on.") No one from CSIS or Canada Post visited Baker in the hospital. He died on the eve of the news of CSIS's "triumph"—the arrest of Ian and Laurie Lambert in May 1996.

Farrell was in Florida when he heard the news of Baker's death. The man in charge of running Operation Vulva for most of southern Ontario had taken a brief respite from his secret duties to try to recover from a death in the family. Farrell hoped that the warm, soothing Florida sun would help ease his grief over the suicide of his oldest sister, Carmelita Rose Farrell. Baker's death caused a whiff of regret in Farrell. In the midst of his own pain and loss, he sent a card of condolence to Mrs. Baker, signing it, "From Don and the boys." But Kenny Baker never got his plaque from CSIS.

12

FEATHERING THEIR NESTS

For more than five years, John Farrell had willingly and enthusiastically done the dirty work for Don Lunau and the service, but he was still getting paid twenty dollars an hour. Meanwhile, some of CSIS's intelligence chiefs appeared to treat the agency's vast resources as a private trust fund. There was vital work to be done, but everywhere Farrell turned, it seemed someone at CSIS was taking the Canadian taxpayer for a ride.

In the wake of Operation Stanley Cup, Farrell's primary job in the SOS unit was to rent apartments across the city to be used as observation posts on CSIS's targets. One place that he rented for the service was a cockroach-infested, two-bedroom apartment in a dilapidated triplex at 4040A Old Dundas Street in the city's west end. The third-floor suite was right across the street from 4033 Old Dundas Street, a tired-looking eight-storey apartment complex that was home to a major counter-terrorism target. Farrell remembers joining Alex Yu and Tommy Birkett on the rooftop of a nearby building to train an antenna on the target's suite. "I was standing there like a human lightning rod, holding the antenna, while Birkett was getting instructions from Yu to have me move a little to the right or a little to the left," Farrell says.

With Lunau in tow, Farrell also regularly visited the service's observation post across from the Chinese consulate in downtown Toronto, where watchers and intelligence officers were supposed to be keeping an eye on Beijing's diplomats and spies. Farrell soon noticed that the basement apartment in the low-rise that faced the Chinese mission also doubled as a refuge for intelligence officers who needed a place to stay for free while they recovered from hangovers or messy divorces.

Lunau and Murphy also asked Farrell to scout for some office space in the Toronto Dominion Tower in the heart of the city's financial district. A friendly Asian government planned to move their consulate into the building, and Farrell says that CSIS wanted to plant bugs and other equipment there to spy on the major trading partner and ally of Canada.

Farrell posed as a business consultant looking for office space. Surprisingly, he was asked to bring someone along: a short, heavy-set man with a shock of white hair and a thick Greek accent, who Farrell thought at first was with Greek intelligence. Later, he learned that the fifty-five-year-old with rough-hewn hands was a close friend of several senior officers, a building contractor who had renovated the homes of some members of the SOS unit. The contractor was playing spy at the taxpayers' expense: he was put on the SOS payroll, not because he had any intelligence training or top-secret security clearance, but because some of the unit's intelligence officers owed him money.

Lunau used Farrell's birth certificate and social insurance number to rent an apartment on The Esplanade in Toronto (as recently as June 2002, the suite's phone was still registered to a John Farrell) and signed a batch of receipts in Farrell's name to cover expenses associated with that observation post. But Farrell never saw much of the money, except for the two hundred dollars that the service paid his mother to clean the already pristine apartment.

The SOS chief also instructed his trusted deputy to rent an apartment at 2142 Bloor Street West. The suite was needed, Lunau explained, because CSIS had to keep a keen eye poised on an important target who lived nearby. Farrell made the trek out to the apartment building, but to Lunau's chagrin, there were no suites available. He had to settle for a two-bedroom apartment at 2146 Bloor Street West. On November 1, 1996, Farrell signed a one-year lease with Robert S. Leung, the physician who owned the aging brick low-rise, to rent Suite 6 for $848 a month. The third-floor apartment in the upscale neighbourhood was spacious and faced High Park, one of the city's largest and most popular green spaces. Lunau asked Farrell to convince Leung's wife, who acted as the landlady, to pay for a new stove and refrigerator for the suite. (Lunau helped deliver both appliances.) Lunau also told Farrell to arrange for cable television and phone service to be installed. He explained that the apartment, with its gleaming hardwood floors and view of busy Bloor Street, was an observation post for a vitally important counter-intelligence operation. Farrell was mystified. The service's techies visited the suite only once and installed a listening device in a living-room armoire as well as a high-security lock on the apartment's front door. Lunau also paid a visit to inspect the new observation post, a rare move for him.

Apart from the two visits, no other CSIS personnel, including technicians, watchers or intelligence officers, ever entered the suite. Farrell and his team of APIs had no mail intercepts in the area. He asked himself who had the service really rented the suite for?

The answer to that question surprised Farrell but also confirmed his belief that his bosses were adept at looking after their own. Farrell discovered that Heather McDonald, the daughter of Keith McDonald, CSIS's national director for the Special Operational Services in Ottawa, had moved into the apartment with a friend and as far as he knew the service was paying the rent and utility bills. The smug arrangement irked Farrell, but he knew that his mission was not to ask questions but to make sure that McDonald's friendly, attractive daughter was as happy and comfortable in her new apartment as possible.

Farrell later learned that Ms. McDonald had been going through a taxing and turbulent time in Ottawa and needed a place where she could just hang out. Toronto is a popular destination for young, adventurous women, but its apartment vacancy rates are notoriously low. CSIS had a novel solution to the challenging problem: turn an apartment supposedly designated for a top-secret counter-intelligence operation into a hostel. Lunau, Farrell says, even hand-picked the furniture for the apartment from CSIS's well-stocked storage facility in Newmarket.

But like many young people with energy to burn, Heather enjoyed playing music loudly, talking to her boyfriend in Ottawa for hours on the phone and partying and dancing on the hardwood floors. The ruckus bothered her sedate neighbours, who preferred the quiet company of their cats and a good book over the incessant thumping of speakers and the jackhammer tapping of high-heeled shoes. When polite requests to turn the music down and to wear slippers failed to do the trick, Farrell was called several times by the landlord's wife. Farrell apologized for all the noise and promised to talk to his "cousins" about their annoying habits. The landlady also demanded to know why Farrell never seemed to be at the apartment. "Look, we rented the place to you, not two girls," Mrs. Leung said. And why had her new tenant changed the locks? Farrell told his inquisitive landlady that he was often away on business in Vancouver and had installed an extra-secure lock because he feared being robbed.

Farrell called Heather and politely asked her to avoid causing any more trouble. But she was in no mood to listen, and accused her neighbours of being stuffy. Heather kept on partying and the neighbours kept on complaining. Farrell worried that soon the police would arrive on Heather's doorstep and ask some ticklish questions. After the second complaint, Farrell called Murphy, who was about to leave for Ottawa to start his new job. Murphy, Farrell says, was more annoyed than angry: "Jesus Christ, can't that girl control herself?"

"Ray, I've already got enough on my plate," Farrell said. He didn't think he'd been hired to billet and mind the children of senior CSIS officers. Murphy told him that Heather's stay in Toronto would soon be over and to just put up with it as best he could.

Farrell learned later why Murphy was reluctant to turf Heather out of the apartment. Senior CSIS officers, Farrell says, had struck a private deal that allowed their children, when they were away from home or studying at university, to stay in apartments that were rented by the service. The children of senior CSIS officers in Ottawa, for example, would stay in apartments in Toronto, and the children of high-ranking intelligence officers in Toronto got to stay in CSIS-controlled "safe houses" or "observation posts" in Ottawa.

Although Farrell kept paying Heather's rent every month, he was soon relieved of the responsibility of chaperoning the SOS boss's daughter. Sandy Brown got that assignment and had about as much success as Farrell in trying to tame Heather and her friend. The bored CSIS officer spent hours sanding down a CSIS-owned armoire in the apartment, which she would later take home. Mercifully, Heather and her friend stayed in the apartment for only about a year.

Farrell kept a separate cheque book to keep track of all the apartments he rented for CSIS. (He listed the postal codes for each unit when he made his entries in order to conceal the actual addresses in case the cheque book was stolen or lost.) His records show that he rented the apartment on Bloor Street for fifteen months, ending in January 1998. In total, the service laid out $12,720 for an apartment used by the daughter of one of its most senior officers. That figure does not include phone bills, cable TV and other miscellaneous expenditures. If McDonald ever reimbursed the service for these expenses, Farrell was never told.

Keith McDonald declined to answer questions about his daughter and the observation post. When the subject of Heather's stay in the apartment was raised with a recently retired SOS member, she said, "Well, everyone was quite aware. There were receipts signed. It was all documented." Asked why Heather was permitted to use an apartment rented ostensibly for a covert operation, the ex-officer said, "I don't know. . . . They were secret operations and I really don't want to discuss them."

Our spy chiefs can behave with such impunity because it is easy for them to evade their watchdog agency, SIRC. The apartment Heather McDonald used was rented under Farrell's name. The phone and television cable bills were made out to Farrell. There was no way to link the apartment to McDonald unless someone blew the whistle. Even if someone did, Farrell was supposedly not an employee of the service but a "contractor" paid by Canada Post. As such, he didn't fall under SIRC's responsibility or mandate. "SIRC is a paper tiger. Lunau knew it. Murphy knew it. McDonald knew it. Bradley knew it and I'm sure Elcock knows it," Farrell says.

SIRC claims access to all of CSIS's files, but that is not the same as real, tangible oversight. "SIRC can look at all the documents they want, but they're not going to find any piece of paper that says, 'Oh, by the way, we are using observation posts to billet the children of senior CSIS agents.' And they're certainly not going to find a piece of paper that shows that I was ordered to steal a Crown key or intercept mail without a warrant or do mail cover checks without a warrant or steal a relay key or steal Kenny Baker's notebooks," Farrell says.

Free apartments weren't the only perks that the children of top CSIS officers enjoyed. They also had access to the service's large fleet of cars. The abuse of CSIS vehicles by high-ranking managers is an open secret at the service. An internal fleet audit conducted in the mid-1990s found that senior CSIS officers routinely used government-owned vehicles for personal reasons, including running errands, driving to and from work and even vacationing with family. The audit provided details of about forty instances where government-owned cars were improperly used by senior intelligence officers. (A veteran officer who helped prepare the audit says he had wanted to provide many more examples of abuse but was ordered by a senior CSIS official to limit the number.) In one case, a top officer in Montreal was discovered to be using a CSIS car for personal purposes when he got a parking ticket. He claimed he was using the car for surveillance, but auditors could find no record of the operation that the vehicle was allegedly being used for.

Serious accidents involving senior CSIS officers who were behind the wheel of government-owned cars have also been routinely covered up. Frank Pratt, the legendary spy catcher who died in late 2001 after a long career with the service, was involved in a near-fatal accident in Toronto. The vehicle was a write-off and Pratt, the service's former head of internal security, ended up in hospital in critical condition. Intelligence sources familiar with the incident said that Pratt may have been drinking before the accident. But Pratt was not charged, and the episode was hushed up to protect the service's reputation.

One of Ray Murphy's daughters was also involved in a serious accident while driving her father's government-issued car. She was headed out for a night on the town when she collided with another car after running a red light at a major intersection in Durham Region, just outside of Toronto. The girl was fine, but the vehicle was badly damaged. Lunau received a frantic call at home from Murphy shortly after the accident. A call to the local police smoothed things over, and Murphy's daughter did not face charges.

Tommy Birkett was driving his company car home to Simcoe, Ontario, one evening in 1996, when he was involved in a mysterious accident. Birkett claimed that a frightened deer jumped into his path and he swerved to avoid hitting the animal. His colleagues doubted that Bambi was responsible for the mishap. Whatever the reason, the car was totalled. David Beazley, the former director-general for the Toronto Region, was involved in as many as three accidents involving CSIS cars, sources said. Senior managers at the spy service tried to cover up for him, but word quickly spread among rank-and-file members that Beazley had been involved in the accidents and that some of the expensive vehicles that the top spy had been driving were headed straight for the scrap heap.

The audit also revealed serious irregularities involving Tony Iachetta, a fast-rising CSIS officer in Edmonton. Iachetta was a star who seemed to have an unmatched ability to cultivate well-placed and valuable sources. But his success failed to impress his colleagues in the prairie region, who strongly suspected that the former Mountie was padding his expense accounts and conjuring up fictitious sources to impress his gullible superiors. They ratted on him, providing auditors with copies of receipts that Iachetta had signed for payments to sources. The chits raised questions about whether, in fact, Iachetta had made up the sources and pocketed the money himself. Auditors also looked into Iachetta's unauthorized use of CSIS vehicles and found a long history of abuse. A report detailing his unsettling transgressions made its way up the chain of command, but the star intelligence officer escaped punishment. In June 1995, Iachetta quit the service. Months later, he committed suicide amid rumours that he was selling Canada's secrets to the highest bidder. A search of his home after his death found scores of secret documents stashed in a safe, even though Iachetta no longer worked for CSIS. One of the auditors involved in exposing Iachetta is still upset that spymasters dismissed the warnings. "We found out about serious problems with Tony a year before his death and they did nothing about it," the veteran officer says.

The exhaustive fleet audit was also supposed to examine the use of a plane purchased by the service to ferry CSIS's director, Ward Elcock, and other top officials across the country. The six-seat, twin-engine Piper was purchased from a U.S. aircraft manufacturer for about $200,000 (U.S.) Just months after the plane was delivered, it had to undergo a major and expensive overhaul and refit because of engine problems and because Transport Canada said the gas tanks didn't conform with Canadian specifications. The plane triggered widespread resentment among rank-and-file intelligence officers, because it was bought in 1990, after the service's budget was slashed by $37 million, and over 700 employees were laid off. Senior CSIS officers tried to justify the plane's purchase by suggesting that it could be used in surveillance operations. But experienced members of watcher units angrily dismissed the idea that a plane could be used to track targets on the ground as foolish, and privately described the purchase as an unnecessary extravagance. The auditors had planned to make reference in their exhaustive review to several trips taken by senior CSIS officers and their wives to Halifax, Montreal and Toronto using the "surveillance" plane. According to a CSIS officer involved in the audit, he was ordered to remove any reference in the document to the controversial plane. "[A senior officer] told me to take the plane out," the officer says. "He said, 'It's not going to be in the audit.'"

Ward Elcock bristles when outsiders, particularly reporters, pry into his expense accounts. Documents made public under the Access to Information Act show that in 1999 the CSIS director spent $29,000 on meals, booze and hospitality and another $19,500 on travel. Where precisely our top spy dines and travels is supposed to be top secret. But I obtained records that reveal that Elcock has continued to indulge his passion for fine food, wine and accommodation on behalf of a government agency that some intelligence experts and politicians insist has been starved for cash.

Since late 1999, Elcock has visited Washington, D.C., London, Paris, Amsterdam, Brussels, China and Brazil, among other destinations. On his travels overseas, Elcock routinely frequents four-star hotels and restaurants. A few months after the September 11 attacks, for instance, he was in Washington and spent close to two thousand dollars on dinner and drinks at the Capital Grille—a place where the powerful and well-heeled go to see and to be seen. He booked accommodations at the Monarch Hotel, a luxury hotel in the heart of the U.S. capital, where discount rates for suites are between three hundred and four hundred dollars a night. In early 2002, he was in London, England, where he dined at J. Sheekey, a restaurant in Covent Garden popular with the rich and famous. His dinner tab topped $515.

At home in Ottawa, Elcock dines at upscale Italian and French restaurants. His haunts include Fiori's, Fratelli's, Cafe Spiga, Trattoria Zingaro, Allegro, Chez Jean Pierre and Les Fougères, a favourite restaurant of diplomats and local swells nestled in the Gatineau hills.

Heather McDonald wasn't the only daughter of a senior CSIS officer that Farrell was ordered to rescue. One was a lot closer to home. Ray Murphy's daughter, Renée, desperately wanted to join the Mounties, and Murphy, a former RCMP sergeant, was equally anxious to see his daughter carry on the family tradition. After graduating from grade twelve, Renée had meandered through odd jobs, including selling horse and riding gear at a shop near the family home in Ajax, Ontario. For Renée, joining the fabled Mounties meant beginning a meaningful career and making her father proud. The trouble was that she enjoyed partying more than studying and had difficulty with the tough entrance exam. She also failed to pass entrance tests for several municipal police forces in Ontario. It appeared that Renée Murphy was not destined to follow in her father's footsteps.

Murphy turned to John Farrell for help. In early 1997, he asked if Farrell could help his daughter gain an advantage over scores of other eager new recruits who also wanted to become Mounties—he wanted him to obtain a copy of the RCMP's well-guarded entrance exam.

Murphy broached the delicate subject carefully, telling Farrell that he was concerned about his twenty-two-year-old daughter's future. "John, she's having a tough time of it," Murphy told Farrell in the underground parking lot at CSIS headquarters. "Do you think you could get your hands on a copy of the exam? It would really help out."

Farrell promised his friend and boss that he would do his best. He contacted a well-placed source inside the police force, and two weeks after Murphy had asked for help, Farrell had a copy of the thirty-five-page exam in his hands. (Farrell's RCMP contact met him at Toronto's main public library on Yonge Street to hand over the document.) Farrell immediately called Murphy with the good news.

Murphy told Farrell that he didn't want to see the exam and that Farrell was not to give Renée the exam, either, but only to share it with her when they met to study. Murphy had just volunteered Farrell to be his daughter's tutor and trainer. The exam was divided into nine sections, with a series of multiple-choice questions on logic, mathematics, memory, grammar, spelling, reading comprehension, vocabulary, judgment and perserverance. And getting hold of the exam was only the first step in the odyssey to win Renée a place in the police force.

Farrell, reluctantly becoming Henry Higgins to Renée's Eliza Doolittle, spent untold hours tutoring her as she tried to memorize the answers to question after question on the exam. Pupil and teacher met regularly at a library in Pickering to painstakingly go over each question on the exam. Renée had trouble concentrating and was overwhelmed by the test's simple mathematics questions. Murphy even hired a math tutor for his daughter.

Renée was also out of shape and overweight, yet needed to pass a gruelling physical examination before she could join the federal police force. Farrell whipped the avid smoker and drinker into shape at a Curzons fitness club in Scarborough, where he briefly arranged a free membership for her (as well as for Billingsley and Lunau). To make sure that his daughter passed the physical exam, Murphy built a pommel horse in the garage of his Ajax home. For convenience, Farrell cajoled the health-club manager into allowing the homemade, wooden-block horse into the club's gymnasium, even though it was bursting with top-of-the-line weight-training and endurance equipment. Farrell patiently guided his uncoordinated student through a makeshift obstacle course he set up at the fitness club. Farrell also enlisted the help of a friend, Stan Gazmin, who had gotten into the RCMP cadet school in Regina and just missed making the cut. Most days, Murphy and his daughter went with Farrell and Gazmin on a long run on Toronto's beachfront boardwalk. Renée had trouble keeping up during the early morning jaunts and often collapsed, gasping for breath. Farrell brought Renée an RCMP T-shirt when her spirits flagged.

After several months of training and studying, Renée had lost sixteen pounds and was ready to write the entrance test. Renée squeaked through by the barest of margins. To show her gratitude, she arrived at Farrell's tiny home carrying a six-pack of Sleeman. Ray Murphy, his wife and daughter celebrated with Farrell at The Keg Steakhouse at 927 Dixon Road, near the airport, on the eve of Renée's departure for the RCMP training academy. At dinner, Renée promised to buy Farrell a sweater for all his trouble and kindness, but she never did.

Renée graduated from the RCMP's arduous twenty-two-week training program at the "Depot" in Regina. No one in the RCMP ever learned that Renée Murphy had studied a copy of the entrance exam through her father's capable and well-connected friend at CSIS.

Constable Renée Murphy is now on maternity leave from a small RCMP detachment in Strathmore, Alberta. She acknowledged that Farrell "may have had" a copy of the exam before she wrote the test, but she denied seeing it. "Not at any time did I see a copy or review an exam with him. No way." She confirmed other details of Farrell's account, including that her father had enlisted Farrell's help to whip her into shape. She declined to provide me with Ray Murphy's number because she said, "I don't know what he is going to tell you."

While Renée Murphy was cheating her way into the RCMP, Farrell was busy completing course after course via correspondence. Perhaps, he thought, if he got the credentials, Lunau would finally honour his commitment to make him a full-fledged member of the SOS unit. By early 1997, Farrell had obtained his BA in general studies from Simon Fraser University and a post-baccalaureate in criminology from the university's School of Criminology.

Lunau had also encouraged Farrell to take advanced courses in how to detect fraud as a way for his lieutenant to cultivate contacts among law-enforcement agents in Canada and the United States, which might prove useful for his SOS work. Lunau had paid the three-hundred-dollar fee for Farrell to enrol in the fraud detection program at George Brown College in Toronto, where he was awarded a certificate for completing the course in 1996. Lunau also gave Farrell four hundred dollars to apply for his certification with the Association of Certified Fraud Examiners based in Austin, Texas. On February 7, 1997, Farrell was awarded the coveted certificate, joining the ranks of fifteen thousand business and government fraud examiners dedicated to fighting white-collar crime. Farrell also joined the International Association of Law Enforcement Intelligence Analysts and became a "member in good standing" with the Canadian Criminal Justice Association, a group of criminologists devoted to preventing crime "and to an improved and humane criminal justice system for Canada."

By the time he was through, Farrell's list of degrees, diplomas and professional memberships in international intelligence and fraud associations exceeded those of all the other members of the SOS unit in Toronto, including Lunau and Murphy. The transformation from crook to criminologist was complete.

Just as Farrell acquired the qualifications that he still hoped would secure his spot in SOS, budget cuts at CSIS suddenly made the once indispensable cog in the elite unit disposable. Since 1994, Farrell had been Lunau's secret and faithful weapon. But in the winter of 1997, Lunau and the service began to ease Farrell out. Money, or more precisely, the lack of it, was once again charting the course of Farrell's life.

Mike Thompson, the former Toronto police officer and divisional manager for Canada Post's Security and Investigation Services, was making the lucrative mail runs to London, Ontario, and exerting more influence over the entire mail intercept program.

The simmering tension over broken promises, the thousands of dollars in unpaid overtime that Farrell insisted the service owed him, and his uncertain future with the service exploded when Lunau dropped off some mail at Farrell's home one evening. Farrell laid into his boss, demanding to know why he wasn't being hired as an intelligence officer inside the SOS unit.

Lunau told Farrell that his hands were tied and that the service was going through a difficult time after enduring heavy cuts to its budget. Farrell wasn't persuaded. He knew that his weekly "expense" cheques hardly put a dent in the service's war chest and that a fraction of the money that the unit spent in bars across the city in any given month would have more than covered his salary as an intelligence officer. Farrell told Lunau that his days of working for twenty dollars an hour were over and that the service had better pay up on unpaid overtime it owed him or there would be trouble.

Lunau tried to appease Farrell by repeating an offer he had first made to him shortly after the successful conclusion of Operation Stanley Cup: a full-time job with the watcher service. Farrell angrily rejected the consolation prize, telling Lunau that the prospect of working under Richard Garland—Garland had been promoted to supervisor—in the PSU left him nauseated.

The force of Farrell's anger surprised Lunau.

"Jesus, John, I've never seen you this mad," Lunau said, and he suggested that Farrell take a week off. Farrell thought Lunau's sudden concern was as hollow as a cave; it reminded him eerily of his oversolicitous behaviour with Kenny Baker after the axe was lowered on the old API's neck.

Word of the spat spread through the SOS unit. Jack Billingsley, the travel agent and spy, called Farrell and suggested they spend a relaxing week in Cancún. At first, Farrell told him to get lost. But Billingsley was persistent and, ultimately, Farrell relented. When he returned from his brief vacation, Farrell met with Lunau and Murphy to discuss his future. As the trio walked down Front Street on a sunny day in 1997, Lunau once again offered Farrell a spot with the watcher service.

"John, really think about this," Murphy said. "We want to take care of you."

"Well, you're not taking care of me," he snapped. "This isn't what I bargained for."

Farrell pointedly reminded Lunau of his pledge that in lieu of all his unpaid overtime, the SOS chief would ensure a spot for him with the unit. "You fucking lied to me, Donnie."

Lunau and Murphy gave Farrell a day to make up his mind. Farrell turned to Cliff Hatcher, the only other SOS member he trusted and respected, for advice. They met in the underground parking lot at CSIS headquarters, and Hatcher candidly told Farrell that he would be a fool to accept the offer.

"You can't take it, John. What a waste of your talents to have you sitting in a car all day. You deserve better. You've got the world by the balls, and there's more to life than being a PSU," Hatcher told Farrell.

Farrell knew Hatcher was right. Working with the watchers was not an option. He was hurt and disappointed. He had done the unit's dirty work without hesitation and this was his reward. Ironically, Farrell says, when he told Lunau and Murphy of his decision, they were also heartbroken.

"They just couldn't understand why I would turn them down," Farrell says.

Farrell believed that Lunau and Murphy were indebted to him for all his years of unwavering loyalty. After all, he was instrumental in the "success" of some of the service's most sensitive and high-profile capers, and Lunau and Murphy—even Murphy's daughter—reaped the rewards of his hard work, perseverance and ingenuity. They had given him their word, and Farrell was determined to keep them to it.

He arranged for a three-month leave of absence from CSIS and, armed with his university degree and intelligence training, began to seriously contemplate joining a police force. Lunau and Murphy encouraged Farrell to make the move; they thought he'd make a great cop.

Farrell narrowed his search to police forces that were prepared to pay for his schooling and allow him to move quickly into an intelligence unit. He researched at least ten municipal forces in Ontario before settling on the Durham Regional Police Service, just outside of Toronto. It would pay for its trainees' textbooks and any courses, regardless of discipline, on one condition: you had to pass. He wasn't alone in wanting to join the small force: hundreds of others had applied for a few openings. Farrell's impressive résumé, however, bowled over recruiters, and he began his constable training course at the Ontario Police College on September 8, 1997.

On the eve of his departure for the police college in Aylmer, Ontario, Farrell learned the real reason why Lunau and Murphy were so eager to arrange his divorce from CSIS. Alan Whitson, a former Mountie and Canada Post's national director of security, was quietly assuming the takeover of the administration of Operation Vulva. Lunau told Farrell at a lunchtime meeting that Canada Post was anxious to distance itself from the service and the mail intercept program. The Crown corporation, Lunau explained, was busy courting private firms, including banks and trust companies, to set up partnerships in the flourishing and lucrative Internet business. Canada Post worried that its relationship with CSIS, if revealed, could prove troublesome. Enter Whitson. "They [Canada Post] want a third party to verify the warrants, and it looks like Whitson is going to get the contract," Lunau told Farrell. "And it looks like you're getting out just in time."

Farrell was dumbfounded. The service and Canada Post appeared well on their way to privatizing the administration of one of the nation's most sensitive and potentially lucrative intelligence-gathering operations. And the front-runner was not Farrell, who had been effectively in charge of the operation for years, but a former Mountie and Canada Post insider.

Lunau told Farrell that Whitson was going to make his money by charging a commission of up to 5 per cent of the total "expenses" claimed by the scores of APIs involved in Operation Vulva right across the country. With hundreds of targets, the secret work was likely to translate into bushels of money for Whitson.

Farrell remembered crossing paths with Whitson when Canada Post sent the former postal inspector for intelligence training in Ottawa. He never envisioned that he might end up working for the overweight, balding ex-Mountie. Lunau, his confidant and mentor, had done nothing to stop it. In fact, Whitson had already incorporated a numbered company—3385710 Canada Inc.—to manage Operation Vulva. The company had two directors: Whitson and his wife, Doris. The firm's head office was listed as 8283 Forest Green Crescent, the Whitson's large, colonial-style home in an exclusive and picturesque section of Metcalfe, Ontario, a forty-minute drive from Ottawa.

A near-mutiny broke out when word of Whitson's new role in Operation Vulva reached the other APIs. "They refused to work with the guy," says Farrell. But when he called Murphy in Ottawa to tell him this, the newly minted director of training for Special Ops told Farrell that the privatization of Operation Vulva was out of his hands.

Farrell packed his bags and headed to the police college. His stay, however, would be brief.

John Farrell arrived at the college resolved, as always, to succeed. The daily, military-like regimen that the potential new recruits endured forged quick but lasting friendships. He stood out among the flock of inexperienced candidates and sailed through the screening process, scoring close to a 90-per-cent average in his courses. But on December 4, 1997, just nine days before his graduation, Farrell was booted out of the college. The charge: he twice "mooned" other cadets during a rowdy party in a private police lounge. Farrell was stunned. The incident was alleged to have taken place on his third day at the college.

Farrell denied the charge, and many of the college's employees rallied to his defence, telling investigators that the young recruit had kept his pants on the entire evening. The lounge manager, Shelly Rice, told investigators, "I didn't see anything out of the ordinary happen in the lounge. No one approached me and said there was a problem in the lounge." She added, "When John came into the lounge, he always treated me with courtesy and respect." Other cadets interviewed by investigators corroborated Rice's view.

The investigators concluded that Farrell was telling the truth and recommended that he not be reprimanded. A second investigation was launched. Again, investigators found that the allegations, were "unsubstantiated" and there were "no direct witnesses and no complainants."

A third probe was ordered, however, after a female Durham police sergeant, who'd heard rumours of the alleged incident, refused to let the matter die. On November 13, Farrell was suspended with pay (nine hundred dollars a fortnight) pending a hearing. Four days later, he was informed that the force would recommend his dismissal. Even the hint of impropriety was enough, it seemed, for senior officers on the force to prevent Farrell from staying on. But the investigator assigned to the case later admitted that he was "under the influence of alcohol" just prior to conducting an interview with Farrell. The female sergeant later confessed that she had altered reports about the incident to make them more damaging to Farrell. (Much later, Farrell learned that senior Durham police officers were anxious to rid themselves of a cadet with links to Canada's intelligence service.)

Farrell was distraught. His hopes of joining the force were dashed by confusing and stale charges that he had pulled a juvenile prank. The incident even made the back pages of the *Toronto Star*. Soon, more serious allegations involving the mishandling of seized weapons, drugs, jewellery, liquor and drug money by senior Durham police officers made the front page of the paper. But it was small consolation for Farrell, who had little alternative but to head back to CSIS, Lunau and Alan Whitson.

13

THE END OF THE AFFAIR

B y the time Farrell returned to Toronto from the Ontario Police College in early 1998, Alan Whitson's takeover of the day-to-day administration of CSIS's mail intercept program was a *fait accompli*. In January of that year, Whitson incorporated another company to manage Operation Vulva, a security consulting firm called Adava Consulting. Whitson was the "sole proprietor" of the firm, described in corporate records as a "division" of the numbered company that the ex-Mountie had set up six months earlier with his wife. Adava Consulting also listed its office address as 8283 Forest Green Crescent. Farrell was strapped for cash and felt he had little choice but to remain part of Operation Vulva.[1]

On January 5, 1998, Farrell signed a contract with 3385710 Canada Inc. to continue working as an API. Whitson's signature is on

---

[1] Farrell searched for other work. He was interviewed by the United Nations via teleconference after being shortlisted for a job as an investigator with the International Criminal Tribunal for the former Yugoslavia at The Hague.

the contract, which was marked secret and listed him as president of the numbered company. Under the terms of the contract, Farrell continued to be paid twenty dollars an hour and to claim a federal government mileage allowance of thirty-three cents per kilometre. But instead of filing his invoices for "fees and expenses" on a weekly basis, Farrell was instructed to submit copies of detailed invoices to Whitson and Lunau every two weeks. The "secret" contract was given a number: ADAVA09. The ten-page document was almost a carbon copy of the series of contracts Farrell had signed with Canada Post since 1992, and it included a non-disclosure clause that barred him from revealing that he had entered into an agreement with 3385710 Canada Inc. Farrell and the other APIs were still not obliged to declare any of the income they were paid by Whitson's numbered company.[2]

Canada Post was no longer the service's proxy—Whitson was. Farrell was now a "contractor" working, on paper at least, for a numbered company controlled by Whitson and his wife. But Farrell was still getting his orders directly from Lunau. Whitson's job was to verify the mail intercept warrants, review the invoices and pay the APIs their so-called expense cheques for professional services rendered. Lunau tried to assure Farrell that Whitson's takeover would mean little discomfort or inconvenience for him and the other APIs. "John, everything is going to remain the same. It's just that now you're going to be getting your cheques from Whitson instead of Canada Post," Lunau said.

But Farrell knew that everything had changed. He would no longer be playing as pivotal a role in Operation Vulva, and that meant less money. There was also the tricky problem of all that unpaid overtime that Farrell claimed the service still owed him. Who was going to make good on that debt, now that Murphy and Lunau had reneged on their promises to make him an official member of the SOS unit? Lunau refused to answer that question, Farrell says.

The bond between the once inseparable colleagues and friends was fraying beyond repair. The quarrels over money and broken promises

---

[2] Whitson did not issue any T4 slips to the APIs working on Operation Vulva.

grew more frequent and intense. Farrell blamed one person above all: himself. "It's a duplicitous world, where loyalty and friendship mean nothing. I betrayed others and now I was being betrayed," he says.

The mercenary wanted his money. Every fortnight, he dutifully filled out his invoices to Whitson and often claimed as much as $1,800 tax-free. (Farrell kept copies of all the invoices.) Whitson raised growing concerns about Farrell's "extravagant" expenses with Lunau. He had little choice but to pay out, however, since Farrell could account for every hour and kilometre. Lunau and Farrell clashed again over the money that Farrell claimed the service still owed him. And he vowed that until the service coughed up the cash, he would no longer get involved in any missions for the SOS unit.

Farrell was enjoying a bowl of vegetable soup at The Sip restaurant in the spring of 1998 when he received an urgent page from Jack Billingsley. He asked the restaurant's manager if he could use their phone.

"John, we need you to rent a place," Billingsley told Farrell.

"Didn't you hear, Jack? I'm not doing that anymore," Farrell said.

"John, we need you to get into a place," Billingsley repeated.

"Does Donnie know about this?" Farrell asked.

"Yeah, of course he does. But he's away."

"So why doesn't he call me and ask me to do the job?" Farrell said. "You guys don't want to pay me the right price. Fuck it."

Billingsley told Farrell that Lunau had dispatched a string of intelligence officers to the apartment, but like the fiasco at Roehampton Avenue, they had all failed miserably.

"We need you, John," Billingsley pleaded. He even suggested that the service was now prepared to pay the outstanding overtime. Hearing that changed Farrell's mind.

The service, Billingsley explained, needed him to rent a two-bedroom basement apartment in the home of a suspected Sikh terrorist. The target ran a newspaper ad to rent out the suite in his two-storey brick home on Nuffield Street in a quiet, middle-class neighbourhood in Brampton. The service wanted to seize the opportunity to get into the target's home and plant listening devices.

Farrell arranged to meet the suspected terrorist just hours after his brief chat with Billingsley. He withdrew two thousand dollars from his chequing account at a nearby bank machine to cover the first and last month's rent and headed out to the apartment. Billingsley had warned Farrell that the target was suspicious of non-Sikhs and that he was potentially dangerous. Farrell was assertive when he met the tall, middle-aged man who sported a long, dark beard, a turban and a ceremonial dagger around his waist. "This place is perfect. I'll take it," he said, as the pair toured the dingy suite.

Farrell calmly told his new landlord that he worked at a nearby postal station. He gave the high-profile CSIS target two references: a friend of his, Don Hammond, and the address and phone number of one of his front companies, Housing Unlimited. (The target did not call either reference.) He signed a lease on the spot, and the target happily gave him a receipt for the rent money (nine hundred dollars per month). Farrell left a message on Lunau's pager saying that the apartment was safely in the service's hands.

A day later, Lunau visited Farrell at his home to congratulate him. But he also had a request: Lunau wanted Farrell to move in and keep tabs on the man whom the service believed to be a highly trained and ruthless terrorist. Farrell and Lunau discussed money. The SOS chief told Farrell that Bob Gordon, the service's regional director-general in Toronto, was only willing to pay for three hours, three days a week. Farrell exploded.

"Donnie, you want me to live in the basement of a fucking terrorist for sixty dollars a day? You're joking," Farrell said. "It's not going to happen."

"John, we're on a tight budget," Lunau explained.

"Fuck off, Donnie," Farrell said.

He told the SOS chief that his travel time to and from the apartment alone would take several hours each week and the idea of sleeping under the very nose of a potentially violent terrorist wasn't appealing. "How do you know that someone won't eventually tip him off to who I really am and he slips into the basement and slits my throat?" Farrell also mentioned Billingsley's promise that he would get his outstanding overtime.

Lunau needed a keen eye trained on the Sikh target, so he promised again to wrestle more money out of the service. Farrell decided to give the SOS chief one last chance to make amends and agreed to move into the apartment.

He gathered a few pieces of CSIS furniture, some clothes that he used for Special Ops work and, with Hammond's help, moved in. Farrell regularly ordered pizza and even sent letters to himself to cement the ruse that he was an ordinary tenant. Once again, his mother charged CSIS two hundred dollars to clean the dank basement apartment.

In preparation for planting a listening device in the target's home, Lunau ordered Farrell to note the number of people who lived in the house, their movements, the location of the electrical box, and the make and models of the door locks and to draw up a detailed diagram of the entire house. Farrell passed on the information to Lunau at one of their regular meetings at the Rose & Crown pub.

Farrell spent several evenings a week at the apartment and every moment was uncomfortable. He often lay awake, listening intently as the target paced overhead. Once, he snapped awake with a rush of adrenalin from an afternoon nap, as the target slipped into his apartment, searching, he claimed, for a tap to turn off the water main. Farrell never slept well in the apartment again.

Four weeks after Farrell moved in, Lunau gave the green light to proceed with the operation to plant the bug. Farrell met Alex Yu, Dean Weber and Sandy Brown at a sprawling parking lot inside the Bramalea Community Park, a short drive from the target's home. After a quick briefing, Farrell paid a brief visit to the house to make sure that the suspected terrorist and his family were away. He returned to the parking lot and gave Brown the all-clear. The SOS team herded into Farrell's car, carrying three black cases and duffle bags filled with tools and equipment. Farrell parked inside the garage and closed the door behind him. The SOS crew crept into Farrell's apartment through a garage door. Yu and Weber removed some panelling from the basement ceiling and, using an electric drill, planted a listening device, while Farrell and Brown stood guard. The mission was over in forty minutes. The crew packed up. As they headed out, the target's wife unexpectedly arrived home and saw the CSIS officer and techies carrying their cases and bags to the small car. Farrell smiled at the woman. Brown nearly fainted.

Days later, Lunau met Farrell at the Mr. Slate Sports Bar to thank him for his crucial role in the sensitive and precarious mission. Farrell demanded his money. Lunau demurred, suggesting that Farrell was, in fact, earning more money than any other SOS member—and there would be no extra cash for the latest caper or the lost overtime. It was the final betrayal.

Money—the absence of it and the need for it—had been Farrell's constant companion since his days in Parma Court. The subject was always guaranteed to trigger his temper. Farrell's father and his brothers stole food, clothing and medicine because they had no money. Farrell's sister Josephine needed money to buy the drugs that led ultimately to an overdose. Farrell watched his mother, Mary, clean the toilets of strangers to earn money. There was never enough money. Farrell was once the leader of a gang that thirsted after money. Canada Post and CSIS had paid him money to break the law. And now Lunau was depriving him of the money he felt he had risked his life for.

Farrell was so angry he wanted to punch Lunau. The SOS boss tried to calm him by offering to buy him lunch and a drink. "No. I only eat and drink with friends, and I'm not among friends right now," Farrell said firmly.

"Johnny, we've been good to you in the past," Lunau reminded him.

"I risked my life. I took care of Ray's daughter. Remember that? I took care of Heather. Remember that? I did everything you asked me to do, and now you won't give me my money," Farrell replied. "This is bullshit. I'm tired of it. I don't want to be part of it anymore. That's it for me." Farrell reminded Lunau of his trip to Buffalo to buy cheap booze for the wedding reception of another of Murphy's daughters, and of a litany of other services he had performed, small and large, that pushed the boundaries of propriety. "Everyone else in SOS is milking the system. I'm the fucking one who does all the work, and you do this."

Lunau looked shaken and worried. Farrell was turning into an espionage agency's worst nightmare: an operative who knew some of its deepest secrets and now seemed beyond its control. If Farrell broke his silence, the consequences were likely to reverberate throughout the service and implicate many of CSIS's most senior officers and officials.

As they left the pub, Lunau, perhaps remembering Farrell's earlier crusades, turned to him and asked, "Hey, Johnny, you're not going to go to the press are you?"

"No. But just watch me," Farrell replied.

A few days later, Lunau instructed him to terminate the Brampton lease, and he was happy to oblige. Juggling his various guises with family, friends and his new girlfriend—a tall, slim native of Switzerland whom he had met on a brief trip to London, England—fuelled his growing estrangement from Lunau. To CSIS, Farrell was a useful tool. To his mother, Farrell was a hard-working son who helped keep the family afloat financially. To his girlfriend and small circle of friends, Farrell was leading a strange life that had him flitting across the city at all hours, running endless errands for his mysterious bosses. It was all taking its toll.

Farrell drafted a note advising his Sikh landlord that he no longer needed the place, that he was suddenly being transferred to Vancouver. And with that lie, Farrell's days in Special Ops were over; he no longer rented apartments for the service or helped execute covert entries. Though he still played a role in coordinating the day-to-day mechanics of Operation Vulva and continued to intercept Holocaust denier Ernst Zundel's mail, even that was about to end. At 10:30 a.m. on January 3, 1999, Farrell and Lunau met in the parking lot of the Boardwalk Cafe in Toronto's east end. The SOS boss arrived in a CSIS car, a blue, four-door Toyota Corolla. Looking ill at ease, he motioned Farrell over to his vehicle, where he explained that since the warrant to seize Zundel's mail had expired, Farrell's services were no longer needed.

Farrell began making phone calls. He decided to leapfrog over the heads of Lunau and Murphy and raise his case directly with other high-ranking CSIS officers and officials. Farrell spoke several times to the service's top spy in Toronto, Bob Gordon (who had succeeded two other long-time CSIS officers, Jack Hooper and David Beazley, as regional director-general). Gordon knew Farrell well from Operation Stanley Cup and tried to disarm him by telling him that other members of the SOS unit had praised his work and spoken highly of his loyalty and patriotism. "Your reputation precedes you," Gordon told Farrell. He listened to Farrell's complaints and promised to call Ottawa to try to settle the dispute over money and perhaps even find him another job in the service.

Farrell reached Keith McDonald on his cellphone in Ottawa to decry his treatment at the hands of the service. The national director for SOS was unmoved by Farrell's protests and abruptly rejected his pleas for money. "Look, John, things happen that we don't like, and we have to be prepared," he said. The veteran CSIS officer told Farrell that his own son had been paralyzed while playing hockey, and that life was full of nasty, sometimes tragic surprises. Farrell wasn't interested in a lecture about how to handle the twists and turns of life, and reminded McDonald of his daughter's comfortable sojourn at the High Park apartment.

"That's not your concern," McDonald said angrily.

"Oh yes, it is. You guys say you don't have the money to pay me, but the service spent thousands of dollars putting your kid up at a Special Ops post in Toronto."

McDonald told Farrell that the service was cash-strapped, and there was little he could do for him. Two weeks later, Lunau called Farrell at home and offered him a mail run in Toronto: sixty dollars a day, five days a week. "You're kidding, Donnie," Farrell responded. "I can make more money working at McDonald's."

Then Gordon called him to say that he was trying to arrange a meeting between Farrell and Lunau to settle the disagreement. "I hope we can get you some cash," he said.

On the morning of March 16, 1999, Lunau had trouble finding a private room for what would be his final official get-together with John Farrell. Convention delegates had invaded Toronto like an occupying army, and there wasn't a hotel to be had. So, as he had done countless times over the past seven years when he needed a problem solved, Lunau called Farrell. And Farrell got in touch with an old friend, Mel George, a reservations manager at the popular SkyDome Hotel, which loomed over CSIS's Front Street headquarters.

"Look, I'm in a jam and I need a favour," Farrell said. He knew George from the times he had booked rooms and luxury boxes at the playground-cum-hotel-cum-baseball-park for parties, where alcohol and drugs had flowed freely. Throwing such parties was a painless way to keep old contacts happy and cultivate new ones, and Farrell would make a bit of change by charging admission.

"No problem, John," George said, and he dispatched a maid to get a room into shape. Farrell thanked him and told the reservations manager that he had just earned himself a fat tip. Farrell called Lunau with the details: The SkyDome Hotel, Room 365, at 11:30 a.m.

Farrell hurried out of his small, two-bedroom house in east-end Toronto and hopped into his car. Foot to the floor, he wove through Toronto's unusually light traffic that March morning. He had made the trip downtown a thousand times before to meet Lunau, Murphy and other SOS members, and he could have done it blindfolded.

He left his car in the care of a bellhop, went to the front desk, checked in at 11:25 a.m. and picked up the pass key for his room. He called Lunau again to remind him that they only had the room for a few hours, so he better get over there ASAP.

Minutes later, there was a knock at the door. Farrell took a quick peek through the peephole and spotted Lunau, looking stern, and accompanied by Al Poulton, CSIS's head of finance and administration in Toronto. Poulton, another ex-RCMP officer, bought the supplies, negotiated and signed the leases and paid the bills, including the receipts filed by the SOS unit. Farrell knew Poulton from his occasional visits to the Beverley Tavern.

He opened the door and motioned to Lunau to come in. His old boss turned on the charm. "Hey, Johnny, how's it going?"

Farrell skipped the pleasantries and sat on the end of the room's queen-sized bed. Lunau and Poulton pulled up chairs to face him.

Lunau asked Farrell if he was wired. Without waiting for a reply, the SOS chief looked under the bed to see if Farrell had planted a bug, then tried to laugh it off. Lunau then headed for the bathroom, Farrell was sure, to check whether his one-time protege had planted bugs there. Farrell silently counted down how long it would take Lunau. He got to thirteen. There were no bugs. Farrell assumed that the briefcase Poulton was carrying was wired for sound, possibly even for video. He wasn't surprised or offended; he would have done precisely the same thing if he had had the time and money. There was no loyalty or trust in this room.

They got down to business. Poulton did the talking. He praised Farrell for his outstanding work for the service but said it was time for an amicable separation. CSIS was prepared to offer him six thousand dollars.

Farrell turned to Lunau. "What the fuck is that, Donnie, a down payment for my lawyer? You can honestly sit there and look me in the face and tell me that I'm worth six thousand dollars?"

"It's not up to me," Lunau said. "If it were up to me, John, I would give you a whole lot more."

Farrell felt an overpowering contempt for Lunau well up in him. He shouted at his former boss, "That's just fucking unacceptable. Six thousand is nothing."

The money, Lunau said, was a "humanitarian" gesture by the service to help tide him over while he looked for a new job, in recognition of his dedication and loyalty. It was a take-it-or-leave-it proposition.

Farrell abruptly changed tack. He asked Poulton and Lunau if they would pay him the six thousand dollars in cash or by cheque. Caught off guard, Poulton told Farrell that they didn't have the money on them but that they were certainly prepared to go to a nearby bank machine and withdraw the cash. Farrell feigned interest.

Poulton calmly added that before he could hand over the money, Farrell had to sign some documents. Lunau sat impassively, though Farrell thought he noticed a hint of fear in his former boss. Farrell vented. He railed about his work on Operation Stanley Cup, Operation Vulva, the covert entries, the thefts, the favours, everything. For ten minutes, Farrell berated Lunau and CSIS for their betrayal. Then, he tacked again and asked if he could get the six thousand dollars in cash.

"Of course," Poulton said, sounding hopeful that Farrell might just take the money.

Poulton pulled a document out of his briefcase. In exchange for the cash, Farrell would have to sign a one-page settlement agreement. There were strict conditions. He could not disclose his connection to the service. He could not sue the service. The money was not an admission that Farrell had even worked for CSIS. Farrell read the settlement agreement over carefully and then threw it at Poulton. It landed on the briefcase.

"Fuck you, and fuck CSIS," Farrell said. "I'm not signing this. This is like signing my life away. No."

Poulton asked Farrell how much it would take. He demanded twenty thousand dollars and a letter of reference. Poulton said he would pass on the request to Ward Elcock.

Farrell made one last appeal to his former friend. "Donnie, put yourself in my position," he said. "Would you take this or would you go to court?"

Lunau paused and said, "I don't know, John. I don't know."

"I think you do know. I'm not signing this," Farrell replied. "That's it. It's over."

The meeting had lasted less than an hour. The trio left the room and silently headed to an elevator together. When Lunau arrived at the front desk, he pulled out his wallet and paid the bill in cash, checking out at 12:26 p.m. He then turned to Farrell and asked if they could still get together for an occasional drink. Farrell shook his head.

Still, he had done Lunau one last favour. The room normally cost about $175. Farrell got it for $75, plus tax. Watching Lunau walk away, Farrell whispered to himself, "Shit! Mel didn't get his tip."

14

ELCOCK AND THE MONEY

Farrell now tapped the same well of determination that had sustained him in his battles with obstinate officials at the Rotherglen Youth Detention Centre, and the York Detention Centre in Toronto. He had prevailed in those sometimes ugly tussles, but CSIS was a very different kind of adversary—a large, powerful institution with the vast resources of the federal Department of Justice behind it. On March 19, 1999, just three days after his meeting with Lunau, Farrell wrote Ward Elcock a conciliatory letter asking the CSIS director to "negotiate a fair and reasonable settlement" of his outstanding claims against the service.

"The extent of my involvement in the intelligence community for the past ten years in my opinion warrants a fair and reasonable offer," Farrell wrote. "During my employment I have proven to be very diligent, untiring and meticulous in my professional duties and obligations." He added, "I have thoroughly enjoyed my past duties and responsibilities and the trust that was placed in me." Farrell claimed that the service owed him fifty thousand dollars in back pay.

Elcock responded to Farrell's letter within days. The 2-page, 317-word response was a meticulously crafted deceit that acknowledged that Farrell had a "working relationship" with CSIS, but absolved the director and the service of any responsibility for the acts he had committed at the behest of senior intelligence officers, including Lunau and Murphy. Elcock's letter was also a carefully constructed cover story to shield senior CSIS officers and officials from any of the consequences of their actions in connection with Farrell's long and remarkable career with the service. Despite its polite, diplomatic tone, the letter's cynical message was clear: in Ward Elcock's view, the service was immune from any meaningful accountability.

But Elcock's letter to Farrell also included some important admissions, which may yet come back to plague Canada's spy chief. In the letter, he admitted that he knew precisely who John Farrell was, and that Farrell was routinely paid directly by CSIS for his clandestine work. The letter confirmed that knowledge of Farrell's "working relationship" with the service reached the highest and most influential levels of Canada's intelligence service.

Elcock began his letter to Farrell with this obtuse reminder: "I accept and appreciate that you are sensitive to your obligations to respect the confidentiality with which you have been entrusted." Simply put, Elcock reminded Farrell that he had sworn to keep his mouth shut. "For the most part," Elcock continued, "your working relationship with the Canadian Security Intelligence Service has been in your former capacity as a contract employee of Canada Post in the Auxiliary Postal Inspector Program." The CSIS director had made his first critical admission: Farrell did indeed have a "working relationship" with the service. But then he attempted to cloud the true nature of Farrell's relationship with the service by describing him as a "contract employee" of Canada Post. Since 1991, Farrell had taken his orders from and reported to two men, both veteran, high-ranking CSIS officers: Don Lunau and Ray Murphy. Still, Elcock insisted, since Farrell was a Canada Post employee, CSIS was not responsible for any of his actions. "The Service is not accountable for and will not provide additional remuneration for any work you performed as an employee of Canada Post," Elcock wrote.

Elcock tried to suggest that Farrell's intimate "working relation-ship" with the service was merely a casual dalliance: "I recognise that you have assisted the service in other ways from time to time and this has been much appreciated. On these occasions you were compensated directly by CSIS, commensurate with the nature of the assistance you provided." This claim was also false. Farrell had been a faithful, dedi-cated and long-standing member of Lunau's elite Special Ops unit. The SOS chief had turned to Farrell for help countless times since 1991. Farrell was Lunau's trusted deputy, doing his bidding when other intelligence officers couldn't or wouldn't.

Elcock's attempt to distance the service and himself from Farrell was not surprising given the fact that, by early 1999, Farrell was becoming a potentially troublesome liability and a threat to the cha-rade of CSIS as a law-abiding intelligence service. The CSIS director did, however, make another significant admission when he acknowledged that the service paid Farrell "directly" for his services. Lunau had, in fact, paid Farrell thousands of dollars in cash and lavished him with expensive gifts, including a leather coat. The handsome cash payments were made throughout Farrell's career with the service. Farrell was not a source or a wannabe spy: he was an integral part of some of this country's most sensitive intelligence operations.

Elcock concluded his letter by reiterating the offer first made to Farrell by Lunau and Poulton at the SkyDome Hotel. "Given that you had gone through a period of unemployment, the Service offered you financial assistance in the amount of $6,000 to assist you in this period of transition. This offer was not intended to represent recognition of what you describe as your long-time commitment to the programs of the Service. Rather it was meant to be a humanitarian gesture for the purpose of assisting you to fulfill financial obligations you have incurred whilst unemployed. You refused to accept that offer," Elcock wrote.

Elcock had now cast himself in an unlikely role: a benefactor reaching out to the unemployed. Canada's spy service had suddenly become a charity and Ward Elcock was its patron. "While not obliged to do so, I am prepared to again provide you with humanitarian assis-tance in the amount previously offered. In the event that you decide to accept, please notify Mr. Bob Gordon at your earliest convenience," he wrote. Ernest Rovet, a lawyer whom Farrell had hired to represent him in his dispute with CSIS, was baffled by Elcock's offer. "In my experience, employers don't go around offering people humanitarian assistance based on no specific claim," Rovet says.

The sentence that stirred the most anger in Farrell was this one: "This offer was not intended to represent recognition of what you describe as your long-time commitment to the programs of the Service." His life since 1991 had been consumed by the needs and demands of CSIS, Lunau and Murphy. And now Canada's top spy was suggesting that it had been a figment of his imagination. Elcock was only the latest and most senior CSIS official, Farrell thought, to invoke a popular and expedient tactic when confronted with unsettling truth: lie, deny and then act surprised.

Elcock closed by wishing Farrell "good luck in your future endeavours."

On April 7, 1999, Farrell sent Elcock a seven-page letter, dissecting the CSIS director's response. Farrell's tone had shifted. The diplomacy that marked his first missive was replaced by hard, unimpeachable facts and sharp accusations.

First, Farrell described the genesis of his relationship with the service. "I received instructions from Mr. Lunau that I was accepted into the CSIS API program and that same CSIS officer has supervised me for the past ten years. I was not taking or receiving direction from [any] official from Canada Post or from Adava Consulting during this time. All of my orders and daily direction came from Mr. Lunau," Farrell wrote.

He offered Elcock a detailed description of his responsibilities for the day-to-day management of Operation Vulva in order to finally disabuse the CSIS director of the notion that he had only "assisted the Service in other ways from time to time." Farrell outlined the maze of front companies that he had set up to rent apartments on the service's behalf. He described in detail his vital involvement in the dangerous counterterrorism operation that targeted the suspected Sikh terrorist in Brampton. "I have been involved in more than a dozen covert apartment rentals as well as setting up fictitious companies and other activities," Farrell wrote. He pointed out his long-standing role in the surveillance of the Lamberts. "In the Stanley Cup operation I invested more than six hours a day, not including sleeping over and conducting surveillance and attending lunch meetings," Farrell wrote.

He also raised serious concerns about why Whitson had been enlisted to administer the mail intercept program. And he offered Elcock a hint of darker secrets about the way Canada's supposedly squeaky-clean intelligence service actually operated. "I also spoke [to Lunau at the SkyDome meeting] about the unethical issues that I felt that Mr. Keith McDonald was committing by allowing his daughter to live in an apartment being paid [for] by the Service and taxpayers." Farrell implored Elcock to settle the dispute "as soon as possible . . . I hope the service will consider my offer reasonable."

Three weeks later, Farrell received a surly reply from Elcock. In his short, one-page letter, the CSIS director did not dispute a word of Farrell's description of the nature and length of his involvement with the service. He made no reference to Farrell's accusation that senior CSIS officers were using apartments meant for sensitive counter-intelligence operations to billet their children. Elcock remained unmoved by Farrell's appeals. "The points you raised in your letter have been the subject of a thorough review. Based on the results of that review, I have concluded that you have been fairly treated in your dealings with this organization and that the Service is under no further obligation to you," Elcock wrote.

Farrell had requested in his letter that Elcock provide him with copies of the proxy agreements he had signed with Canada Post and Adava Consulting. Elcock told Farrell the service didn't have the information. The CSIS director added that "there are no signed agreements between you and the Canadian Security Intelligence Service in regard to any other forms of assistance you provided in the past." Translation: there was no paper trail to back up Farrell's claims about the nature and extent of his relationship with the service.

Elcock closed his letter by suggesting that Farrell take his complaints to SIRC. The CSIS director was confident, it seemed, that the watchdog agency would cause the service little harm.

As a final resort, Farrell tried to reach Elcock by phone. Standing in the middle of the huge parking lot of the Scarborough Town shopping centre, Farrell used his cellphone to call CSIS headquarters in Ottawa. A CSIS operator patched him through to the service's assistant director, Tom Bradley, a career civil servant who had spent time with the Canadian International Development Agency before joining the world of espionage.

"It's John Farrell from Toronto," Farrell said.

"Oh, I know all about you," Bradley chuckled.

Farrell told Elcock's deputy that he had been treated unfairly by the service and that the six-thousand-dollar offer was unacceptable.

"Look, John, like it or leave it," Bradley said. "If you don't like our decisions, I frankly don't care. I suggest you give SIRC a call if you have a complaint."

Farrell wondered whether Bradley, safely ensconced in his sixth-floor office at CSIS's Xanadu-like headquarters just outside Ottawa, had ever risked his life to protect Canada's national security. He wondered whether Bradley had ever lived in the basement of a suspected terrorist or spied on Russian intelligence officers. Farrell thought about responding in kind to Bradley's curt, cavalier tone, but he let the temptation pass.

Instead, he called an operator in Ottawa. "Can I have the main number for the Security Intelligence Review Committee please?"

SIRC and CSIS are twins. When Ottawa passed the CSIS Act in 1984, which gave birth to Canada's new civilian spy service, it made room in the legislation for SIRC. The review committee's job is to keep watch over the spies and ensure that our intelligence officers play their secret games by the rules. The watchdog agency is also an avenue of appeal for Canadians who believe that they have been abused or wronged by the service. (Much of SIRC's energies are consumed by complaints from would-be Canadian citizens or landed immigrants who claim that in its zeal to protect national security, the service has unjustly denied them vital security clearances.) SIRC must also review policy directives issued by the solicitor general to CSIS. The watchdog's responsibilities are not only crucial to the governance of Canada's secret service but clearly onerous.

The tricky relationship between the two agencies is both adversarial and co-operative. SIRC is obliged to pry into the service's secret world and disclose what it has discovered to Canadians through the solicitor general. In its annual reports and special audits, SIRC must satisfy the public's right to know what CSIS is up to, while trying to avoid making powerful enemies at the service or undermining the nation's security.

The two agencies are not equals. CSIS's budget and size dwarf SIRC's. CSIS has thousands of employees, wields immense powers and has a multi-million-dollar budget. SIRC has five part-time committee members (mostly lawyers and ex-politicians with little previous exposure to the intelligence trade) and only sixteen clerical, administrative, legal and research staff who sometimes double as the agency's spokespersons. Given the tipped scales, SIRC paradoxically relies heavily on CSIS for information about how it is doing its job. That dependency can breed a close relationship between the two agencies. David Peel, a former inspector general, warns that watchdog agencies like SIRC are prone to being co-opted by the intelligence services they keep watch over. It's a sort of Stockholm Syndrome within the intelligence community.

In fact, SIRC often acts as a shield for CSIS and the federal government when the service is forced out of the shadows and into the uncomfortable spotlight. When unsettling intelligence scandals rock CSIS—often triggered by the work of journalists, not SIRC—the service's spymasters and the government invariably refuse to answer questions, assuring Canadians that the watchdog agency is on the case. Given its relatively meagre resources, SIRC takes months to report its findings, by which point the media's and the political opposition's attention is consumed by other pressing matters. Yesterday's scandal, however important, is consigned to the back pages, forgotten by all but a few pesky reporters and interested academics. SIRC, ironically, is often CSIS's best friend.

While John Farrell was girding for a long, lonely battle with CSIS in the spring of 1999, Jean-Luc Marchessault, his wife, Brigitte, and their two infant sons, were still reeling from the traumatic aftershocks of their own duel with Canada's secret service. Marchessault had been a proud and productive CSIS officer, dedicated to his secret work, popular with most of his colleagues for his quirky sense of humour, admired for his loyalty and patriotism. Now he was a beaten man, the victim of a well coordinated campaign by senior CSIS officers to destroy his reputation, raise doubts about his allegiance and force him out of the service he loved.

While high-ranking and well-connected CSIS officers escaped punishment for their corruption and law-breaking, Marchessault was essentially fired from the service after a decade-long career because a handful of senior officers deemed the francophone agent's performance to be not quite up to CSIS's exacting standards. And yet the same CSIS officers who passed judgment on Marchessault tolerated widespread drinking, laziness, abuse of service cars, gambling on government computers, stealing from the agency's coffers and using safe houses for private soirees, when the culprits were the favoured "fair-haired boys."

Jean-Luc Marchessault was not a "fair-haired boy" but one of the new breed of intelligence officer that the service told the country it wanted to recruit into its ranks in its early years. Born in Montreal in 1959, Marchessault was the son of a world-renowned pediatrician. His youth was unremarkable, save for losing the sight in his left eye because of a congenital defect. Perfectly bilingual and with a degree in political science and journalism from the University of Montreal, he was enthralled by the vision of a new intelligence service being born out of the ashes of the discredited RCMP Security Service. Marchessault applied to become a spy in 1985. He underwent a rigorous security screening, psychological assessment and mandatory polygraph test. Then a moratorium on hiring new recruits was declared, and Marchessault had to wait until it was lifted. He was finally hired on April 3, 1989. He had just been married, and it was his first full-time job.

He revelled in the service's three-month training regimen. The days were long and filled with a broad menu of classes on counter-intelligence and counter-terrorism operations, surveillance techniques and interviewing skills. Marchessault knew that good intelligence work had little in common with the comic-book, superhero world of James Bond, and was instead the product of patience, diligence and perseverance. In his first display of the stubbornness that would frustrate and anger his superiors, Marchessault joined six other members of his graduating class to protest their planned transfer to Toronto, upset that other, well-connected recruits were able to pick their postings. The gambit didn't work. Most of the fresh recruits were shipped to Toronto, another to B.C., and only one remained in Ottawa.

He spent his first two years working in security screening, the service's sweatshop. He conducted security assessments on endless diplomats and bureaucrats, and enjoyed the work. Soon, interesting cases began to cross his path. One file involved an associate of Gerald Bull, the Canadian engineer and arms dealer, who was bidding on a government contract. In 1990, Bull was shot five times in the head by suspected Mossad agents outside his apartment door in Brussels to prevent him from selling the "Supergun" he had developed to Iraq. Another intriguing case that Marchessault came across involved a government official with possible links to biker gangs.

In July 1991, he was transferred to Toronto and found himself among the first wave of francophone officers to move into an anglophone work environment where the service was dominated by RCMP dinosaurs. He didn't receive a particularly warm welcome. He was a university graduate and a francophone—doubly cursed in his new post. An undercurrent of suspicion and thinly veiled discrimination greeted many of the francophone officers who worked for the service outside of Quebec. When Marchessault heard a snide reference to "frogs," he immediately challenged the offender. But he tried not to let the petty insults prevent him from befriending his colleagues. In order to get ahead at CSIS, an officer had to be liked.

Marchessault rotated through a series of jobs in Toronto, moves designed to give recent recruits a taste of every vein of intelligence work. He did a three-week stint as acting supervisor in the counterterrorism branch. His boss on the busy and high-profile Russian desk was Joe Fluke.[1] Marchessault enjoyed working for the hard-driving Fluke, whose reputation for aggressiveness and risk-taking endeared him to younger recruits.

Marchessault was party to several sensitive cases while working alongside Fluke on the Russian desk. In early 1991, a Russian man and his son arrived at Toronto's Pearson International Airport and claimed refugee status. During routine questioning by immigration officers, the Russian, who was in his mid-forties, intelligent and soft-spoken, said he had information that might be of interest to Canadian and British intelligence officials. A CSIS counter-intelligence officer was quickly dispatched to debrief the promising refugee claimant. The Russian told his inquisitor that he was linked to the KGB and had information that the Soviet espionage agency had successfully infiltrated the British and Canadian embassies in Moscow. Two KGB officers, the Russian said, had been planted inside the high-profile diplomatic missions as local hires and were busy targeting key Canadian and British diplomats. He was prepared to identify the spies in return for special consideration of his refugee application.

Ottawa and CSIS agreed to deal, knowing the dynamite information was likely to trigger a major diplomatic spat. The Russian was sequestered in a downtown hotel and questioned at length by the service. CSIS concluded that he was telling the truth. The British sent a team of intelligence officers to Canada, including two officers from its domestic spy service, MI5, and an officer from its foreign espionage agency, MI6, to question the man. Marchessault's job was to chaperone his British counterparts during their stay in Canada.

The Russian was shown pictures of every employee inside both legations and, true to his word, he plucked out the two KGB officers.

---

[1] The star intelligence officer was suspended in 1997 after he was ensnared in corruption allegations. In August 1998, Fluke was charged with accepting gifts from businessmen without official approval. Three more corruption charges were later tacked on. Then, as if a magic wand had been waved over the brewing scandal, the charges were dropped. Fluke subsequently resigned from the service and today works as a consultant with a security firm that offers protection to VIPs.

CSIS scored valuable points with its British brethren, who were grateful at being tipped off. Marchessault, Fluke and other members of the Russian desk celebrated their success with the MI5 and MI6 agents at Alice Fazooli's Italian Crabshack on Adelaide Street, near the service's downtown headquarters. In exchange for his invaluable service, CSIS paid the refugee claimant one thousand dollars. Insulted, he decided to return to the Soviet Union with his son.

Marchessault's early performance appraisals were filled with superlatives about his positive attitude, eagerness and loyalty. He was turning into a capable, if unspectacular, investigator who appeared destined to enjoy a long and successful career. In 1995, he was transferred from the Russian desk into the service's counter-terrorism branch to keep tabs on suspected Armenian, Sudanese, Islamic and Irish terrorists living in Canada. He bemoaned the move because he had cultivated a string of precious sources, the lifeblood of any intelligence service, and now had to start from scratch in another branch.

Marchessault also began to take note of the service's sordid underbelly. He saw some senior officers routinely return from lunch unsteady on their feet, while others didn't return at all. "Some supervisors that I worked with would go out for two- to three-hour lunches and come back smelling like a brewery," he says. "And by four o'clock, the office was a ghost town." He learned of senior officers who were involved in serious car crashes with CSIS vehicles. The accidents were covered up to protect reputations and careers. He saw officers embellish their reports with information from questionable sources to curry favour with superiors. He learned that some money for intelligence operations had been used to buy stereo equipment instead. He saw safe houses used by officers for nightly trysts or weekend getaways. He learned that an officer had invited his mother along to a debriefing with a source. He knew of a female officer who had been placed under house arrest after suffering a psychological breakdown and who was later arrested at the airport allegedly carrying a weapon and passport. In effect, he saw the same corrupt, unseemly world that Farrell saw. (The two men have never met.)

"There is an understanding, a culture at CSIS that says that to get along, you have to belong," Marchessault says. "The drinking, the laziness, the vices were all secrets of that fraternity."

In the summer of 1996, the service's methodical assault on Marchessault's reputation began after he attended a meeting in Ottawa between CSIS employee association representatives from its seven regions and senior CSIS managers, including Elcock. (The service's employee association is an informal union made up of intelligence officers and PSU members.) Marchessault went to the meeting against the wishes of some of his colleagues in Toronto, who wanted to be represented by an empty chair to symbolize their displeasure with the way senior officers were managing the service. Marchessault thought a voice raised in protest would be more effective than no voice at all. At the meeting, he brought up many of the concerns percolating in Toronto, especially the perception that promotions were being handed out not on merit but as a result of nepotism and favouritism. The pointed criticism wasn't well-received.

Retribution was swift. His performance appraisals began to include questions about his writing skills and analytical abilities. The service's psychologist suggested that he was suffering from "perceptual deficits." Marchessault was perplexed. Months earlier, he had received an award from the regional director-general in Toronto, David Beazley, in recognition of his "efforts and enthusiastic commitment to the Service's corporate endeavours."

Anxious, Marchessault sought the advice of Michel Gingras, the head of the employee's association. Gingras told him to get out of Toronto. He had seen other careers implode at the whim of capricious and vindictive managers. Marchessault found himself caught in a no man's land, having alienated both managers and some influential rank-and-file intelligence officers. But he decided to stay put. "I had done nothing to deserve being treated that way," he says.

The service's campaign against him gathered momentum. His performance appraisals were deemed "unsatisfactory." He was ordered to complete a work schedule that seemed designed, he says, to see him fail. He was the subject of an avalanche of "reviews," including a Special Evaluation Review, a Breach of Conduct and Discipline Review and a

Performance Evaluation Report. A mountain of paper was generated by an intelligence service that had decided to rid itself of a young, capable officer. Still, Marchessault didn't fully understand the root of the service's animus toward him, beyond the repeated references in the reviews to his "poor" memo-writing.

Then came the final blow. On July 17, 1997, Marchessault became the target of an internal security investigation. "It was," he says, "the kiss of death." The accusations: he had examined 8,500 classified documents without permission and made copies of 471 of the documents. Réal Allard, an investigator with the service's internal security branch in Montreal, travelled to Toronto to conduct the probe. Elcock was advised of the potential breach of security and approved the investigation. Marchessault was suspended pending the outcome. "I cannot adequately express the depth of pain, worry and anxiety those allegations caused me and my family," Marchessault says. "It's one thing to be told you're not doing a good job, it's quite another to be accused of being a traitor."

On July 21, 1997, Allard concluded that "no breach of security occurred." In a report marked "secret," Al Smith, the service's director-general of internal security, accepted Allard's findings. "I am satisfied that Réal Allard's thorough investigation has examined this incident sufficiently and that I can state that it is highly unlikely that sensitive Service information has been disclosed to unauthorized parties outside of the Service," Smith wrote.

Marchessault returned to work vindicated—or so he thought. But nothing had changed. With the help of his lawyer, an uncle, he fought to keep his job, filing grievance after grievance. It was useless. On Christmas Eve, 1997, Marchessault was told that he was going to be fired. In his letter informing Marchessault of this fact, his once-proud boss, David Beazley, wrote, "Mr. Marchessault's presence in this Region is now a disruptive force impairing operational effectiveness and efficiency."

Marchessault appealed to Ward Elcock to overturn his dismissal. In an impassioned six-page letter to the director, Marchessault claimed that he had been unjustly singled out for punishment and intimidation while some senior officers who had committed egregious offences enjoyed immunity. "I have an eerie feeling that the Service is falling back to the old habits of the RCMP," Marchessault wrote. "No doubt, in view of this trend, the Service will be the subject of increasing controversy."

Elcock rejected Marchessault's warning and his appeal. As his colleagues watched in silence, Marchessault cleaned out his desk, handed in his CSIS ID and was escorted out of the service's Front Street headquarters on January 21, 1998. "I was numb," he says, recalling the scene. The career he loved was over, but his battle wasn't. "I was a loyal employee, dedicated to my job, in early, out late, worked evenings, never claimed overtime, because I enjoyed the job. I thought it was important."

Marchessault filed request after request under the Privacy Act and the Access to Information Act to amass key documents in one final bid to win his job back by appealing to the Public Service Staff Relations Board (PSSRB). CSIS claimed it couldn't find many of the documents that Marchessault had requested; those documents were crucial to Marchessault's argument that he had been unfairly singled out and was the victim of a campaign by senior CSIS officers to destroy his reputation. During twelve days of hearings, he tried to make the point that managers abused service privileges and acted with impunity. He reported that Beazley used the service cars for non-official purposes and had been in two accidents involving service cars. Beazley admitted that was true. A small but significant victory, Marchessault thought. The PSSRB ultimately ruled that it didn't have jurisdiction over the wrongful dismissal dispute. Marchessault was crushed. He had mortgaged his house and spent thirty thousand dollars in legal fees for nothing.

After the board issued its decision, some of the missing documents magically appeared. On January 12, 1999, Marchessault received a letter from CSIS informing him that "as a result of further searching regarding [your] personal information bank, additional information was located." Among the documents that were "located" was a short note written by a senior CSIS officer, which referred to the service's strategy on dealing with Marchessault as "turning the screws." So Marchessault filed a complaint with Bruce Phillips, Canada's no-nonsense privacy commissioner. On

December 14, 1999, Phillips issued an unprecedented and pointed rebuke of the service. He found that senior CSIS officers had broken the law by destroying documents related to Marchessault's work performance. Some of the information that Marchessault had requested had been destroyed in clear violation of the service's own rules governing the handling of documents. Phillips also found that the service's top spy in Toronto, David Beazley, had illegally obtained sensitive personal information about Marchessault, including his medical and psychological records, credit history, and correspondence between the young intelligence officer and his lawyer. "I have concluded that the disclosure of your personal information to [Beazley] was not a consistent use of the information and that your confidentiality rights under the Privacy Act were contravened," Phillips wrote in his six-page ruling.

Phillips told Marchessault that he could take some solace in knowing that the ruling might prevent CSIS from breaking the law in the future. "Unfortunately, my findings do not change the fact that another individual was made aware of your personal information. You may, however, find some satisfaction in knowing that as a result of your complaint, others may be spared from having their privacy invaded," Phillips wrote.

Marchessault had lost his job, apparently because he couldn't write a report properly. And yet Elcock and Beazley escaped punishment despite the fact that the privacy commissioner of Canada had found that the service broke the law. Beazley was sent to London as the service's liaison officer, and Elcock's term as director was renewed for another five years, allowing him to remain comfortably perched in his sixth-floor office at the "Big House" in Ottawa.

Still, Marchessault remains defiant. "They wanted to break me, but they couldn't. The service said I couldn't do my job, but it was a lie. They believe they are above the law, but they are not. They play by their own rules, and they make them up as they go along. They have absolutely no respect for the law, and it's time that CSIS was held to account. It may sound naive, but I truly believe that the rule of law is at stake here."

Marchessault's ordeal upset many of his colleagues. They watched with a mixture of resignation and trepidation as the career of an eager, bright and dedicated intelligence officer was systematically crushed by senior CSIS managers, including David Beazley. Dick Lewis, the former head of the employees' association, and Robert Christopher, another intelligence officer in Toronto, testified on Marchessault's behalf at the PSSRB hearing. But most of his colleagues remained silent, fearing retribution if they spoke out.

One veteran intelligence officer who witnessed it all agreed to speak out on condition that his name not be used. The retired officer has built a new life for himself far from the secret world he once inhabited. But he still fears the reach of Canada's secret service. "It is a vindictive organization that will stop at nothing to crush its critics," the quiet ex-officer says. He believes that Marchessault was precisely the kind of intelligence officer that the service needs to keep within its fold. "Unlike many of the officers he worked for, Jean-Luc was a sincere, honest, professional intelligence officer, with unquestionable integrity." He watched as Marchessault applied those qualities during delicate and sometimes dangerous forays into Canada's immigrant communities to elicit information and recruit sources. "He won people's trust and confidence," the former officer says. "He was a good intelligence officer, but he was singled out and then forced out of a job simply because he alienated the wrong people."

Marchessault had soldiered on, he says, in a region that was suffering from "a serious malaise" that drained the morale of scores of rank-and file intelligence officers. Many officers, he says, believed that much of the information that was generated by the service's counter-intelligence and counter-terrorism branches was routinely rejected by timid politicians, who wanted desperately to avoid alienating voters in high-profile and powerful ethnic groups. "We would often present information to the minister and the response would be that they would wait until the election was over before acting on it. And then the election would come and go and we would present the evidence again, but they still wouldn't act upon it," he says. "It was very frustrating."

The lingering friction between new recruits and old-guard RCMP still causes damage. "The ex–RCMP officers were insecure and intimidated by the university graduates that were entering the service.

Unfortunately, the hostility between the two camps never waned."

The retired officer says that beyond the malaise that pervaded the Toronto region, a much more serious disease infected CSIS: laziness. "There were officers that put their feet up on their desk and read the newspaper all day. There were officers who spent three or four hours a day in the gym. There were people who ran businesses while they were at work. There were officers who would just go to the bar and drink. There were others who simply refused to go out into the field. And they were never punished," he says angrily. "It was all unbelievable."

The former officer says that while he was never asked to engage in unethical conduct, he knew other intelligence officers who were recruited to spy on their colleagues. "They were asked to keep records on their co-workers," he says. "The managers were asking the good friends of employees to spy on their friends and they did it." The ex-officer says that Gerry Baker, a veteran counter-terrorism officer, was asked by senior CSIS managers to commit perjury while he was being questioned by SIRC about the conduct of his co-workers. "They [the managers] told Baker, 'This is the position that the agency is taking and this is the position we want you to take as well.' Baker refused to do it. And he was in the doghouse for a long time because of that."

The dishonesty and lack of accountability gnawed at him. "People who had a keen interest in wanting to do good would cave in to the corruption, either by being silent or following orders in the interest of being promoted. I was disgusted," he says. "That's why I left. I simply couldn't stomach it anymore."

15

THE RECKONING

John Farrell's expensive, frustrating and, at times, infuriating duel with CSIS began in earnest when he contacted Sylvia MacKenzie, a senior complaints investigator with SIRC in Ottawa. In a calm but firm voice, Farrell sketched the broad outlines of his career with CSIS for MacKenzie as he stood in the middle of the Scarborough Town Centre's sprawling parking lot with a cellphone pressed to his ear. He wondered whether he was wasting his time. He knew that Lunau, Murphy and many of the SOS members scoffed at SIRC. "Lunau thought SIRC was about as annoying as a twenty-four-hour flu," Farrell says. He remembered how the SOS chief routinely made intelligence officers rehearse their stories well in advance of the arrival of SIRC's young, often inexperienced investigators.

Farrell asked MacKenzie if SIRC would pay for a quick trip to Ottawa so they could meet to discuss his complicated and alarming story. He offered her a few appetizing hints of the "professional services" he had provided for CSIS since 1991. But MacKenzie didn't bite. The review committee's small budget, she explained, didn't cover the travel expenses of potential complainants. The busy investigator then told Farrell that she had to deal with an important call on the other line and would get back to him later. Farrell was poised to reveal some of the service's most troubling and damning secrets, and he was already getting the cold shoulder. Lunau was right, Farrell thought. SIRC was a joke.

Eventually, MacKenzie got back to Farrell. It turned out she planned to attend a conference in Toronto and they could rendezvous at the Royal York hotel. Farrell cautiously agreed to the meeting. Still, it felt surreal. Just as the former gang leader had never imagined that he would become a spy, Farrell had never envisioned telling all to a government lawyer.

Farrell was late for the meeting. MacKenzie grew so impatient she had Farrell paged over the hotel's public address system—not a wise move. CSIS's headquarters was a stone's throw away and the landmark hotel was often teeming with intelligence officers. The service routinely used rooms at the hotel to debrief sources, and paid bellmen, the concierge and security guards fat tips to keep informed about the comings and goings of unsavoury characters.

Farrell had wanted MacKenzie to book a room so that they could meet privately, but SIRC's investigator was in a hurry and took him to a ground-floor café. MacKenzie was tiny, barely five-foot-two, with shoulder-length brown hair and a soft, high-pitched voice. She spoke English with a thick French accent, which had Farrell straining to make out some of her questions. For her part, MacKenzie was surprised by Farrell's youth.

Farrell went over the arc of his career with the service, from his tentative beginnings in Operation Vulva to his intimate involvement in the SOS unit. He told MacKenzie that the service owed him thousands of dollars in unpaid overtime. He patiently recounted the front companies he had set up for the service, his involvement in covert entries, and the orders he was given to break the law, including stealing Baker's notebooks. He also raised his concerns about CSIS being permitted to privatize its mail intercept program.

Finally Mackenzie sounded a little excited: "These are very serious allegations."

Farrell nodded.

She paused for a moment, thinking, and then completely astonished Farrell. She was unsure, she said, as to whether his complaint fell within the watchdog's mandate.

"What do you mean, you don't know if this falls within your mandate? What more do you want?"

Well, she said, she had the power to review all of CSIS's records, and SIRC had just completed an audit that handed the service another clean bill of health. Since the committee had the "absolute authority" to peruse all of the service's files, it knew precisely what was happening within CSIS's murky bowels—and Farrell's allegations, although interesting, just didn't fit.

"You're joking, right? Of course they keep things from you," Farrell said.

"I've been an investigator for years and we see everything," MacKenzie shot back, clearly offended by Farrell's remark.

"Don't try to pull rank with me. I worked for CSIS for ten goddamn years and I don't need a lecture from you. They hide stuff from SIRC all the time."

MacKenzie suggested that SIRC might be able to mediate the dispute over money. In the meantime, she told Farrell, he should write another letter to Elcock.

"At that point, I thought these guys aren't watchdogs, they're lapdogs," Farrell says.

The meeting was over in less than an hour. MacKenzie was anxious to catch the hotel's shuttle bus to the airport for her flight back to Ottawa. "We'll get back to you," she said. Farrell would just have to take a number and wait.

Farrell had taken up Bradley's challenge and filed a complaint against CSIS with SIRC. His first brush with SIRC had left him disillusioned. So he bought a cheap airline ticket and flew off to visit his girlfriend in Zurich. He was also physically and emotionally exhausted, and the looming battle with his former allies weighed on his mind. He hoped that despite MacKenzie's hesitancy the committee would take up his case, do the job they were empowered to do—hold CSIS to account—and help him recoup some of his money. He was in for a very long wait.

On June 1, 1999, Farrell received a letter from Maurice Archdeacon, SIRC's gentlemanly and officious executive director, informing him that the review committee was busy making a "preliminary review" of his complaint to determine whether it had "jurisdiction" over the matter.

On the same day, Archdeacon alerted CSIS that Farrell had lodged a complaint. In his letter to the service, Archdeacon noted that Farrell had tried unsuccessfully to settle the dispute by contacting Elcock. "The complainant wrote the Committee that since 1990 he has worked on the CSIS/API program and has assisted in the coordination of this highly classified program until 2 January 1999 when his contract was terminated without justifiable cause," the executive director wrote. "The complainant also claims that along with his duties as a CSIS/API coordinator, he has worked as a human undercover source directly for the Service (verbal contract) and as such has not been paid according to his agreement. The complainant feels the Service's recent humanitarian offer of $6,000 is insufficient . . . the complainant believes that the reason his contract was terminated as an API was due to his refusal to continue performing covert investigations for the SOS branch of the Service and because he had been very outspoken when the Service arbitrarily gave the contract to a private company."

While Archdeacon was writing letters, Farrell was busy calling MacKenzie from pay phones in Zurich, pestering her about the status of his complaint. MacKenzie told Farrell that the committee needed more information in order to decide whether to proceed. Farrell was confused and disappointed and felt she didn't comprehend the risk he had taken by agreeing to meet her and then betray secrets CSIS had never intended for public consumption. Farrell was SIRC's ticket into the real workings of this country's secret service and the watchdog agency appeared unsure about how to deal with him.

Worried that SIRC was about to abandon him, Farrell wrote to several Liberal politicians, asking for an "independent review" of his allegations. He contacted his local member of Parliament, Tom Wappel, who told Farrell there was little he could do. On May 3, 1999, Farrell had written Prime Minister Jean Chrétien, pointing out that his attempts to reach a "mutual agreement" with CSIS were greeted by "constant resistance." Significantly, Farrell provided Chrétien with a copy of his seven-page letter to Elcock, detailing his long career with the service. "Without dragging this matter before the courts and the public, I would like your office to review this matter," Farrell wrote.

On June 7, 1999, Farrell received a perfunctory reply from Angela Gillis, the prime minister's executive correspondence officer. "On behalf of the Prime Minister, I would like to acknowledge your correspondence of May 3 regarding your previous affiliation with the Canadian Security Intelligence Service," Gillis wrote. "You may be assured that your views have been given careful consideration. A copy of your correspondence has been forwarded to the Honourable Lawrence MacAulay, Solicitor General of Canada." Farrell's letter was now riding Ottawa's bureaucratic merry-go-round. Gillis failed to point out who precisely in the Prime Minister's Office (PMO) had given Farrell's letter "careful consideration." Nor did she suggest what steps the PMO had taken in response to Farrell's important letter, apart from slipping it into the inter-office mail. (The prime minister and the solicitor general cannot say that Farrell didn't give them fair warning.)

Farrell kept pushing for a settlement that would shield the government from embarrassment, but he was rebuffed at every turn. Finally, on July 21, 1999, he received a two-paragraph letter from MacAulay. Predictably, the solicitor general sought refuge behind SIRC's skirt. "I have been advised," he wrote, "that the Security Intelligence Review Committee is currently reviewing this matter at your request."

Month after month slipped by and still the committee hadn't made up its mind whether to act on Farrell's case. Exasperated, on August 4, 1999, Farrell wrote MacKenzie a long letter spelling out, yet again, the nature of his work for the service. "I have set up, operated and maintained a number of front companies for CSIS. I set up covert apartment rentals that senior CSIS managers allowed their daughters to live in with friends. I regularly investigated people at the request of Don Lunau. I was asked by a CSIS officer to break into a car and retrieve and destroy written information that could harm the Service," Farrell wrote. SIRC's inaction puzzled him. "I wondered whether I needed to carry a neon sign saying, 'Agent ordered by CSIS to break law' before they emerged from their coma," he says.

Farrell's lawyer, Ernest Rovet, was also troubled by SIRC's idleness. "They have been passive throughout. Whatever John told them, it didn't whet their appetite to know more," Rovet says. "My impression was that they kept putting him off. They kept raising the hurdles all the time and they seemed not terribly interested in what he had to say."

While SIRC and the Liberal government dithered, Farrell's correspondence certainly caught the service's attention. In his lengthy August letter to MacKenzie, Farrell pointed out that he was still in possession of a laptop computer that CSIS had given him and that was registered to the solicitor general. The computer and, more important, the mountain of classified information stored in it, give the lie to Elcock's claim that Farrell had only worked with the service from "time to time." Copies of all of Farrell's correspondence with government officials, agencies and politicians were forwarded to Elcock at his request.

After reviewing the letters, a senior CSIS officer noted in an internal memorandum that while Farrell's "various allegations appear to be unchanged, I would draw your attention to Farrell's claim that he has a laptop belonging to CSIS."

On October 14, 1999—seven months after his meeting with MacKenzie at the Royal York—Farrell finally received the news he had been hankering for. In the interim, Maurice Archdeacon had left SIRC to become inspector general for CSIS, and the acting executive director, Maurice Klein, informed Farrell by letter that the committee had decided to investigate his complaint: "After having conducted a preliminary review of your complaint, the Committee has determined that it has jurisdiction in your case, and is proceeding with its investigation."

The long delay, however, had eroded Farrell's already anemic confidence in the watchdog agency, and he wondered how long an investigation might take. He decided to cut his losses, and wrote CSIS, agreeing to accept the six-thousand-dollar offer. But the service was no longer in the mood to make "humanitarian" gestures. In a brusque letter to Farrell on November 22, 1999, Tom Bradley pointed out that SIRC "has, at your request, initiated an inquiry into the issues you have raised," and it was clear he was piqued by the former operative's actions. "In view of the ongoing SIRC inquiry and the significant time which has elapsed since this offer was last extended, the Service will not be acting upon your latest request for assistance," Bradley wrote.

SIRC was now Farrell's only hope, and at the time, I was reporting stories that shook any remnant of faith he had in the review committee and its relationship to CSIS. On November 12, 1999, I revealed in a front-page story in the *Globe and Mail* that a trio of drug addicts had stolen a top-secret CSIS document from an officer's van while she was watching a hockey game in Toronto. The "operational planning document" detailed the service's battle plans for the coming year. Phil Gibson, a CSIS spokesman, described the theft as the most serious breach of security in the service's history. The service went on to grudgingly acknowledge that the lost information could have posed a profound threat to Canada's national security if it had fallen into the wrong hands.

I was a reporter, not an intelligence insider, but I learned of the highly classified document's theft before SIRC did. Ward Elcock didn't bother to inform SIRC's head, Paule Gauthier, about the theft; the Quebec City lawyer only learned of the grave security lapse when she picked up her morning paper. Later, it was revealed that the solicitor general had also failed to alert SIRC to the security breach.

The spy scandal was not only a slap in the face to the watchdog agency but looked like proof that SIRC was an irrelevant player in the intelligence game. Gauthier tried to regain some lustre by launching a probe into the incident and arguing that SIRC would have eventually discovered the theft of the document.

But the stolen-document fiasco wasn't the only CSIS controversy that SIRC seemed to be completely in the dark about. The watchdog agency had to rely on a string of my reports in the *Globe* to learn that over a hundred current and former intelligence officers had set up a company called the X-MP Fund to sue CSIS for back pay and benefits; that the RCMP and CSIS were at war with each other over the fate of a joint probe, code-named Project Sidewinder, into Chinese espionage in Canada; that the service's former chief psychologist, Brian Lynch, was claiming that senior CSIS officers routinely pressured him to divulge the confidential medical records of rank-and-file officers; that a former officer confessed to destroying key evidence related to the service's probe into the 1985 bombing of an Air-India plane that killed all 329 people on board; and that Michel Simard, a thirty-five-year veteran of both the RCMP Security Service and CSIS, claimed that morale at the agency was plummeting and described the service as a "rat hole."

CSIS was reeling from revelations that had ordinary citizens, prominent journalists, politicians, veteran intelligence officers and even Reid Morden, a former CSIS director, referring to the embattled agency as the Keystone Kops of the spy business. Ron Atkey, a former SIRC chair, and other intelligence experts, called on Ward Elcock to resign. A *Globe* editorial writer suggested that the service was imploding under the weight of the embarrassing exposés. In a plaintive year-end message to CSIS employees, Elcock acknowledged that the flood of unflattering stories had "dampened spirits" within the service. But he vowed to soon "set the record straight."

SIRC, meanwhile, was lurching from one investigation to the next, trying to keep pace with the steady stream of stories that had put the watchdog agency on the defensive.

While the review committee was busy reacting to the almost daily crises swirling around the intelligence service, the probe into Farrell's complaint languished. SIRC claimed that Farrell's reluctance to provide it with more details about his tenure at CSIS made him responsible, in part, for its moribund investigation. But it was clear that in the wake of leaks, scandals and a simmering revolt within CSIS ranks, Farrell wasn't a priority for SIRC. For months, the watchdog let his complaint gather dust.

Farrell was so discouraged and strapped for cash that he briefly toyed with the idea of joining the RCMP, going so far as to take the force's entrance exam (without cheating). He was offered a spot, but the urge to become a Mountie soon passed. He chose instead to renew his offensive against CSIS, with or without SIRC's help. Farrell had his lawyer draft a letter to CSIS on December 17, 1999, threatening to sue the agency unless it paid him the outstanding overtime. "[Farrell's] duties went far beyond mere mail interception. His additional duties involved significant risk to his health and safety. He believed, based on representations made to him, that he would be compensated in a fair and reasonable manner for these additional and hazardous assignments," Rovet wrote.

Three weeks later, the service delivered its reply and a warning. On January 10, 2000, Mary MacFadyen, a Department of Justice lawyer writing on Elcock's behalf, cautioned Farrell that if he went public with his allegations, he would be prosecuted under the Official Secrets Act. "Anyone who without authorization discloses information entrusted to him by an employee of the Crown or which he obtained by his contractual relationship with the Crown is guilty of an offence under the Official Secrets Act," MacFadyen noted. The lawyer also reminded Farrell that since he had "signed several 'non-disclosure' agreements"—although she didn't say with whom—CSIS encouraged him to keep his mouth shut. In any event, she wrote, if Farrell launched a lawsuit against the service, Ottawa would try to quash the case by arguing that it could damage Canada's "national security." MacFadyen kept to the line that since Farrell had signed contracts with Canada Post, he wasn't a CSIS employee. She then took the charade one step further, alluding in her letter to Farrell's "alleged involvement with the Canadian Security Intelligence Service." Even Elcock had the sense to acknowledge that Farrell had a "working relationship" with CSIS. MacFadyen closed her letter by contradicting herself. "Mr. Farrell has been treated fairly in his dealings with the Service," she wrote. Apparently, Farrell did have "dealings" with CSIS after all.

Rovet quickly fired back. The service, he charged, was trying to "obfuscate" its relationship with Farrell in order to "mislead" SIRC and "avoid accountability" in the courts and with the watchdog agency. "Mr. Farrell's ostensible employer has been either Canada Post or an . . .

agency created by a former senior employee of Canada Post for the specific purpose of adding one more layer of blurring between CSIS and the persons it wished to employ," Rovet wrote in a March 15 letter to MacFadyen.

He insisted that Farrell was not going to be intimidated by threats of prosecution under the Official Secrets Act. "My client will not be deterred from pursuing his legal rights," Rovet wrote. "Nor will my client be reluctant to make public his concerns about the way in which CSIS conducts its business on behalf of the people of Canada." Despite the threats, Rovet told MacFadyen, Farrell was still prepared to "explore . . . a negotiated settlement."

Two weeks later, MacFadyen rejected Rovet's offer and suggested that Farrell take his chances with SIRC. "I understand that Mr. Farrell's complaint with the Security Intelligence Review Committee relating to the same matter is still formally outstanding," she wrote on March 31.

By this point, Farrell had approached Lunau, Murphy, McDonald, Gordon, Bradley and Elcock to try to resolve the dispute. When he was rebuffed, he went to the prime minister, the solicitor general and SIRC. At every turn, Farrell was told either to get lost or wait. Now he was being threatened with jail if he spoke out. Finally, his patience had run out and he called me at the *Globe and Mail* to arrange for a meeting at the Royal York hotel.

The press had always been Farrell's avenue of last resort. At Rotherglen, he had gone up the chain of command to resolve his concerns about the treatment of prisoners, before leaking information to the press. At the York Detention Centre, he had appealed to provincial cabinet ministers and Ontario's premier to investigate serious allegations of corruption and sexual abuse at the jail before blowing the whistle. Despite CSIS's warnings of retribution, Farrell decided not only to speak out but to take the service to small claims court. "They declared war on me," Farrell says. "I may be a Catholic but I had never turned the other cheek and I wasn't about to start now."

Farrell was late for the meeting, but unlike SIRC, I had booked a room, ordered food and drinks and set aside several hours for him to tell his story. And what a tale it was. At first, Farrell was tentative as he silently sized me up along with a *Globe* colleague of mine from Ottawa. Then he slowly peeled away the layers of his work with CSIS. In the end, he told us the same story he had repeatedly told CSIS's watchdog. "This is just the tip of the iceberg," he said. Farrell promised that, in time, he would expose it all if we won his trust.

Following the meeting, Farrell showed us documents to corroborate much of his tale of intrigue, betrayal, deceit and law-breaking inside CSIS. In a front-page story on July 7, 2000, the newspaper revealed that Canada's secret service operated a "dirty tricks" unit with Farrell as its key member. It was, as Farrell said, just the tip of the iceberg, but it was enough to send a tremor through CSIS. In a bid to snuff out yet another controversy, the service issued a short statement "categorically" denying "that any of its employees broke the law or instructed anyone else to break the law on behalf of the service." CSIS also warned us that the naming of service employees was "an indictable offence." Farrell wasn't surprised. "Remember CSIS's motto," he said. "Lie, deny, then act surprised."

Don Lunau quickly changed his phone number at CSIS's Toronto headquarters, and his wife shooed me away from their home. I reached MacAulay on his cellphone while driving to a political event in his native Prince Edward Island. "You don't want me to get a ticket or into an accident?" he said nervously, as he fended off persistent questions about Farrell's relationship with the service. The junior cabinet minister promised to read the news report and comment later. He never did.

Maurice Archdeacon, CSIS's new inspector general, said he was troubled by Farrell's allegations. But, he assured me, SIRC had the matter well in hand. The usually unflappable chair of SIRC, Paule Gauthier, denied that the review committee had ignored Farrell's damning allegations. "The file is still there and we know what we have to do," she said, her voice rising in anger and frustration.

Farrell's file had, in fact, been in SIRC's hands for over a year, and the watchdog agency had done very little with it. Again, it took a newspaper report to spur the agency into action. Two days after Farrell went public, MacKenzie began trying to reach him. "In the space of twenty-four hours, she left me at least four messages on my answering machine," Farrell says. "She said she was prepared to fly down to Toronto to meet with me as soon as possible."

MacKenzie refused to answer my questions about her sudden enthusiasm to interview Farrell. Gauthier, stung by accusations that SIRC had dragged its feet, defended her agency's handling of the complaint and again suggested that Farrell was to blame for any delays in the case. The accusation incensed his lawyer. "His complaint was active. He filed everything he had to file. There was disclosure. Then, [SIRC] was supposed to investigate but they did nothing," Rovet says.

On June 29, 2000, just days after I first approached SIRC for comment about Farrell's allegations, Susan Pollak, the agency's executive director, wrote him a letter acknowledging that there was "some confusion about the status" of his complaint. Pollak also informed Farrell that SIRC had unilaterally "suspended" its probe into his complaint in late 1999, though SIRC had never informed Farrell that it had done so. "I trust that any ambiguity or misunderstanding that may exist can be clarified," Pollak wrote. The letter was SIRC's first correspondence with Farrell in months. Why the committee waited more than six months to contact Farrell to "clarify" the status of his complaint remained a mystery since, like CSIS, SIRC refused to answer questions about its dealings with the former operative.

On July 10, Farrell sent a bitter reply to Pollak, in which he rebuked the review committee for its "complacent" and "outrageous" behaviour. "If there was any confusion, it was clearly on your part," he wrote. "I wanted this investigation to proceed." He told Pollak that he had "lost faith" in the committee's ability to probe the service's "wrongdoings." "I stepped forward because I felt that I had been wronged by CSIS and [that] there needed to be a public airing of these very important . . . issues," he wrote. The review committee, he insisted, only showed a renewed interest in his complaint because he had gone public. "Recent media accounts of my complaint have prompted you to take action you should have taken months ago," Farrell wrote.

At the same time, Farrell was chasing, through small claims court, the six thousand dollars CSIS had once offered him. In a six-page statement of claim, which he drafted himself, Farrell argued that he had rejected the service's original offer because Elcock had insisted that, in exchange for the money, he had to waive his right to sue CSIS in the future. The service and its director, Farrell alleged, "have acted in an unreasonable and dishonest [manner] and should refrain from engaging in conduct that is unfair." On the face of it, Farrell's lawsuit appeared to be a prank. But he was dead serious, and Ottawa certainly had to take the case seriously. The possibility that Farrell might be able to compel Lunau, Murphy, McDonald, Gordon and perhaps even Elcock to testify in court or swear out affidavits must have filled CSIS with dread. Charleen Brenzall, another Department of Justice lawyer acting on CSIS's behalf, filed several motions, citing court precedents and legal tomes, to have the case thrown out before the government filed a statement of defence.

Farrell went to small claims court for two reasons: cases are usually dealt with swiftly, and therefore cheaply, and he had a reasonably good chance of getting his money. When the Department of Justice finally filed its statement of defence, Farrell discovered that the government had changed its story. Justice Minister Anne McLellan denied the existence of any contract between Farrell and Canada Post or "any servant or agent of the Crown." It was a stunning about-face. Elcock and the service consistently denied that Farrell was a CSIS employee, insisting instead that he had signed "contractual arrangements" with Canada Post and Adava Consulting. Now the government was claiming those contracts didn't exist. According to McLellan, Farrell had never been a CSIS employee, nor had he signed contracts with Canada Post and Adava Consulting. So who precisely had John Farrell worked for, then? The mounting contradictions in Ottawa's story left Farrell shaking his head. "They were all lying, trying to get away from me as fast as possible, like rats off a sinking ship. So they started making it up as they went along."

CSIS and Brenzall employed every tool in their legal arsenal to drag the case out in the hope that Farrell would run out of patience or cash. At one point, Brenzall tried unsuccessfully to have the court proceedings adjourned because she was going on vacation. But CSIS and the

Department of Justice had underestimated Farrell's resolve. Fifteen months after having filed his statement of claim, Farrell persuaded a judge to set a trial date. While CSIS was fighting hard to stay out of court, Brenzall offered Farrell the six thousand dollars he was seeking on one condition: he had to sign a secret settlement drafted by a senior Department of Justice lawyer and agree to keep his mouth shut. Curiously, according to the first settlement agreement, the offer was "in no way an admission or acknowledgment of the existence of any form of relationship" between Farrell and CSIS. Once again, the Department of Justice was apparently unaware that Elcock had already acknowledged that Farrell had a "working relationship" with the service.

While CSIS and the Department of Justice were still trying to get their stories straight, Farrell confronted a crisis that suggested his battle with the service had taken a sinister turn. The laptop computer he'd referred to in one of his many letters to the powers-that-be was stolen just days after he went public with his story of CSIS wrongdoing.

Just as Kenny Baker had kept a written diary of his work for the service, Farrell had methodically made a detailed electronic record of his clandestine work. The names and addresses of high-profile targets, as well as a daily account of his intimate involvement in Operation Vulva and Operation Stanley Cup, were stored on the computer. Ironically, in June 1999, Farrell had written Bradley, asking the service to make arrangements to retrieve the computer—which had CSIS bar code number 000634196 affixed to its side—along with a cellphone and two secure briefcases used by the SOS unit. "The above items were assigned to me from SOS—Don Lunau," Farrell wrote Bradley. "I will be leaving for Zurich so please make arrangements for the return of the above CSIS property." Bradley never bothered to respond to Farrell's request. So the former CSIS operative hid the computer in a closet in the two-bedroom flat of his friend, Don Hammond.

It remained there until Farrell discovered it was missing on the morning of July 12. He promptly reported its disappearance to police. Farrell told Constable Al Dorkin of 54 Division that the computer was the property of Canada's intelligence service and contained highly classified information about CSIS operations and methods. When Dorkin finally realized that Farrell wasn't joking, he promised to make note of the lost computer in the Canadian Police Information Centre (CPIC) databank. (CSIS has access to the databank.)

Then Farrell faxed a short note to Elcock and Bradley asking them to immediately contact his new lawyer, Paul Copeland, "as this matter requires urgent attention as it pertains to national security." Copeland, a highly respected criminal and civil lawyer in Toronto, was a persistent thorn in the service's side. Farrell had turned to him for help when he could no longer afford to pay Rovet. (Copeland agreed to substantially reduce his fees.) Farrell then faxed a second, more detailed letter to Elcock and Bradley, informing them that he had reported the theft of the computer to Toronto Police. "I contacted CSIS several times," Farrell wrote, "to arrange the return of this equipment and no one expressed any interest in retrieving it."

Elcock and Bradley waited seven days to reply to Farrell's urgent letters and when they did, they confidently insisted through MacFadyen, that their former operative had never reported the loss of a computer to police. "We understand that no computer was reported stolen to the police as suggested by [Farrell]," MacFadyen told Copeland in a July 19, 2000, letter. This time, she did concede that Farrell was, in fact, given a computer by the service, adding that it "contained no information of a sensitive nature." Then the befuddled lawyer asked Farrell to "describe in detail the sensitive information allegedly contained in the computer." After recovering from a fit of laughter, Farrell and his lawyer agreed that the Keystone Kops were still very much hard at work. Copeland called Constable Dorkin and confirmed Farrell's story. The helpful police officer even provided Farrell's lawyer with the occurrence number: 2000/115 224.

On August 1, Copeland faxed a letter to MacFadyen. "I do not understand where or how CSIS gets its information," Copeland began. "Today I spoke with Constable Dorkin . . . he confirmed to me that on July 12, 2000, a computer was reported stolen." He then went in for the kill. "Perhaps you would be good enough to explain to me how CSIS concluded that no computer was reported stolen to the police. If CSIS cannot obtain that type of information from the Toronto Police Service,

I wonder about its ability to gather information in matters of national security." The truth was, the service's crack investigators hadn't bothered to call the Toronto Police or check the CPIC. If they had, they would have quickly learned that Farrell was telling them the truth. Instead, in yet another display of the arrogance that typified the service's senior ranks, Farrell's pleas were airily dismissed.

On August 3, MacFadyen did an about-face. "The computer is described as having a bar code that the Service recognizes," she wrote to Copeland. CSIS finally realized it was missing one very important computer.

To try to assess the damage, MacFadyen asked Copeland if Farrell would be kind enough to write CSIS a note detailing the sensitive information contained in the lost computer. Farrell had already provided Elcock and Bradley with much of the information, so he told the Department of Justice to get lost. The computer with all that highly classified information is still missing.

Three weeks earlier, Farrell had met with CSIS and handed over its secure briefcases and a cellphone that Lunau had given him. The brief but telling encounter, witnessed by myself and a colleague and captured by a photographer, revealed just how anxious CSIS had become to retrieve some of the tools of the trade that Farrell had been trying to return to the service for more than a year.

The hastily arranged meeting took place on a hot summer's day, July 14, just steps from the service's Toronto headquarters, amid a gaggle of peanut vendors, rickshaw drivers and curious tourists. Farrell made all the arrangements. He called Bob Gordon's secretary on her private line and asked to be put through to CSIS's top spy in Toronto. Gordon immediately took Farrell's call. Farrell told Gordon that he wanted to hand back a briefcase and cellphone in front of the Front Street offices. Gordon said he would arrange to have an officer meet him in a quarter of an hour.

Farrell drove down to CSIS headquarters and waited. Within minutes, a tall, well-dressed intelligence officer moved toward Farrell. He asked the officer if he could see his CSIS identification and then handed over the briefcase and cellphone. The officer refused to explain to me why the service was suddenly interested in meeting a man whom CSIS claimed it had only a fleeting and trifling relationship with.

By the time SIRC resurrected its dormant probe into Farrell's complaint, the former CSIS operative was facing a big problem: money. Farrell had spent several thousand dollars of his savings to enrol in the Bachelor of Education program at Toronto's York University. He had decided to become a teacher. No more living on the fringes of legality, supposedly helping out the good guys. Though Copeland had agreed to take a cut in pay, he started pressing Farrell for a retainer, and unless Farrell came up with the money, he would have to face CSIS alone. Farrell and Copeland repeatedly appealed to SIRC to help cover the costs of his legal fees, but the review committee said no. "The Committee does not consider it appropriate to alter its long-standing practice not to provide such assistance," Susan Pollak told Copeland in a July 26, 2000, letter. Pollak reminded Farrell that "many complainants submit and pursue their complaints without legal representation." Pollak's argument—that since some people can't afford to hire lawyers to protect their rights, then Farrell should forgo the privilege—was a telling example of the committee's skewed thinking.

In an impassioned letter to Copeland, Farrell pointed out that CSIS would likely appear before the review committee with a posse of government lawyers in tow—all paid for from the public purse. He, on the other hand, seemed destined to stand alone. Farrell would have to prepare his case, question witnesses, submit to questioning, and cross-examine the service's witnesses, all without the benefit of a lawyer.

"Any process which pits an individual against state bureaucracy, any hearing which allows everyone but the complainant to have counsel at public expense is inherently a process that is, in the end, a farce," Farrell wrote. "It is a process which will attempt to make me look like a disgruntled, disaffected troublemaker whose sole aim is to embarrass his betters. Getting at the truth is the least of its concerns. It should be clear to SIRC and the government that if it creates a process whereby wrongdoing by public officials will be investigated, it must do everything in its power to make the process fair. It makes it fair by ensuring that all those who come before a committee or board have equal access to representation . . . What the refusal of SIRC to underwrite my legal costs says is that SIRC is not truly interested in hearing what I have to say. It is not truly interested in carrying out its mandate to the public."

Farrell faced another, perhaps graver, problem. If he testified, he risked prosecution not only under the Official Secrets Act but also under the Criminal Code. SIRC assured Farrell that his testimony before the committee could not be used against him by police to lay criminal charges. But Copeland wasn't convinced that Farrell enjoyed blanket immunity. The two sides met on July 12, 2000—the very day Farrell reported the missing computer to police—to discuss the status of the complaint and Farrell's immunity.

Sylvia MacKenzie was joined by Gordon Cameron, a former police officer and a lawyer with Blake, Cassels & Graydon, a high-profile law firm, who often acted as counsel for SIRC at its hearings. The meeting took place at the law firm's posh offices in Commerce Court in the heart of Toronto's financial district. MacKenzie, who had dyed her hair blond, assured Farrell that the room had been swept for bugging devices. Copeland asked Farrell to keep his temper in check. But when MacKenzie introduced Cameron as SIRC's lawyer, he exploded. "You can afford to hire outside counsel for yourself, but you can't help me with my legal fees!" His outburst rattled MacKenzie, who insisted that the CSIS Act prevented the committee from assisting complainants with their legal costs.

The meeting, already tense, rapidly deteriorated. MacKenzie suggested that Farrell hadn't provided the review committee with very much information to go on. "You're a Mickey Mouse investigator," he fired back. Farrell reminded her that he had sent the committee two letters detailing his accusations against the service. Copeland asked MacKenzie if Farrell had told her about the theft of Kenny Baker's notebooks.

"Yes," she replied.

"What more do you need?" Copeland asked.

MacKenzie suggested that CSIS may have, in fact, obtained a

warrant to break into Baker's car and steal the notebooks.

"Did they have one?" Copeland asked.

MacKenzie refused to answer the question.

"It's outrageous and preposterous to believe that CSIS could obtain a judicial warrant to break into a car and steal notebooks with the intent to destroy evidence," said Copeland.

"I couldn't believe it," Farrell says. "She actually suggested that CSIS had obtained a warrant to break into the car of one of their own operatives."

MacKenzie then shocked them by offering to recuse herself from the case, and Copeland and Farrell slipped into a nearby closet to discuss their next move. When they emerged, Copeland shifted the discussion to the issue of immunity for Farrell, urging SIRC to approach Ontario's attorney general to help engineer an immunity deal for his client. Cameron and MacKenzie listened carefully but were noncommittal. MacKenzie was certain that Farrell's testimony before the review committee could not be used against him by the police. Copeland, however, still had his doubts.

The meeting settled nothing. SIRC had refused to help Farrell with his legal bills and now the watchdog agency was being coy about immunity. "I just didn't understand why they were so reluctant to give me any sort of hand," Farrell says. Despondent, he approached Tom Bradley again to settle the dispute. The service's assistant director rejected the overture.

Copeland began negotiations with the Ontario attorney general to try to strike an immunity deal for Farrell. On July 17, 2000, he wrote Murray Segal, a senior official in the attorney general's office, to lay the foundation for the immunity request. "In my view it is an important public issue that the representatives of Canada's security agencies comply with the laws of Canada," Copeland wrote. "The granting of immunity to Mr. Farrell will allow him to participate in an investigation of [the] conduct of CSIS personnel without Mr. Farrell at the same time being left with the concern that at the end of the day he may be the only one who would suffer any consequences from the evidence he gave to SIRC."

The attorney general's office was prepared to consider granting Farrell immunity in exchange for his information. But before it entered into serious negotiations, it wanted more details about the crimes Farrell had allegedly committed as well as input from SIRC. The committee, however, was reluctant to make representations to the attorney general in support of the immunity request unless Farrell provided it with more information.

Farrell faced an unenviable quandary. If he provided more information and the negotiations went nowhere, he would expose himself to prosecution. But if he didn't provide the information, there would be no immunity deal. Farrell agonized over his decision. He was unemployed, going to teacher's college, sharing a small flat with his friend Don Hammond and facing bankruptcy. It wasn't the best position to be in to make perhaps the most important decision of his life. In the end, he reluctantly gave Copeland the green light to draft letters to SIRC and the attorney general, providing more details about the illegal acts he had committed on the orders of senior CSIS officers. On January 3, 2001, Copeland wrote Farrell to inform him that the letters were ready. All he needed was Farrell's consent to send them off. He also reminded his cash-strapped client that he needed his retainer or "I will not act as your counsel at any SIRC hearings." Farrell understood Copeland's frustration. The prominent attorney had spent hours on his case for free and now he wanted to be paid. Since Farrell couldn't raise the money for Copeland's retainer, the immunity negotiations promptly collapsed.

Farrell was broke but not broken. He appealed to Rovet to take up his cause again. "John is a very charming and persuasive young man," Rovet says; he agreed to help for a fraction of his regular fee.

On May 16, 2001, almost two years after he first approached SIRC, Farrell and Rovet were party to a conference call with Ray Speaker, one of the committee's five part-time members. Speaker, a soft-spoken and respected former Conservative cabinet minister from Enchant, Alberta, was joined on the call by Tom Dastous, the committee's senior counsel; Mary MacFadyen; two unidentified CSIS officers and other SIRC officials. The teleconference had been arranged to discuss, yet again, the status of Farrell's complaint and a possible immunity deal with Ontario's attorney general. Farrell had been longing to make his case directly to Speaker. "It was a chance for me to hopefully get some answers to a few unanswered questions," he says. But it was Dastous who asked the first question.

"Mr. Farrell, do you intend to proceed with the complaint that you filed with SIRC?" he asked.

"Yes," Farrell said emphatically, then demanded to know why he had to try to cobble together an immunity deal alone. "It is in the best interest of the public and in the mandate of SIRC to get to the bottom of this investigation," Farrell said. "I feel I am left out on a limb if I am not granted immunity." The committee was unmoved by Farrell's plea. Dastous insisted that SIRC wasn't able to act on behalf of complainants and, in any event, the CSIS Act already provided him with a measure of immunity. Farrell reminded SIRC's lawyer that the Department of Justice, acting on CSIS's behalf, had warned him not to speak out. "Ms. MacFadyen has already threatened me, in a letter with regards to the Official Secrets Act, not to divulge any wrongdoing or anything I have done in the performance of my duties," Farrell said. Dastous said nothing.

Rovet then asked the committee the question at the heart of Farrell's dispute with CSIS and SIRC. "There is one other matter that has been troubling me," Rovet said, "and it is related to the whole issue of a lone citizen coming forward. What troubles me is that Mr. Farrell has information and issues related to the manner in which CSIS has conducted its affairs, and whether in fact those affairs have been conducted lawfully in Canada. And that is an issue that goes beyond him, of course. It affects the integrity of our institutions and the way in which we are governed . . . but he is a lone individual and what I want to know from you, as we proceed, which we will, is whether the mandate of SIRC is simply to listen to him as an individual, or does SIRC have some overriding independent motivation to get at the truth."

For a moment, silence fell as the profundity of Rovet's question settled in. Then Dastous offered up this response: "SIRC has two mandates: first, to investigate complaints; and second, to review all the activities of the Service. And if in the course of a hearing we learn facts that could lead to a research project, SIRC will act accordingly."

Before everyone hung up, Farrell made one final request: "I have a question for Mr. Speaker. I want his word and his commitment that he is dedicated to getting at the truth and to the bottom of this complaint."

"The assignment that I took on was to do just that, and that is my intention," Speaker said.

Despite that promise from Speaker, the many months since the teleconference call have been filled with more procedural delays and accusations. Farrell is not very much closer to having the review committee hear his complaint than when he first called Sylvia MacKenzie from a shopping centre parking lot in Toronto. MacKenzie has moved on to another job with Transport Canada, joining an exodus of other key SIRC staff.

Spurred on by his success in small claims court (after months of wrangling, the two sides settled out of court), Farrell filed a $185,000 wrongful dismissal suit against CSIS. In its four-page statement of defence, the service repeated its position: "The plaintiff's services were provided as an independent contractor to the third parties, not as an employee."

Then, in early September 2001, the service made a submission to SIRC, requesting that Farrell and Rovet be barred from hearing any of the intelligence agency's testimony to the committee for "national security" reasons. "The relationship between the Service and the Complainant was related to the mandate of the Service to investigate threats to the security of Canada," CSIS wrote. "The evidence to be offered by the Service within this proceeding will be of such a nature that revealing the evidence to Mr. Farrell or his counsel will compromise the security of that information and hence the security of Canada."

Farrell laughed when he read the document.

John Farrell fulfilled a dream on Tuesday, September 4, 2001. It was the first day of a new school year; a warm, sunny day, filled with hope and possibilities. As he walked through the same set of pockmarked school doors that he had once raced through as a troubled young boy, Farrell was filled with thoughts about the adventures, surprises, frustrations and disappointments that lay ahead. Farrell was returning to a Catholic primary school in the heart of Parma Court, this time as a teacher, after graduating from York University with distinction. He and his classmates had often wondered about the moment when they would stand in their own classrooms, before their own students. And that day had finally arrived for Farrell. As he walked into tiny Room 134, crammed with desks and rambunctious twelve-year-olds, the petty, duplicitous world of spies seemed a long way away.

John Farrell had found a new life in old, familiar surroundings.

16

LESSONS LEARNED

Ward Elcock is a lucky man. The intelligence service he has commanded since 1994 has been wracked by one scandal after another: from purloined secret documents, law-breaking and incompetence, to corruption and nepotism by senior CSIS officers. Until now, most of these offences have been carefully concealed from Canadians. Through it all, Elcock and his loyalists within the service, including his former assistant director, Tom Bradley, have never been truly held to account.[1]

Elcock has deflected critics, parliamentarians and inquisitive reporters with a wave of his hand and has dismissed questions about his controversial tenure as CSIS director with bluff assurances and monosyllabic answers. He has emerged unscathed, in part because he has skilfully forged alliances with journalists—particularly in Ottawa's incestuous orbit—and academics, who have, in exchange for his ear and his information,

---

[1] Bradley retired from the public service in April 2002.

defended him and the service.[2] But in large measure, Elcock and CSIS have been shielded from accountability by less-than-tenacious watch-dogs and a succession of junior ministers who prefer to play the role of marionette rather than defend the public interest.

Elcock's luck, however, may have finally run out. The stain on his administration has been exposed not by the Security Intelligence Review Committee or the inspector general, but by a young man who faithfully served CSIS and Elcock for close to nine years: John Farrell. The former CSIS operative's tale of life inside the intelligence agency is so damning it demands one immediate consequence: Elcock's resignation.

It is important to recall that CSIS's first director, Ted Finn, was forced to resign in 1987 after the service provided a federal court judge with a fraudulent affidavit in support of an application for a wiretap warrant. There was no evidence that Finn was either directly or indirectly involved in the legal transgression, but he knew he had little alternative but to quit. By resigning, Finn drew a line in the sand to mark the service's respect for the law in pursuit of security threats. Elcock and company haven't just crossed that line, they've obliterated it.

It is clear from the documentation Farrell has tucked away that senior CSIS officers and officials, including Elcock and Bradley, were intimately familiar with the young CSIS operative and the long-time role he played for the service. The litany of shocking misdeeds that have occurred under Elcock's watch stretches over years and involves much more than an error-filled affidavit. Both men should take their cue from Finn and accept responsibility for the service's grievous conduct under their leadership. If Elcock won't go voluntarily, then he should promptly be shown the door.

The resignation of a haughty intelligence official should only be the beginning of the necessary accounting that desperately needs to

---

[2] Elcock often lunches with key members of the parliamentary press gallery in Ottawa. In recent years, Stewart Bell, a reporter with the *National Post*, has been the recipient of "exclusive" interviews with the CSIS director when the service has been thrust into the public spotlight by other, less agreeable, reporters.

take place as the ripples of Farrell's clandestine work as a paid government operative move beyond CSIS.

Farrell's systematic spying on union leaders at the behest of his superiors at Canada Post shatters the myth that the Crown corporation respects the rights of its workers and abides by the law. What is central to Farrell's troubling story about the nature and extent of the intelligence-gathering on key union officials is his admission that he was directly and deeply involved in the spying. Farrell is pointing an accusatory finger not only at Canada Post but at himself.

His revelations may trigger criminal investigations and lawsuits. What is certain, however, is that André Ouellet, the president and chief executive officer of Canada Post, and his boss, the minister responsible for Crown Corporations, David Collenette, will have to answer some tough questions about what Farrell was up to as divisional intelligence officer.

Elcock's nominal boss, Solicitor General Lawrence MacAulay, is said to be one of Prime Minister Jean Chrétien's favourites in cabinet, in part because of his ability to parry questions in the House of Commons about CSIS by strictly adhering to a nonsensical script that reads, "I can't get involved in the day-to-day operations of CSIS." Meanwhile, the intelligence service that MacAulay is obliged by law to oversee has continued to break the law and treat the rights and liberties of Canadians like inconvenient obstacles to be quashed in the name of national security. Although it is unlikely, given the culture of cronyism that increasingly defines the Chrétien government, MacAulay must be replaced by a politician who understands the gravity of the solicitor general's responsibilities, and acts like a public servant, rather than a servant of CSIS.

Canadians also have a right to know why the administration of one of the service's most sensitive intelligence-gathering operations—the mail intercept program—was handed over to private firms controlled by a recently retired Canada Post executive. Canadians have a right to know who precisely Alan Whitson, his wife and their small but powerful companies are accountable to. The service has refused to answer these questions. Not surprisingly, SIRC and the inspector general appeared to be completely in the dark about the intimate relationship between CSIS and Whitson's two firms: 3385710 Canada Inc. and Adava Consulting.

These questions must be answered because Canadians rightly believe that the handling of their mail is a sacred trust. What assurances can there be that CSIS is intercepting mail in compliance with the law when the administration of the program has been farmed out to a private firm?

If one undeniable truth has emerged from Farrell's long journey in the world of this country's intelligence service, it is this: he was casually ordered to break the law in pursuit of suspected villains. He was ordered to intercept mail without judicial warrants; he was ordered to steal a Crown key; he was ordered to conduct mail cover checks on scores of Canadians without a judicial warrant.

How can Canadians expect there to be any meaningful oversight of a security agency such as CSIS, which pledges to uphold the rule of law while protecting Canadians, when it is quietly handing over critical responsibilities to firms who are apparently accountable to no one but the secret service they work for?

Whitson refused to answer that question when I ventured to the ex-Mountie's house to inquire about his working relationship with CSIS. The former Canada Post executive opened the front door slightly and shouted: "You are not welcome on my property. Please leave now," as three dogs nipped at my heels. Asked why so much secrecy surrounded his firm's relationship with CSIS, Whitson sputtered with anger. "I'm not being secretive. You have no business in my life. Just get out of it. I don't want to talk to you."

I asked Whitson why the service had effectively privatized the administration of Operation Vulva. "I don't know what you are talking about. Goodbye. Thank you very much. And I'm telling you, get off my property now," Whitson said, and slammed the door.

SIRC also needs to be asked a few pointed questions. It's time for members of Parliament to take a long, hard look at the review body's leadership and performance. With hesitancy and inaction, SIRC failed Farrell miserably and, in so doing, failed Canadians. The important and necessary business of watching over the watchers cannot be left to a handful of part-time, political appointees, who are often preoccupied with their business interests, legal careers and other pursuits.

Historically, the review body has been a dumping ground for former politicians and political party insiders looking for something intriguing to do in their spare time. With the notable exception of Ron Atkey—SIRC's tenacious first chairman—the review body's leadership has been largely accommodating to CSIS, careful not to alienate its formidable adversary. The committee's latest appointed member was Gary Filmon, the former long-time premier of Manitoba. He joined two other former premiers—Ontario's Bob Rae and New Brunswick's Frank McKenna—on the review body[3]. Why Filmon was chosen to fill the post remains a mystery. What is clear, however, is that his appointment was made with no input or debate by the public or parliamentarians and, as such, is at odds with the agency's alleged commitment to transparency.

The SIRC chair, Paule Gauthier, and the other committee members have impressive-looking résumés, represent Canada's major political parties and regions and undoubtedly share a desire to keep CSIS in check. But ensuring that the intelligence service abides by the law and does not trample on the rights of Canadians, landed immigrants and refugees is a full-time job, not a part-time assignment to be squeezed in between other engagements.

Indeed, Gauthier acknowledged at a parliamentary hearing considering the federal government's so-called anti-terrorist legislation, that the resources Ottawa showered on the police and CSIS after September 11 will likely result in much more work for the understaffed watchdog agency. And yet, inexplicably, she has failed to admonish the federal government for failing to provide the review body with more money so it can perform its duties.

SIRC lacks the expertise and resources to do its job. Gauthier and her colleagues on the committee have had to rely on a minuscule staff to keep watch over CSIS. This is a recipe for continued failure. Many

---

[3] Rae and McKenna stepped down from SIRC in April 2002.

of SIRC's staff, like the committee members themselves, have little or no previous experience as investigators or knowledge of the world of intelligence. This is yet another example of the regrettable timidity that has marked Gauthier's tenure as head of the committee.

SIRC's chair could learn a lesson from George Radwanski, who took over from Bruce Phillips as the country's privacy commissioner, or the equally outspoken John Reid, the nation's information commissioner. Radwanski and Reid have been robust and trenchant critics of Ottawa's move, since September 11, to shroud CSIS's work in even more secrecy. They have effectively used their bully pulpits and, if necessary, taken the government to court to challenge government policy and legislation to protect Canadians' privacy and rights.

SIRC has become a meek, ineffectual body that offers the service an occasional slap on the wrist. And Paule Gauthier has shown little resolve to take on CSIS's powerful bureaucracy. Like Elcock, it is time for her to go. Her committee's woeful handling of Farrell's complaint is a telling example of its ineptness. Rather than recognize that Farrell had an urgent story to tell, the review body dithered and alienated him. Rather than assure Farrell that it would do everything in its power to protect him from prosecution in exchange for his unprecedented testimony, it made lukewarm gestures of support. Rather than accept responsibility for its sorry handling of Farrell's complaint, it tried to lay the blame at his feet.

SIRC has touted itself as an "independent body" that has the "absolute authority" to examine "all information concerning CSIS's activities." Farrell's long association with CSIS gives the lie to that assertion. CSIS and the solicitor general, the record shows, have routinely kept Gauthier and the review body in the dark about much of the service's activities. Rather than protest loudly, the SIRC chair and her colleagues have remained largely silent. They have opted, instead, to adopt many of CSIS's disquieting habits. Gauthier and Susan Pollak have increasingly exhibited a siege mentality, bristling at any hint of criticism of SIRC's performance. Their sudden retreat into silence after questions were raised about the watchdog agency's handling of Farrell's complaint mirrors CSIS's penchant for unreasonable secrecy.

Properly directed, financed and constituted, SIRC could play a vital role in watching over CSIS and its omnipotent leadership. As a first step, membership on the committee must be a full-time occupation rather than a part-time pastime. Members should be recruited from the well of qualified Canadians who have a profound knowledge of the world of intelligence, human rights and civil liberties. Finally, the review body should badger Ottawa into increasing its budget so it can hire a team of experienced investigators who know where to look, how to look and what to look for.

But if those reforms were ever enacted, they would do John Farrell little good. In a fundamental way, SIRC has forfeited the right to pursue his complaint. Farrell was prepared to help the watchdog agency excise the cancer inside CSIS. He was castigated.

He chose instead to make some startling admissions in this book. He knows the enormous risk he has taken, and it has caused him many troubled nights. His future and perhaps even his freedom are at stake. But in the end, he decided to blow the whistle yet again on some very powerful government agencies and officials. Yes, he was a willing mercenary in the pay of the government of Canada and a Crown corporation. And yet Farrell has done what his former employers dare not do: tell Canadians the truth.

Like many whistle-blowers, Farrell will likely be excoriated by the service's faithful allies as a disgruntled misfit. His character, record and memory will likely come under withering assault in an effort to undermine his credibility and make him more vulnerable to attack. The service and Canada Post will vilify Farrell because, ultimately, they fear him. They will try to destroy Farrell to save themselves. This cannot be permitted to happen.

One person who promises to back Farrell up is Don Lunau. Farrell paid his old boss an impromptu visit at his home in Pickering on a hot, humid day in July 2002. Lunau greeted Farrell with a smile, a handshake and a commitment, assuring Farrell that he would tell the truth about Farrell's involvement with CSIS. "I'll tell exactly what went on," Lunau said, emphatically. "Whatever I'll say, it will be the truth, but I might not be able to say everything." Senior CSIS officials wouldn't let him tell all. "Remember I told you, right at the beginning, that if you went this route [going public] it's out of my hands. . . . Believe me, it's all out of my control. . . . That's why they don't tell me anything, because they don't want to get me involved."

Lunau seemed to relish the opportunity to see Farrell again, and insisted with a hint of nostalgia in his voice that he'd always known their paths would cross again. He told him that his former comrades in the SOS unit, including Cliff Hatcher and Jack Billingsley, often inquired about his welfare: "Everyone has been asking." Despite the friendly tone of the encounter, Lunau said he would have to inform his superiors that Farrell had dropped by. "I have to follow orders," he said. "I have a lot of service to go."

John Farrell should not be prosecuted or persecuted for stepping forward to tell us the truth. He should not be made the scapegoat for the sins of others. The Ontario attorney general's office should move speedily to do what in 2000 it had tentatively taken steps toward: grant Farrell immunity in exchange for his help, guidance and testimony. Only then will the culture of impunity that pervades the senior ranks of CSIS begin to be stripped away. Only then will this country's spy chiefs realize that they are not above the law.

In 1981, the McDonald Commission into wrongdoing by the RCMP Security Service had this warning for Canadians: "to permit a national police force or security intelligence agency to adopt a policy which entails systematic violations of 'minor' laws puts these organizations at the top of a slippery slope." CSIS, its watchdogs and Ottawa have failed to heed that warning. As a result, the service has violated the law with abandon and has slid to the bottom of that slippery slope. The question is, do Canadians have the will to hold CSIS to account?

A NOTE ON SOURCES

This book is the product of interviews with eighty-nine people. Some of these individuals spent many hours with the author and agreed to be interviewed on several occasions to corroborate information provided by other sources or to clarify remarks they had made in earlier interviews. Many of the individuals interviewed, including current and former employees of CSIS and Canada Post, agreed to talk only on a background or not-for-attribution basis. Under these well-established ground rules, the information can be used, but the source cannot be identified. Others, however, agreed to be identified.

The heart of the book is based on interviews conducted with John Farrell over two years. The interviews were conducted primarily in Toronto and Ottawa. Mr. Farrell also provided the author with original documentation, notes, banking records, logs, invoices, taped conversations and items that verified events and information that he described in extraordinary detail in interviews. Other documents confirming sensitive information described in this book were obtained through a variety of confidential sources.

ACKNOWLEDGEMENTS

A book of this nature could not have been written without the support of my family and friends. Without my father Xhelal's profound belief in the public duty and responsibility of a journalist, I would never have embarked upon a career as an investigative reporter. My mother, Feruze, continues to teach me the rewards of hard work and determination. If I have been fortunate to have inherited a measure of her seemingly bottomless well of courage and strength, then I hope those qualities are reflected in this book. Greg, my late father-in-law, never wavered in his conviction that my work needed to be done, and he never once doubted my ability to do it. I am also indebted to Patricia, my kind and thoughtful mother-in-law, for her encouragement along the way.

The other members of my large family all played, without fail, a vital role in helping me complete this book. To Darlene, Steve, Kayla, Arno and Maedla, Liane, Jerry, Eva, Dervish, Kimete, Ydriz, Aurélie, Sarah, Lolita, Nderim, Ilire, Kupi and finally Paul, I offer my deepest thanks.

Beyond my immediate family, there are fiercely loyal friends whose kind words of encouragement often cemented my determination to finish this book. I am fortunate indeed to count Elliott Shiff, Jim Bronskill at Southam News and Rod Ellis at *CTV News* among that small but precious group. Peter Bouroukis and his wonderful wife, Gina, and their two boys, Dean and Theo, shared their hearts and home in good times and bad. Without the help of my devoted family physician, Dr. Vanna Schiralli, completing this book would have been much more difficult. To Michel Juneau-Katsuya I owe an enormous debt of thanks. A former veteran CSIS officer, Michel is a man of unrivalled principle and integrity. He is, simply put, the kind of man that Canada's intelligence service desperately needs. Like Michel, Jean-Luc Marchessault is a man of conviction. He and his wife, Brigitte, put their faith in me. I hope I have not let them down.

Of course, this book would never have been written without the encouragement of my agent, Helen Heller. Helen instantly understood why this book needed to be published. And wise woman that she is, Helen called the most gifted editor in the country, Anne Collins, who shepherded this book from genesis to publication. With her supremely skilled eye and deft touch, Anne turned my bulky manuscript into a book. I am also indebted to my publisher, Random House Canada, for showing such faith, patience and understanding. Stacey Cameron and Pamela Murray took great care in copy-editing, and Pamela Robertson, Anne's former executive assistant, was always helpful and kind.

I am grateful to a small stable of students who patiently transcribed hours of taped interviews conducted for this book: Alexis, Rosella, Maria and Michelle. There are also a number of people, who cannot be named because of the positions they hold in government, who offered me their wise counsel, trust and guidance. I am thankful to you all.

I want to thank John Farrell for allowing me to tell his story. By stepping forward, John is taking the kind of risk few people dare to take. Not once during the research and writing of this book did John ever prevent me from telling the truth. For that, I, and Canadians, owe him a debt of gratitude. And John wishes to thank his family and friends, especially his mother, Mary, and his longtime friend, Don, for their support, encouragement and belief that he has done the right thing.

Finally, I must thank my wife, Sharon, and my daughter, Sabrije. Without you, nothing would be possible.

APPENDIX

The letter from Mike
Thompson offering Farrell
a job as a postal inspector

Farrell drafted this letter for
Thompson, requesting that
his top secret security clearance
be expedited

Farrell's first contact with CSIS. The form CSIS officer Gordon Bell filled out, assessing the security risks involved in the post office hiring a young man with a criminal record

The notice that Farrell had been pardoned

						PROTECTED	
Security & Investigation Services							
Canada Post Corporation					DATE:	92-01-30	
Xerox Building							
785 Carling Ave.					INVOICE #	JF-47	
OTTAWA, Ontario							
K1A 0B1							
For services rendered to Canada Post Corporation							
By:	John FARRELL, P.O.Box 51017 Eglinton Square Post Office						
	Scarborough, Ontario M1L 4T2						
Contract No:							
Expenditure Code:	308870-830-000-1430						
WARRANT NO:	CSIS	91-1					
Week Ending: 92-01-30	Date	Day	Time Started	Time Finished	# Hours	Km Travelled	
	92-01-27	Monday	700	1030	3.5	84 km	
	92-01-28	Tuesday	700	1030	3.5	84 km	
	92-01-29	Wednesday	700	1200	5.0	143 km	
	92-01-30	Thursday	600	1130	5.5	153 km	
		Friday	DAY	OFF			
	Totals:						
OTHER EXPENSES						$900	
Total Kms @ .27 per km						$125.28	
Hours (Minimum 3 hrs. @ $20.00)						$350.00	
TOTAL Claimed This Week						$484.28	
			Reviewed By:				
					Michael Thompson		
					Divisional Manager		
					Security & Investigation Services		

One of Farrell's early invoices for his work doing mail intercepts for CSIS. The CSIS warrant number appears in the middle of the invoice. Farrell suggested to Don Lunau that for security's sake they should eliminate this information from the invoices

The first page of one of Farrell's contracts to provide services as an API

The first page of Farrell's contract with Adava Consulting, the privately owned firm run by Alan Whitson, a former RCMP officer and Canada Post manager. Adava took over the running of CSIS's top secret mail-intercept program

Farrell's security clearance renewal listing the other Toronto-area APIs who did mail intercepts for CSIS, including Mike Thompson, his former boss at Canada Post

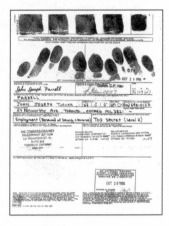

The forms indicating that Farrell's top secret security clearance had been renewed

Bradley's letter to Jesse Barnes, which confirms that Barnes met with a CSIS officer (Angela Jones) to discuss the missing surveillance files

345

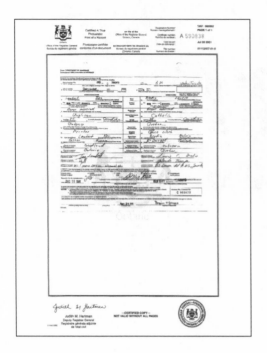

Ian and Laurie Lambert's Canadian marriage licence, in which Ian entered the wrong occupation and in which Laurie listed as "unknown" her parents' country of origin

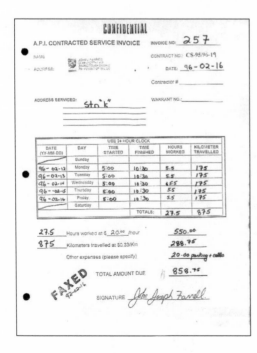

An invoice for Farrell's work intercepting mail from the Lamberts' Roehampton apartment building

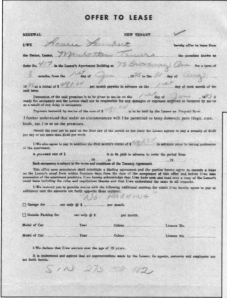

A copy of the lease for an apartment Farrell rented as John Turner to keep an eye on Laurie Lambert when she moved to the Manhattan Towers, along with a copy of Laurie's lease

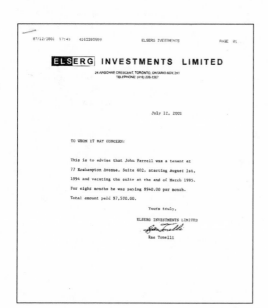

A letter from the landlord confirming that Farrell rented the Roehampton apartment

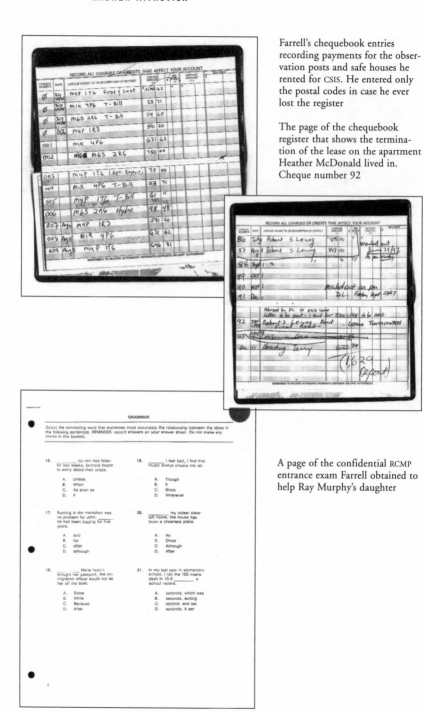

Farrell's chequebook entries recording payments for the observation posts and safe houses he rented for CSIS. He entered only the postal codes in case he ever lost the register

The page of the chequebook register that shows the termination of the lease on the apartment Heather McDonald lived in. Cheque number 92

A page of the confidential RCMP entrance exam Farrell obtained to help Ray Murphy's daughter

Canadian Security
Intelligence Service

Service canadien du
renseignement de sécurité

Director - Directeur

Mr. John Farrell
24 Kenworthy Avenue
Toronto, Ontario
M1L 3B2

Dear Mr. Farrell:

This will acknowledge receipt of your letter dated
March 19, 1999.

I accept and appreciate that you are sensitive to your
obligations to respect the confidentiality with which you have
been entrusted.

For the most part, your working relationship with the
Canadian Security Intelligence Service (CSIS) has been in your
former capacity as a contract employee of Canada Post in the
Auxiliary Postal Inspector Program. In January, 1999, you chose,
of your own volition, to discontinue working in that capacity.
The Service is not accountable for and will not provide
additional remuneration for any work you performed as an employee
of Canada Post.

I recognise that you have assisted the Service in other ways
from time to time and this has been much appreciated. On those
occasions you were compensated directly by CSIS, commensurate
with the nature of assistance provided. However, the Service is
under no further obligation to you in that regard.

Given that you had gone through a period of unemployment,
the Service offered you financial assistance in the amount of
$6,000 to assist you in this period of transition. This offer

.../2

P.O. Box 9732, Station 'T', Ottawa, Ontario K1G 4G4   C.P. 9732, Succursale 'T', Ottawa (Ontario) K1G 4G4

- 2 -

was not intended to represent recognition of what you describe as
your long term commitment to the programs of the service. Rather
is was meant to be a humanitarian gesture for the purpose of
assisting you to fulfill financial obligations you would have
incurred whilst unemployed. You refused to accept that offer.

For the reasons explained above, I do not share your view
that your services merit a payment of $50,000. While not obliged
to do so, I am prepared to again provide you with humanitarian
assistance in the amount previously offered. In the event that
you decide to accept, please notify Mr. Bob Gordon at your
earliest convenience.

I wish you good luck in your future endeavours.

Yours sincerely,

W.P.D. Elcock

CSIS director Ward Elcock's letter, offering Farrell $6,000 in "humanitarian assistance"

Canadian Security
Intelligence Service

Service canadien du
renseignement de sécurité

NOV 2 2 1999

Mr. John J. Farrell
3003 Danforth Avenue
Suite 3 - 557
Toronto Ontario
M4C 5R4

Dear Mr. Farrell:

This will acknowledge receipt of your letter dated
November 7, 1999.

As your records will show, the offer of financial
support was intended to assist you with the transitional
difficulties you were experiencing during your period of
unemployment in March 1999. Since that time, the Security
Intelligence Review Committee (SIRC), has, at your request,
initiated an inquiry into the issues you have raised.

In view of the ongoing SIRC inquiry and the
significant time which has elapsed since this offer was last
extended, the Service will not be acting upon your latest request
for assistance.

Yours sincerely,

T.S. Bradley
Assistant Director
Secretariat

P.O. Box 9732, Station 'T', Ottawa, Ontario K1G 4G4   C.P. 9732, Succursale 'T', Ottawa (Ontario) K1G 4G4

Former CSIS assistant director Tom Bradley's letter rejecting Farrell's appeal

INDEX

INDEX